"*The American Statesmen Series was a pathbreaking venture in its time; and the best proof of its continuing vitality for our time lies in the testimony of the introductory essays written by eminent scholars for the volumes of the Chelsea House edition—essays that not only explain the abiding value of the texts but in many cases represent significant scholarly contributions on their own.*

"*Chelsea House is contributing vitally to the scholarly resources of the country—and, at the same time, helping us all to understand and repossess our national heritage.*"
—*Professor Arthur M. Schlesinger, jr.*

Other titles in this Chelsea House series:

CHARLES FRANCIS ADAMS, *Charles Francis Adams, Jr.*
JOHN ADAMS, *John Quincy Adams and Charles Francis Adams*
JOHN QUINCY ADAMS, *John T. Morse, Jr.*
SAMUEL ADAMS, *James K. Hosmer*
JUDAH P. BENJAMIN, *Pierce Butler*
JOHN C. CALHOUN, *Hermann E. von Holst*
LEWIS CASS, *Andrew C. McLaughlin*
SALMON P. CHASE, *Albert Bushnell Hart*
HENRY CLAY, *Carl Schurz*
ALBERT GALLATIN, *Henry Adams*
ALEXANDER HAMILTON, *Henry Cabot Lodge*
ANDREW JACKSON, *William Graham Sumner*
JOHN JAY, *George Pellew*
THOMAS JEFFERSON, *John T. Morse, Jr.*
JAMES MADISON, *Sydney Howard Gay*
JOHN MARSHALL, *Albert J. Beveridge*
JAMES MONROE, *Daniel Coit Gilman*
GOUVERNEUR MORRIS, *Theodore Roosevelt*
JOHN RANDOLPH, *Henry Adams*
CHARLES SUMNER, *Moorfield Storey*
MARTIN VAN BUREN, *Edward M. Shepard*
GEORGE WASHINGTON, *John Marshall*
DANIEL WEBSTER, *Henry Cabot Lodge*

Forthcoming titles in this Chelsea House series:

JOHN P. ALTGELD, *Harry Barnard*
THOMAS HART BENTON, *Theodore Roosevelt*
JAMES G. BLAINE, *Edward Stanwood*
DANIEL BOONE, *Reuben G. Thwaites*
WILLIAM JENNINGS BRYAN, *M. R. Werner*
AARON BURR, *James Parton*
PETER COOPER, *R. W. Raymond*
STEPHEN A. DOUGLAS, *Allen Johnson*
DAVID FARRAGUT, *Alfred Thayer Mahan*
ULYSSES S. GRANT, *Louis A. Coolidge*
NATHANIEL GREENE, *Francis Vinton Greene*
MARCUS ALONZO HANNA, *Herbert D. Croly*
SAM HOUSTON, *Marquis James*
HENRY KNOX, *Noah Brooks*
LUTHER MARTIN, *Paul S. Clarkson and R. Samuel Jett*
ROBERT MORRIS, *Ellis Paxson Oberholtzer*
FRANKLIN PIERCE, *Nathaniel Hawthorne*
WILLIAM H. SEWARD, *Thornton K. Lothrop*
JOHN SHERMAN, *Theodore E. Burton*
WILLIAM T. SHERMAN, *B. H. Liddell Hart*
THADDEUS STEVENS, *Samuel W. McCall*
ROGER B. TANEY, *Carl Swisher*
TECUMSEH, *Glenn Tucker*
THURLOW WEED, *Glyndon G. VanDeusen*

PATRICK HENRY
MOSES COIT TYLER

INTRODUCTION BY
LANCE BANNING

GENERAL EDITOR
ARTHUR M. SCHLESINGER, JR.
ALBERT SCHWEITZER PROFESSOR OF THE HUMANITIES
THE CITY UNIVERSITY OF NEW YORK

CHELSEA HOUSE
NEW YORK, LONDON
1980

Copyright © 1980 by Chelsea House Publishers, a division of
Chelsea House Educational Communications, Inc.
All rights reserved
Printed and bound in the United States of America

Library of Congress Cataloging in Publication Data

Tyler, Moses Coit, 1835-1900.
    Patrick Henry.

    Reprint of the ed. published by Houghton,
Mifflin, Boston, which was issued as v. 3 of Ameri-
can statesmen.
    Bibliography: p.
    Includes index.
    1. Henry, Patrick, 1736-1799.   2. Virginia--
Politics and government--Revolution, 1775-1783.
3. Legislators--United States--Biography.
4. United States. Continental Congresses--Biog-
raphy.   5. Virginia--Governors--Biography.
I. Title.   II. Series: American statesmen ; v. 3.
[E302.6.H5T92 1980]   973.3'092'4 [B]   80-18577
ISBN 0-87754-190-6

Chelsea House Publishers
Harold Steinberg, Chairman & Publisher
Andrew E. Norman, President
A Division of Chelsea House Educational Communications, Inc.
70 West 40 Street, New York 10018

CONTENTS

ILLUSTRATIONS
FOLLOWING PAGE 188

BLAZING THE WAY
Arthur M. Schlesinger, jr.

THE ORIGINAL AMERICAN STATESMEN SERIES consisted of thirty-four titles published between 1882 and 1916. Handsomely printed and widely read, the Series made a notable contribution to the popular appreciation of American history. Its creator was John Torrey Morse, Jr., born in Boston in 1840, graduated from Harvard in 1860 and for nearly twenty restless years thereafter a Boston lawyer. In his thirties he had begun to dabble in writing and editing; and about 1880, reading a volume in John Morley's English Men of Letters Series, he was seized by the idea of a comparable set of compact, lucid and authoritative lives of American statesmen.

It was an unfashionable thought. The celebrated New York publisher Henry Holt turned the project down, telling Morse, "Who ever wants to read American history?" Houghton, Mifflin in Boston proved more receptive, and Morse plunged ahead. His intention was that the American Statesmen Series, when complete, "should present such a picture of the development of the country that the reader who had faithfully read all the volumes would have a full and fair view of the history of the United States told through the medium of the efforts of the men who had shaped our national career. The actors were to develop the drama."

In choosing his authors, Morse relied heavily on the counsel of his cousin Henry Cabot Lodge. Between them, they enlisted an impressive array of talent. Henry Adams, William Graham Sumner, Moses Coit Tyler, Hermann von Holst, Moorfield Storey and Albert Bushnell Hart were all in their early forties when their volumes were published; Lodge, E. M. Shepard and Andrew C. McLaughlin in their thirties; Theodore Roosevelt in his twenties. Lodge took on Washington, Hamilton and Webster, and Morse himself wrote five volumes. He offered the authors a choice of $500 flat or a royalty of 12.5¢ on each volume sold. Most, luckily for themselves, chose the royalties.

Like many editors, Morse found the experience exasperating. "How I waded among the fragments of broken engagements, shattered pledges! I never really knew when I could count upon getting anything from anybody." Carl Schurz infuriated him by sending in a two-volume life of Henry Clay on a take-it-or-leave-it basis. Morse, who had confined Jefferson,

John Adams, Webster and Calhoun to single volumes, was tempted to leave it. But Schurz threatened to publish his work simultaneously if Morse commissioned another life of Clay for the Series; so Morse reluctantly surrendered.

When a former Confederate colonel, Allan B. Magruder, offered to do John Marshall, Morse, hoping for "a good Virginia atmosphere," gave him a chance. The volume turned out to have been borrowed in embarrassing measure from Henry Flanders's *Lives and Times of the Chief Justices*. For this reason, Magruder's *Marshall* is not included in the Chelsea House reissue of the Series; Albert J. Beveridge's famous biography appears in its stead. Other classic biographies will replace occasional Series volumes: John Marshall's *Life of George Washington* in place of Morse's biography; essays on John Adams by John Quincy Adams and Charles Francis Adams, also substituting for a Morse volume; and Henry Adams's *Life of Albert Gallatin* instead of the Series volume by John Austin Stevens.

"I think that only one real blunder was made," Morse recalled in 1931, "and that was in allotting [John] Randolph to Henry Adams." Half a century earlier, however, Morse had professed himself pleased with Adams's *Randolph*. Adams, responding with characteristic self-deprecation, thought the "acidity" of his account "much too decided" but blamed the "excess of acid" on the acidulous subject. The book was indeed hostile but nonetheless stylish. Adams also wrote a life of Aaron Burr, presumably for the Series. But Morse thought Burr no statesman, and on his advice, to Adams's extreme irritation, Henry Houghton of Houghton, Mifflin rejected the manuscript. "Not bad that for a damned bookseller!" said Adams. "He should live for a while at Washington and know our *real* statesmen." Adams eventually destroyed the work, and a fascinating book was lost to history.

The definition of who was or was not a "statesman" caused recurrent problems. Lodge told Morse one day that their young friend Theodore Roosevelt wanted to do Gouverneur Morris. "But, Cabot," Morse said, "you surely don't expect Morris to be in the Series! He doesn't belong there." Lodge replied, "Theodore . . . *needs the money*," and Morse relented. No one objected to Thomas Hart Benton, Roosevelt's other contribution to the Series. Roosevelt turned out the biography in an astonishing four months while punching cows and chasing horse thieves in the Badlands. Begging Lodge to send more material from Boston, he wrote that he had been "mainly evolving [Benton] from my inner consciousness; but when he leaves the Senate in 1850 I have nothing whatever to go by. .... I hesitate to give him a wholly fictitious date of death and to invent all the work of his later years." In fact, T.R. had done more research than he pretended; and for all its defects, his *Benton* has valuable qualities of vitality and sympathy.

Morse, who would chat to Lodge about "the aristocratic upper crust in which you & I are imbedded," had a fastidious sense of language. Many years later, in the age of Warren G. Harding, he recommended to Lodge that the new President find someone "who can clothe for him his 'ideas' in the language customarily used by educated men." At dinner in a Boston club, a guest commented on the dilemma of the French ambassador who could not speak English. "Neither can Mr. Harding," Morse said. But if patrician prejudice improved Morse's literary taste, it also impaired his political understanding. He was not altogether kidding when he wrote Lodge as the Series was getting under way, "Let the Jeffersonians & the Jacksonians beware! I will poison the popular mind!!"

Still, for all its fidelity to establishment values, the American Statesmen Series had distinct virtues. The authors were mostly from outside the academy, and they wrote with the confidence of men of affairs. Their books are generally crisp, intelligent, spirited and readable. The Series has long been in demand in secondhand bookstores. Most of its volumes are eminently worth republication today, on their merits as well as for the vigorous expression they give to an influential view of the American past.

Born during the Presidency of Martin Van Buren, John Torrey Morse, Jr., died shortly after the second inauguration of Franklin D. Roosevelt in 1937. A few years before his death he could claim with considerable justice that his Series had done "a little something in blazing the way" for the revival of American historical writing in the years to come.

New York
May, 1980

INTRODUCTION
TO THE
CHELSEA HOUSE EDITION
Lance Banning

MOSES COIT TYLER was uniquely qualified to write a biography of Patrick Henry. This was less than obvious to publishers concerned to meet a deadline, and John T. Morse, Jr., the editor of the American Statesmen Series, was forced to withdraw the contract before the dawdling author finally delivered a completed manuscript. Yet the finished work was ample vindication of the editor's first instinct. Immediately acclaimed as one of the best of a distinguished series, Tyler's *Henry* was definitive for sixty years. Recent scholarship has added further information and altered certain shadings of the portrait, but it has not rejected Tyler's most important findings or surpassed his gift for capturing the Virginian's greatness.

Though very distantly related to Virginia's Tylers, Moses was of Yankee stock, an abolitionist and temperance man who joined the new Republican party in 1856 and the Congregational clergy in 1859. Physically and temperamentally unsuited to the pulpit, though drawn toward religion so strongly that he entered the Episcopal priesthood in 1883, Tyler resigned his ministry in 1862 and traveled overseas to promote the regimen of "musical gymnastics" to which he credited the restoration of his health. On the English lecture circuit, he also proved an able advocate of the Union, but Tyler was a liberal, not a radical, Republican and bore no lasting grudge against the South.

Returning to the United States, Tyler joined the faculty at the University of Michigan. As a scholar, he inclined to let his subjects speak for themselves. One of the signal contributions of his greatest work, *The Literary History of the American Revolution,* was his sympathetic presentation of the Loyalist position. His tolerance for all historical combatants, his admiration for the English, his deep religiosity, and his familiarity with both the Anglican and the dissenting points of view would all find outlets in his study of Virginia's Revolutionary titan.

Perhaps Morse sensed as much when he invited Tyler to undertake the first scholarly biography of Henry in March 1881. But there were other, equally compelling reasons for the choice. Three years before, Tyler had published

A History of American Literature, 1607-1765.
That masterpiece, still widely used, had placed
him at the forefront of the new generation of
"critical" historical scholars. He soon accepted
Cornell's offer of a chair in American history,
the first such in the country. In 1884 he helped
to found the American Historical Association.
Tyler was already working on the Revolutionary years, and his history of colonial literature
had displayed his talent for verbal portraiture.
Morse's invitation was a natural one. Few
American statesmen were more colorful than
Henry. None was more enveloped in historical
misinformation.

The myths about the revolutionary hero
had two sources. In the first place, Patrick
Henry had but slight concern for the historical
record. Unlike Washington or Jefferson, he
saved few papers. We do not even have an absolutely reliable transcript of any of his famous
speeches. In consequence, no one will ever
clear the haze completely from the man. When
records fail, moreover, legends take their place.
In Henry's case the mists that always hide the
past were thickened—not maliciously, but most
successfully—by William Wirt, his first biographer.

Frustrated by the paucity of written evidence, Wirt leaned heavily and uncritically on

the untrustworthy recollections of Henry's aging contemporaries, then filled remaining gaps as best he could. He relied particularly on Thomas Jefferson, whose views were strongly biased by the lingering effects of ancient battles with his sometime friend. Jefferson later denounced Wirt's book, which praised the brilliant orator extravagantly. Still, if Wirt had altered the colors of the portrait, he had nonetheless retained a Jeffersonian outline. However faulty, the resulting picture was compelling and pernicious, both because its author was a powerfully attractive stylist and because the hero he presented was the sort in which Americans of the expansive nineteenth century wanted to believe.

Wirt's *Sketches of the Life and Character of Patrick Henry* (1817) went through twenty-five editions in its first fifty years. The Henry it portrayed was an untutored "child of nature" who rose by force of natural genius from a frontier background to spur his colony to revolution and challenge an entrenched elite with principles of liberty and democracy. If not the "avaricious," "rotten-hearted" demagogue Jefferson remembered, he was still by Wirt's account a legal ignoramus whose success as an attorney and importance as a Revolutionary leader rested on native shrewdness, not on trained intelligence, and most of all on his gift of speech. He did not know the law, would not apply himself to legislative business, and could not draft a proper bill. But he could move the coolest men to tears or laughter and lead a legislature on whatever path he chose.

Moses Tyler thoroughly demolished this received impression of Patrick Henry as a rude, uneducated backwoods lout. With the aid of Henry's grandson, William Wirt Henry, who had long been working on a compilation of his grandfather's papers, Tyler uncovered many records Wirt had missed. These he used with critical acuity. He showed beyond a doubt that Henry's education, though no match for that of several of his colleagues, was not to be despised and was not irrelevant to his success. He demonstrated that young Henry worked assiduously as an attorney and overcame his skimpy early training enough to impress men whose legal knowledge was universally admired. In legislative bodies he did not shun service on the committees where hard work was done, nor did he uniformly take the easy, popular positions. As Revolutionary Governor he fully upheld the dignity of an exalted office.

All this Tyler showed, and showed within the framework of a tale superbly told. He wrote with flair and humor. "He could not

dig," Tyler said of the failed young farmer and
storekeeper, "neither could he traffic, but perhaps he could talk." Indeed he could, and
Tyler nearly manages to carry us into the
presence of that unexampled tongue.

No biography, of course, can stand without
challenge through a century of historical research. Recent scholarship suggests that Tyler
skirted Henry's flaws and overstressed his virtues. The book is laudatory and defensive. The
ugliness and avarice that impressed Jefferson
are missing from the picture. We must turn to
later studies for a fuller understanding of
Henry's drive for wealth and its political consequences. Tyler does not mention troublesome
relationships within the Henry home. Nor is
the work without occasional mistakes. Henry
did not write the article on religious freedom in
Virginia's Declaration of Rights. George Mason
drafted the first version, and Henry introduced
a substitute that was the work of young James
Madison—quickly backing away when warned
that it was worded in a manner that would immediately disestablish the Anglican Church.
Both of Henry's most respected modern students also question his responsibility for all of
Virginia's Stamp Act Resolutions.

Tyler's arguments do not persuade in every
case. A notable example is his description of

Henry's transformation from bitter critic of the Constitution into defender of the Federalist regime. For Jefferson, the explanation was simple: Henry profited from Alexander Hamilton's financial schemes. The causes for the switch were probably less crude than that, yet neither can we rest with Tyler's explanation that the Bill of Rights had answered Henry's objections to the new Constitution. Henry worried that the Bill of Rights would quiet demands for alterations of structural provisions left untouched by Madison's amendments: the six-year term for Senators, the power of direct taxation, and much else.

Here, as elsewhere, it seems clear that Tyler was unable to escape entirely from the net William Wirt had cast. His Henry was still the champion of the democracy, a consistent liberal who challenged the Old Dominion's aristocratic elite as he challenged the British Empire. Modern scholarship increasingly insists that these are faulty terms in which to analyze the Revolutionary struggle. Henry did not overturn an old elite, he entered it. As he rose in wealth and social stature, he grew more conservative, as many do. Nor was he ever quite so liberal or democratic on domestic issues as Tyler suggested. He opposed a democratic suffrage and resisted a revision of Virginia's con-

stitution although the latter was notoriously
defective and had been put into effect by legislative fiat. He favored tax support for churches.
His enemies perceived him as a rather auto-
cratic Governor.

Historians today are hesitant to write in
terms of a confrontation between democracy
and aristocracy in Revolutionary Virginia or to
identify persistent legislative factions earlier
than the 1780s. When factions did appear,
Henry seems to have maintained an essential
independence. His powers of persuasion were
so great that other legislators waited nervously
for any hint of his position, but they could
seldom guess where he would stand. The great
man could be counted on to favor measures he
conceived to be in the interests of his section
of Virginia or his state, but who could know
his grounds for judging where those interests
lay? With others of his generation, he believed
that "virtue," in its broadest sense, was indispensable in any people who intended to remain
republican and free. Henry shared that vision
of the difference between America and a corrupt, declining England which has seemed to
recent scholars such a critical dimension of the
Revolutionary struggle. His determination to
preserve the sources of this special way of life
and to guard against generally accepted dangers

to republican society—the advance of public immorality, the establishment of a large professional army, or the impoverishment of the lesser landowners, for example—helps us understand his advocacy of tax support for churches, his reluctance to approve a universal suffrage, his opposition to the Constitution, and his fear of foreign influence later on. Beyond this, the surviving records are too sparse for anyone to reconstruct his thought with enough confidence to say what were the fundamental principles that guided him.

Tyler may attribute more consistency to Henry than seems justified today, although it should be mentioned that he was the first to show that Henry's opposition to an increase of federal authority was a gradually developed thing. For explanations of the hero's conduct, Tyler turned more often toward principle and less often toward self-interest than later writers have. And yet the flaws and errors it is possible to discern after ninety years of further study seem less heavy in the balance than the undeniable accomplishments of this fine work. Every later writer has accepted Tyler's demolition of the mythical Patrick Henry as a lazy, half-illiterate, crude-mannered creature better qualified to play the fiddle at a country dance than to call the moves in Williamsburg or Richmond.

No subsequent biographer has equaled Tyler in ability to reconstruct the aura of these moments when the mesmerizing giant spoke. None has exceeded his capacity to capture the appealing qualities that won Henry the affection of Virginia's ordinary people. Even from today's perspective Tyler's *Patrick Henry* is—I use the word advisedly—a stirring book.

Lexington, Kentucky
April, 1980

BIBLIOGRAPHICAL NOTE

For information about Tyler I have depended mostly on Howard Mumford Jones, *The Life of Moses Coit Tyler* (Ann Arbor, 1933) and on the same author's article in the *Dictionary of American Biography*.

The principal printed collection of Henry's writings is still *Patrick Henry: Life, Correspondence, and Speeches*, 3 vols. (New York, 1891) by William Wirt Henry, who shared his materials generously with Tyler. The fullest modern biography is Robert Douthat Meade, *Patrick Henry*, 2 vols. (Philadelphia, 1957-1969). A shorter but more persuasive interpretation is Richard R. Beeman, *Patrick Henry: A Biography* (New York, 1974).

For Henry's factional position during the 1780s and 1790s readers may consult Norman K. Risjord, *Chesapeake Politics, 1781-1800* (New York, 1978), though Beeman would insist that Risjord's categories are too rigid. For current understandings of the Revolutionary ethos, the indispensable works are Bernard Bailyn, *The Ideological Origins of the American Revolution* (Cambridge, 1967) and Gordon S. Wood, *The Creation of the American Republic* (Chapel Hill, 1969). These may be supplemented for Henry's final years by my own *The Jeffersonian Persuasion* (Ithaca, 1978).

AUTHOR'S PREFACE
TO THE
1899 EDITION

I HAVE gladly used the opportunity afforded by a new edition of this book to give the text a minute revision from beginning to end, and to make numerous changes both in its substance and in its form.

During the eleven years that have passed since it first came from the press, considerable additions have been made to our documentary materials for the period covered by it, the most important for our purpose being the publication, for the first time, of the correspondence and the speeches of Patrick Henry and of George Mason, the former with a life, in three volumes, by William Wirt Henry, the latter also with a life, in two volumes, by Kate Mason Rowland. Besides procuring for my own pages whatever benefit I could draw from these texts, I have tried, while turning over very frequently the writings of Patrick Henry's contemporaries, to be always on the watch for the means of correcting any mistakes I may have made concerning him, whether as to fact or as to opinion.

In this work of rectification I have likewise been aided by suggestions from many persons, of whom I would particularly mention the Right Rev. Joseph Blount Cheshire, Jr., D. D., Bishop of North Carolina, and Mr. William Wirt Henry.

M. C. T.

CORNELL UNIVERSITY, 31 March, 1898.

AUTHOR'S PREFACE
TO THE
1887 EDITION

In this book I have tried to embody the chief results derived from a study of all the materials known to me, in print and in manuscript, relating to Patrick Henry, — many of these materials being now used for the first time in any formal presentation of his life.

Notwithstanding the great popular interest attaching to the name of Patrick Henry, he has hitherto been the subject of but one memoir founded on original investigation, and that, of course, is the Life by William Wirt. When it is considered, however, that Wirt's book was finished as long ago as the year 1817, — before the time had fairly come for the publication of the correspondence, diaries, personal memoranda, and official records of every sort, illustrating the great period covered by Patrick Henry's career, — it will be easy to infer something as to the quantity and the value of those printed materials bearing upon the subject, which are now to be had by us, but which were not within the reach of Wirt. Accordingly, in his lack of much of the detailed testimony that then lay buried in inaccessible documents, Wirt had to trust largely to the somewhat imaginative traditions concerning Patrick Henry which he found floating in the air of Virginia; and especially to the supposed recollections of old people, — recollections which, in this case, were nearly always vague, not always disinterested, often inaccurate, and generally made up of emotional impressions rather than of facts. Any one who will take the trouble to ascertain the enormous disadvantages under which Wirt wrote, and which, as we now know, gave him great discouragement, will be inclined to applaud him for making so good a book, rather than to blame him for not making a better one.

It is proper for me to state that, besides the copious printed materials now within reach, I have been able to make use of a large number of manuscripts relating to my subject. Of these may be specified a document, belonging to Cornell University, written by a great-grandson of Patrick Henry, the late Rev. Edward Fontaine, and giving, among other things, several new anecdotes of the great orator, as told to the writer by his own father, Colonel Patrick Henry Fontaine, who was much with Patrick Henry during the later years of his life. I may add that, through the kindness of the Hon. William Wirt Henry of

Richmond, I have had access to the manuscripts which were collected by Wirt for the purposes of his book, but were only in part used by him. With unstinted generosity, Mr. Henry likewise placed in my hands all the papers relating to his illustrious grandfather, which, during the past thirty years or more, he has succeeded in bringing together, either from different branches of the family, or from other sources. A portion of the manuscripts thus accumulated by him consists of copies of the letters, now preserved in the Department of State, written by Patrick Henry, chiefly while governor of Virginia, to General Washington, to the president of Congress, to Virginia's delegation in Congress, and to the Board of War.

In the very front of this book, therefore, I record my grateful acknowledgments to Mr. William Wirt Henry; acknowledgments not alone for the sort of generosity of which I have just spoken, but for another sort, also, which is still more rare, and which I cannot so easily describe, — his perfect delicacy, while promoting my more difficult researches by his invaluable help, in never once encumbering that help with the least effort to hamper my judgment, or to sway it from the natural conclusions to which my studies might lead.

Finally, it gives me pleasure to mention that, in the preparation of this book, I have received

courteous assistance from Mr. Theodore F. Dwight
and Mr. S. M. Hamilton of the library of the
Department of State; from the Rev. Professor
W. M. Hughes, of Hobart College; and from the
Rev. Stephen H. Synnott, rector of St. John's,
Ithaca.

M. C. T.

CORNELL UNIVERSITY, 3 June, 1887.

PATRICK HENRY

CHAPTER I

EARLY YEARS

On the evening of October 7, 1732, that merry Old Virginian, Colonel William Byrd of Westover, having just finished a journey through King William County for the inspection of his estates, was conducted, for his night's lodging, to the house of a blooming widow, Mistress Sarah Syme, in the county of Hanover. This lady, at first supposing her guest to be some new suitor for her lately disengaged affections, "put on a Gravity that becomes a Weed;" but so soon as she learned her mistake and the name of her distinguished visitor, she "brighten'd up into an unusual cheerfulness and Serenity. She was a portly, handsome Dame, of the Family of Esau, and seem'd not to pine too much for the Death of her Husband, who was of the Family of the Saracens. . . . This widow is a person of a lively & cheerful Conversation, with much less Reserve than most of her Countrywomen. It becomes her very well, and sets off her other agreeable Qualities to Advantage. We tost off a Bottle of honest Port, which we relisht with a broil'd Chicken. At Nine I retir'd to my Devotions, And then Slept so Sound that Fancy itself was Stupify'd, else I shou'd have dreamt of my most obliging Landlady." The next day being Sunday, "the courteous Widow invited me to rest myself there that good day, and go to Church with Her, but I excus'd myself by telling her she wou'd certainly spoil my Devotion. Then she civilly entreated me to make her House my Home whenever I visited my Plantations, which made me bow low, and thank her very kindly." [1]

Not very long after that notable visit, the sprightly widow gave her hand in marriage to a young Scotchman of good family, John Henry, of Aberdeen, a protégé and probably a kinsman of her former husband; and continuing to reside on her estate of Studley, in the county of Hanover, she became, on May 29, 1736, the mother of Patrick Henry.

Through the lineage of both his parents, this child had some claim to an inheritance of brains. The father, a man of firm and sound intellect, had been liberally educated in Scotland; among the country gentlemen of his neighborhood in Virginia, he was held in high esteem for superior intelligence and character, as is shown by the positions he long held of county surveyor, colonel of his regiment, and presiding judge of the county court; while he

---

[1] *Byrd Manuscripts*, ii. 79, 80.

could number among his near kinsmen at home
several persons of eminence as divines, orators, or
men of letters, — such as his uncle, William Robertson, minister of Borthwick in Mid Lothian
and afterward of the Old Greyfriars' Church
in Edinburgh; his cousin, David Henry, the successor of Edward Cave in the management of
the "Gentleman's Magazine;" and especially his
cousin, William Robertson, principal of the University of Edinburgh, and author of the "History of
the Reign of the Emperor Charles V." Moreover,
among the later paternal relatives of Patrick Henry
may be mentioned one person of oratorical and
forensic genius very brilliant and in quality not
unlike his own. Patrick Henry's father was second cousin to that beautiful Eleanor Syme of
Edinburgh, who, in 1777, became the wife of
Henry Brougham of Brougham Hall, Westmore-
land. Their eldest son was Lord Brougham, who
was thus the third cousin of Patrick Henry. To
some it will perhaps seem not a mere caprice of
ingenuity to discover in the fiery, eccentric, and
truculent eloquence of the great English advocate
and parliamentary orator a family likeness to that
of his renowned American kinsman; or to find in
the fierceness of the champion of Queen Caroline
against George IV., and of English anti-slavery reform and of English parliamentary reform against
aristocratic and commercial selfishness, the same
bitter and eager radicalism that burned in the
blood of him who, on this side of the Atlantic,

was, in popular oratory, the great champion of the colonies against George III., and afterward of the political autonomy of the State of Virginia against the all-dominating centralization which he saw coiled up in the projected Constitution of the United States.[1]

Those, however, who knew the mother of Patrick Henry, and her family, the Winstons, were accustomed to think that it was from her side of the house that he derived the most characteristic traits not only of his genius, but of his disposition. The Winstons of Virginia were of Welsh stock; a family marked by vivacity of spirit, conversational talent, a lyric and dramatic turn, a gift for music and for eloquent speech, at the same time by a fondness for country life, for inartificial pleasures, for fishing and hunting, for the solitude and the unkempt charms of nature. It was said, too, of the Winstons that their talents were in excess of their ambition or of their energy, and were not brought into use except in a fitful way, and under the stimulus of some outward and passing occasion. They seem to have belonged to that very considerable class of persons in this world of

[1] I have from private sources information that Brougham was aware of his relationship to Patrick Henry, and that in recognition of it he showed marked attentions to a grand-nephew of Patrick Henry, the late W. C. Preston, of South Carolina, when the latter was in England. Moreover, in his *Life and Times*, i. 17, 18, Brougham declares that he derived from his maternal ancestors the qualities which lifted him above the mediocrity that had always attached to his ancestors on the paternal side.

whom more might have been made. Especially
much talk used to be heard, among old men in
Virginia, of Patrick Henry's uncle, his mother's
own brother, William Winston, as having a gift
of eloquence dazzling and wondrous like Patrick's,
nay, as himself unsurpassed in oratory among all
the great speakers of Virginia except by Patrick
himself.[1]

The system of education prevailing in Virginia
during Patrick Henry's early years was extremely
simple. It consisted of an almost entire lack of
public schools, mitigated by the sporadic and ir-
regular exercise of domestic tuition. Those who
could afford to import instruction into their homes
got it, if they desired; those who could not, generally went without. As to the youthful Patrick,
he and education never took kindly to each other.
From nearly all quarters the testimony is to this
effect, — that he was an indolent, dreamy, frolic-
some creature, with a mortal enmity to books,
supplemented by a passionate regard for fishing-
rods and shot-guns; disorderly in dress, slouching,
vagrant, unambitious; a roamer in woods, a loi-
terer on river-banks; having more tastes and aspirations in common with trappers and frontiersmen
than with the toilers of civilized life; giving no
hint nor token, by word or act, of the possession
of any intellectual gift that could raise him above
mediocrity, or even up to it.

During the first ten years of his life, he seems

[1] Wirt, 3.

to have made, at a small school in the neighborhood, some small and reluctant progress into the
mysteries of reading, writing, and arithmetic;
whereupon his father took personal charge of the
matter, and conducted his further education at
home, along with that of other children, being
aided in the task by the very competent help of
a brother, the Rev. Patrick Henry, rector of St.
Paul's parish, in Hanover, and apparently a good
Scotch classicist. In this way our Patrick acquired some knowledge of Latin and Greek, and
rather more knowledge of mathematics, — the latter being the only branch of book-learning for
which, in those days, he showed the least liking.
However, under such circumstances, with little
real discipline, doubtless, and amid plentiful in-
terruptions, the process of ostensible education
went forward with the young man; and even this
came to an end by the time that he was fifteen
years old.

At that age, he was duly graduated from the
domestic schoolroom into the shop of a country
tradesman hard by. After an apprenticeship there
of a single year, his father set him up in trade,
joining with him in the conduct of a country store
his elder brother, William, a youth more indolent,
if possible, as well as more disorderly and uncom-
mercial, than Patrick himself. One year of this
odd partnership brought the petty concern to its
inevitable fate. Just one year after that, having
attained the ripe age of eighteen, and being then

entirely out of employment, and equally out of money, Patrick rounded out his embarrassments, and gave symmetry to them, as it were, by getting married, — and that to a young woman quite as impecunious as himself. The name of this damsel was Sarah Shelton; her father being a small farmer, and afterward a small tavern-keeper in the neighborhood. In the very rashness and absurdity of this proceeding on the part of these two interesting young paupers, irresistibly smitten with each other's charms, and mutually resolved to defy their own helplessness by doubling it, there seems to have been a sort of semi-ludicrous pathos which constituted an irresistible call for help.

The parents on both sides heard the call, and by their joint efforts soon established the young couple on a little farm near at hand, from which, by their own toil, reënforced by that of half a dozen slaves, they were expected to extort a living. This experiment, the success of which depended on exactly those qualities which Patrick did not then possess, — industry, order, sharp calculation, persistence, — turned out as might have been predicted. At the end of two years he made a forced sale of some of his slaves, and invested the proceeds in the stock of a country store once more. But as he had now proved himself to be a bad farmer, and a still worse merchant, it is not easy to divine by what subtle process of reasoning he had been able to conclude that there would be any improvement in his circumstances by getting out of agriculture and back into merchandise.

When he undertook this last venture he was still but a youth of twenty. By the time that he was twenty-three, that is, by the autumn of 1759, he had become convinced that his little store was to prove for him merely a consumer of capital and a producer of bad debts; and in view of the necessity of soon closing it, he had ample excuse for taking into consideration what he should do next. Already was he the happy father of sundry small children, with the most trustworthy prospect of a steady enlargement and multiplication of his paternal honors. Surely, to a man of twenty-three, a husband and a father, who, from the age of fifteen, had been engaged in a series of enterprises to gain his livelihood, and had perfectly failed in every one of them, the question of his future means of subsistence must have presented itself as a subject of no little pertinence, not to say urgency. However, at that time Patrick seems to have been a young fellow of superabounding health and of inextinguishable spirits, and even in that crisis of his life he was able to deal gayly with its problems. In that very year, 1759, Thomas Jefferson, then a lad of sixteen, and on his way to the College of William and Mary, happened to spend the Christmas holidays at the house of Colonel Nathan Dandridge, in Hanover, and there first met Patrick Henry. Long afterward, recalling these days, Jefferson furnished this picture of him: —

" Mr. Henry had, a little before, broken up his store, or

rather it had broken him up ; but his misfortunes were
not to be traced either in his countenance or conduct."
" During the festivity of the season I met him in society
every day, and we became well acquainted, although I
was much his junior. . . . His manners had something
of coarseness in them. His passion was music, dancing,
and pleasantry. He excelled in the last, and it attached
every one to him." [1]

Shortly after Jefferson left those hilarious scenes
for the somewhat more restrained festivities of the
little college at Williamsburg, Patrick succeeded
in settling in his own mind what he was going to
do next. He could not dig, so it seemed, neither
could he traffic, but perhaps he could talk. Why
not get a living by his tongue? Why not be a
lawyer?

But before we follow him through the gates of
that superb profession, — gates which, after some
preliminary creaking of the hinges, threw open to
him the broad pathway to wealth, renown, unbounded influence, — let us stop a moment longer
on the outside, and get a more distinct idea, if we
can, of his real intellectual outfit for the career on
which he was about to enter.

[1] In a letter to Wirt, in 1815, *Life of Henry*, 14, 15; also
Writings of Jefferson, vi. 487, 488, where the letter is given, apparently, from the first draft.

CHAPTER II

WAS HE ILLITERATE ?

CONCERNING the quality and extent of Patrick Henry's early education, it is perhaps impossible now to speak with entire confidence. On the one hand there seems to have been a tendency, in his own time and since, to overstate his lack of education, and this partly, it may be, from a certain instinctive fascination which one finds in pointing to so dramatic a contrast as that between the sway which the great orator wielded over the minds of other men and the untrained vigor and illiterate spontaneity of his own mind. Then, too, it must be admitted that, whatever early education Patrick Henry may have received, he did, in certain companies and at certain periods of his life, rather too perfectly conceal it under an uncouth garb and manner, and under a pronunciation which, to say the least, was archaic and provincial. Jefferson told Daniel Webster that Patrick Henry's "pronunciation was vulgar and vicious," although, as Jefferson adds, this "was forgotten while he was speaking."[1] Governor John Page "used to relate, on the testimony of his own ears," that Pat-

[1] Curtis, *Life of Webster*, i. 585.

rick Henry would speak of "the yearth," and of
"men's naiteral parts being improved by larnin'; "[1]
while Spencer Roane mentions his pronunciation
of China as "Cheena."[2] All this, however, it
should be noted, does not prove illiteracy. If,
indeed, such was his ordinary speech, and not, as
some have suggested, a manner adopted on particular occasions for the purpose of identifying himself with the mass of his hearers, the fact is evidence merely that he retained through his mature
life, on the one hand, some relics of an old-fash-
ioned good usage, and, on the other, some traces
of the brogue of the district in which he was born,
just as Edmund Pendleton used to say "scaicely"
for scarcely, and as John Taylor, of Caroline,
would say "bare" for bar; just as Thomas Chalm-
ers always retained the brogue of Fifeshire, and
Thomas Carlyle that of Ecclefechan. Certainly
a brogue can never be elegant, but as it has many
times coexisted with very high intellectual cultivation, its existence in Patrick Henry does not prove
him to have been uncultivated.

Then, too, it must be remembered that he himself had a habit of depreciating his own acquaintance with books, and his own dependence on them.
He did this, it would seem, partly from a consciousness that it would only increase his hold on
the sympathy and support of the mass of the people of Virginia if they should regard him as absolutely one of themselves, and in no sense raised

[1] Randall, *Life of Jefferson*, i. 20.   [2] MS.

above them by artificial advantages. Moreover,
this habit of self-depreciation would be brought
into play when he was in conversation with such
professed devourers of books as John Adams and
Jefferson, compared with whom he might very
properly feel an unfeigned conviction that he was
no reader at all, — a conviction in which they
would be quite likely to agree with him, and which
they would be very likely to express. Thus, John
Adams mentions that, in the first intimacy of their
friendship begun at the Congress of 1774, the
Virginian orator, at his lodgings, confessed one
night that, for himself, he had "had no public
education;" that at fifteen he had "read Virgil
and Livy," but that he had "not looked into a
Latin book since."[1] Upon Jefferson, who of course
knew Henry far longer and far more closely, the
impression of his disconnection from books seems
to have been even more decided, especially if we
may accept the testimony of Jefferson's old age,
when his memory had taken to much stumbling,
and his imagination even more to extravagance
than in his earlier life. Said Jefferson, in 1824,
of his ancient friend: "He was a man of very little
knowledge of any sort. He read nothing, and had
no books."[2]

On the other hand, there are certain facts concerning Henry's early education and intellectual
habits which may be regarded as pretty well estab-

[1] *Works of John Adams*, ii. 396.
[2] Curtis, *Life of Webster*, i. 585.

lished. Before the age of ten, at a petty neighborhood school, he had got started upon the three primary steps of knowledge. Then, from ten to fifteen, whatever may have been his own irregularity and disinclination, he was member of a home school, under the immediate training of his father and his uncle, both of them good Scotch classical scholars, and one of them at least a proficient in mathematics. No doubt the human mind, especially in its best estate of juvenile vigor and frivolity, has remarkable aptitude for the repulsion of unwelcome knowledge; but it can hardly be said that even Patrick Henry's gift in that direction could have prevented his becoming, under two such masters, tolerably well grounded in Latin, if not in Greek, or that the person who at fifteen is able to read Virgil and Livy, no matter what may be his subsequent neglect of Latin authors, is not already imbued with the essential and indestructible rudiments of the best intellectual culture.

It is this early initiation, on the basis of a drill in Latin, into the art and mystery of expression, which Patrick Henry received from masters so competent and so deeply interested in him, which helps us to understand a certain trait of his, which puzzled Jefferson, and which, without this clue, would certainly be inexplicable. From his first appearance as a speaker to the end of his days, he showed himself to be something more than a declaimer, — indeed, an adept in language. "I have been often astonished," said Jefferson, "at his

command of proper language; how he obtained the
knowledge of it I never could find out, as he read
little, and conversed little with educated men." [1]
It is true, probably, that we have no perfect report
of any speech he ever made; but even through
the obvious imperfections of his reporters there
always gleams a certain superiority in diction, —
a mastery of the logic and potency of fitting words;
such a mastery as genius alone, without special
training, cannot account for.   Furthermore, we
have in the letters of his which survive, and which
of course were generally spontaneous and quite un-
studied effusions, absolutely authentic and literal
examples of his ordinary use of words.   Some of
these letters will be found in the following pages.
Even as manuscripts, I should insist that the letters of Patrick Henry are witnesses to the fact and
quality of real intellectual cultivation: these are
not the manuscripts of an uneducated person.   In
penmanship, punctuation, spelling, syntax, they
are, upon the whole, rather better than the letters
of most of the great actors in our Revolution.
But, aside from the mere mechanics of written
speech, there is in the diction of Patrick Henry's
letters the nameless felicity which, even with great
natural endowments, is only communicable by genuine literary culture in some form.   Where did
Patrick Henry get such literary culture?   The
question can be answered only by pointing to that
painful drill in Latin which the book-hating boy

[1] Curtis, *Life of Webster*, i. 585.

suffered under his uncle and his father, when, to his anguish, Virgil and Livy detained him anon from the true joys of existence.

Wirt seems to have satisfied himself, on evidence carefully gathered from persons who were contemporaries of Patrick Henry, that the latter had received in his youth no mean classical education; but, in the final revision of his book for publication, Wirt abated his statements on that subject, in deference to the somewhat vehement assertions of Jefferson. It may be that, in its present lessened form, Wirt's account of the matter is the more correct one; but this is the proper place in which to mention one bit of direct testimony upon the subject, which, probably, was not known to Wirt. Patrick Henry is said to have told his eldest grandson, Colonel Patrick Henry Fontaine, that he was instructed by his uncle "not only in the catechism, but in the Greek and Latin classics."[1] It may help us to realize something of the moral stamina entering into the training which the unfledged orator thus got that, as he related, his uncle taught him these maxims of conduct: "To be true and just in all my dealings. To bear no malice nor hatred in my heart. To keep my hands from picking and stealing. Not to covet other men's goods; but to learn and labor truly to get my own living, and to do my duty in that state of life unto which it shall please God to call me."[2]

Under such a teacher Patrick Henry was so

[1] MS.   [2] MS.

thoroughly grounded, at least in Latin and Greek grammar, that when, long afterward, his eldest grandson was a student in Hampden-Sidney College, the latter found "his grandfather's examinations of his progress in Greek and Latin" so rigorous that he dreaded them "much more than he did his recitations to his professors."[1]   Colonel Fontaine also states that he was present when a certain French visitor, who did not speak English, was introduced to Governor Henry, who did not speak French.   During the war of the Revolution and just afterwards a similar embarrassment was not infrequent here in the case of our public men, among whom the study of French had been very uncommon; and for many of them the old colonial habit of fitting boys for college by training them to the colloquial use of Latin proved to be a great convenience.   Colonel Fontaine's anecdote implies, what is altogether probable, that Patrick Henry's early drill in Latin had included the ordinary colloquial use of it; for he says that in the case of the visitor in question his grandfather was able, by means of his early stock of Latin words, to carry on the conversation in that language.[2]

This anecdote, implying Patrick Henry's ability to express himself in Latin, I give for what it may be worth.   Some will think it incredible, and that impression will be further increased by the fact that Colonel Fontaine names Albert Gallatin as the visitor with whom, on account of his ignorance

[1] MS.   [2] MS.

of English, the conversation was thus carried on in Latin. This, of course, must be a mistake; for, at the time of his first visit to Virginia, Gallatin could speak English very well, so well, in fact, that he went to Virginia expressly as English interpreter to a French gentleman who could not speak our language.[1] However, as, during all that period, Governor Henry had many foreign visitors, Colonel Fontaine, in his subsequent account of that particular visitor, might easily have misplaced the name without thereby discrediting the substance of his narrative. Indeed, the substance of his narrative, namely, that he, Colonel Fontaine, did actually witness, in the case of some foreign visitor, such an exhibition of his grandfather's good early training in Latin, cannot be rejected without an impeachment of the veracity of the narrator, or at least of that of his son, who has recorded the alleged incident. Of course, if that narrative be accepted as substantially true, it will be necessary to conclude that the Jeffersonian tradition of Patrick Henry's illiteracy is, at any rate, far too highly tinted.

Thus far we have been dealing with the question of Patrick Henry's education down to the time of his leaving school, at the age of fifteen. It was not until nine years afterward that he began the study of the law. What is the intellectual record of these nine years? It is obvious that they were years unfavorable to systematic training of any

---

[1] Henry Adams, *Life of Gallatin*, 59, 60.

sort, or to any regulated acquisition of knowledge.
During all that time in his life, as we now look
back upon it, he has for us the aspect of some law-
less, unkempt genius, in untoward circumstances,
groping in the dark, not without wild joy, towards
his inconceivable, true vocation; set to tasks for
which he was grotesquely unfit; blundering on
from misfortune to misfortune, with an overflow
of unemployed energy and vivacity that swept him
often into rough fun, into great gusts of innocent
riot and horseplay; withal borne along, for many
days together, by the mysterious undercurrents of
his nature, into that realm of reverie where the
soul feeds on immortal fruit and communes with
unseen associates, the body meanwhile being left
to the semblance of idleness; of all which the man
himself might have given this valid justification: —

> " I loafe and invite my soul,
> I lean and loafe at my ease, observing a spear of summer
> grass."

Nevertheless, these nine years of groping, blundering, and seeming idleness were not without their
influence on his intellectual improvement even
through direct contact with books. While still a
boy in his teens, and put prematurely to uncon-
genial attempts at shopkeeping and farmkeeping,
he at any rate made the great discovery that in
books and in the gathering of knowledge from
books could be found solace and entertainment; in
short, he then acquired a taste for reading. No
one pretends that Patrick Henry ever became a

bookish person. From the first and always the habit of his mind was that of direct action upon every subject that he had to deal with, through his own reflection, and along the broad primary lines of common sense. There is never in his thought anything subtle or recondite, — no mental movement through the media of books; but there is good evidence for saying that this bewildered and undeveloped youth, drifting about in chaos, did in those days actually get a taste for reading, and that he never lost it. The books which he first read are vaguely described as "a few light and elegant authors,"[1] probably in English essays and fiction. As the years passed and the boy's mind matured, he rose to more serious books. He became fond of geography and of history, and he pushed his readings, especially, into the history of Greece and of Rome. He was particularly fascinated by Livy, which he read in the English translation; and then it was, as he himself related it to Judge Hugh Nelson, that he made the rule to read Livy through "once at least in every year during the early part of his life."[2] He read also, it is apparent, the history of England and of the English colonies in America, and especially of his own colony; for the latter finding, no doubt, in Bever-

[1] Wirt, 9.
[2] Wirt, 13. This is the passage on which Jefferson, in his extreme old age, made the characteristically inaccurate comment: "His biographer says, 'He read Plutarch every year.' I doubt if he ever read a volume of it in his life." Curtis, *Life of Webster*, i. 585.

ley and in the grave and noble pages of Stith, and
especially in the colonial charters given by Stith,
much material for those incisive opinions which he
so early formed as to the rights of the colonies,
and as to the barriers to be thrown up against the
encroaching authority of the mother country.

There is much contemporaneous evidence to show
that Patrick Henry was throughout life a deeply
religious person. It certainly speaks well for his
intellectual fibre, as well as for his spiritual tendencies, that his favorite book, during the larger
part of his life, was "Butler's Analogy," which
was first published in the very year in which he
was born. It is possible that even during these
years of his early manhood he had begun his endur-
ing intimacy with that robust book. Moreover,
we can hardly err in saying that he had then also
become a steady reader of the English Bible, the
diction of which is stamped upon his style as un-
mistakably as it is upon that of the elder Pitt.

Such, I think it may fairly be said, was Patrick
Henry when, at the age of twenty-four, having
failed in every other pursuit, he turned for bread
to the profession of the law. There is no evidence
that either he or any other mortal man was aware
of the extraordinary gifts that lay within him for
success in that career. Not a scholar surely, not
even a considerable miscellaneous reader, he yet
had the basis of a good education; he had the
habit of reading over and over again a few of the
best books; he had a good memory; he had an

intellect strong to grasp the great commanding features of any subject; he had a fondness for the study of human nature, and singular proficiency in that branch of science; he had quick and warm sympathies, particularly with persons in trouble, — an invincible propensity to take sides with the under-dog in any fight. Through a long experience in offhand talk with the men whom he had thus far chiefly known in his little provincial world, — with an occasional clergyman, pedagogue, or legislator, small planters and small traders, sportsmen, loafers, slaves and the drivers of slaves, and, more than all, those bucolic Solons of old Virginia, the good-humored, illiterate, thriftless Caucasian consumers of tobacco and whiskey, who, cordially consenting that all the hard work of the world should be done by the children of Ham, were thus left free to commune together in endless debate on the tavern porch or on the shady side of the country store, — young Patrick had learned somewhat of the lawyer's art of putting things; he could make men laugh, could make them serious, could set fire to their enthusiasms. What more he might do with such gifts nobody seems to have guessed; very likely few gave it any thought at all. In that rugged but munificent profession at whose outward gates he then proceeded to knock, it was altogether improbable that he would burden himself with much more of its erudition than was really necessary for a successful general practice in Virginia in his time, or that he would permanently content himself with less.

CHAPTER III

BECOMES A LAWYER

SOME time in the early spring of 1760, Thomas Jefferson, then a lad in the College of William and Mary, was surprised by the arrival in Williamsburg of his jovial acquaintance, Patrick Henry, and still more by the announcement of the latter that, in the brief interval since their merrymakings together at Hanover, he had found time to study law, and had actually come up to the capital to seek an admission to the bar.

In the accounts that we have from Henry's contemporaries respecting the length of time during which he was engaged in preparing for his legal examination, there are certain discrepancies, — some of these accounts saying that it was nine months, others six or eight months, others six weeks. Henry himself told a friend that his original study of the law lasted only one month, and consisted in the reading of Coke upon Littleton and of the Virginia laws.[1]

Concerning the encounter of this obscure and raw country youth with the accomplished men who examined him as to his fitness to receive a license

[1] Wirt, 16.

to practice law, there are three primary narratives, — two by Jefferson, and a third by Judge John Tyler. In his famous talk with Daniel Webster and the Ticknors at Monticello, in 1824, Jefferson said: "There were four examiners, — Wythe, Pendleton, Peyton Randolph, and John Randolph. Wythe and Pendleton at once rejected his application; the two Randolphs were, by his importunity, prevailed upon to sign the license; and, having obtained their signatures, he again applied to Pendleton, and after much entreaty, and many promises of future study, succeeded also in obtaining his. He then turned out for a practicing lawyer."[1]

In a memorandum[2] prepared nearly ten years before the conversation just mentioned, Jefferson described somewhat differently the incidents of Henry's examination: —

"Two of the examiners, however, Peyton and John Randolph, men of great facility of temper, signed his license with as much reluctance as their dispositions would permit them to show. Mr. Wythe absolutely refused. Rob. C. Nicholas refused also at first; but on repeated importunities, and promises of future reading, he signed. These facts I had afterwards from the gentlemen themselves; the two Randolphs acknowledging he was very ignorant of law, but that they perceived him to be a young man of genius, and did not doubt he would soon qualify himself."[3]

[1] Curtis, *Life of Webster*, i. 584.
[2] First printed in the Philadelphia *Age*, in 1867; and again printed, from the original manuscript, in *The Historical Magazine*, August, 1867, 90–93. I quote from the latter.
[3] Jefferson's memorandum, *Hist. Mag.* for August, 1867, 90.

Long afterward, and when all this anxious affair
had become for Patrick Henry an amusing thing
of the past, he himself, in the confidence of an
affectionate friendship, seems to have related one
remarkable phase of his experience to Judge John
Tyler, by whom it was given to Wirt. One of
the examiners was "Mr. John Randolph, who was
afterwards the king's attorney-general for the
colony,— a gentleman of the most courtly elegance
of person and manners, a polished wit, and a profound lawyer. At first, he was so much shocked
by Mr. Henry's very ungainly figure and address,
that he refused to examine him. Understanding,
however, that he had already obtained two signatures, he entered with manifest reluctance on the
business. A very short time was sufficient to sat-
isfy him of the erroneous conclusion which he had
drawn from the exterior of the candidate. With
evident marks of increasing surprise (produced, no
doubt, by the peculiar texture and strength of Mr.
Henry's style, and the boldness and originality of
his combinations), he continued the examination
for several hours; interrogating the candidate, not
on the principles of municipal law, in which he no
doubt soon discovered his deficiency, but on the
laws of nature and of nations, on the policy of the
feudal system, and on general history, which last
he found to be his stronghold. During the very
short portion of the examination which was devoted
to the common law, Mr. Randolph dissented, or
affected to dissent, from one of Mr. Henry's an-

swers, and called upon him to assign the reasons of his opinion. This produced an argument, and Mr. Randolph now played off on him the same arts which he himself had so often practiced on his country customers; drawing him out by questions, endeavoring to puzzle him by subtleties, assailing him with declamation, and watching continually the defensive operations of his mind. After a considerable discussion, he said, 'You defend your opinions well, sir; but now to the law and to the testimony.' Hereupon he carried him to his office, and, opening the authorities, said to him: 'Behold the force of natural reason! You have never seen these books, nor this principle of the law; yet you are right and I am wrong. And from the lesson which you have given me (you must excuse me for saying it) I will never trust to appearances again. Mr. Henry, if your industry be only half equal to your genius, I augur that you will do well, and become an ornament and an honor to your profession.' " [1]

After such an ordeal at Williamsburg, the young man must have ridden back to Hanover with some natural elation over his success, but that elation not a little tempered by serious reflection upon his own deficiencies as a lawyer, and by an honest purpose to correct them. Certainly nearly everything that was dear to him in life must then have risen before his eyes, and have incited him to industry in the further study of his profession.

[1] Wirt, 16, 17.

At that time, his father-in-law had become the keeper of a tavern in Hanover; and for the next two or three years, while he was rapidly making his way as a general practitioner of the law in that neighborhood, Patrick seems occasionally to have been a visitor at this tavern. It was in this way, undoubtedly, that he sometimes acted as host, especially in the absence of his father-in-law, — receiving all comers, and providing for their entertainment; and it was from this circumstance that the tradition arose, as Jefferson bluntly expressed it, that Patrick Henry "was originally a bar-keeper,"[1] or, as it is more vivaciously expressed by a recent writer, that "for three years" after getting his license to practice law, he "tended travelers and drew corks."[2]

These statements, however, are but an exaggeration of the fact that, whenever visiting at the tavern of his father-in-law, he had the good sense and the good feeling to lend a hand, in case of need, in the business of the house; and that no more than this is true may be proved, not only from the written testimony of survivors,[3] who knew him in those days, but from the contemporary records, carefully kept by himself, of his own earliest business as a lawyer. These records show that, almost at once after receiving his license to practice law,

[1] Curtis, *Life of Webster*, i. 584.

[2] McMaster, *Hist. of U. S.* i. 489.

[3] I have carefully examined this testimony, which is still in manuscript.

he must have been fully occupied with the appropriate business of his profession.

It is quite apparent, also, from the evidence just referred to, that the common history of his life has, in another particular, done great injustice to this period of it. According to the recollection of one old man who outlived him, "he was not distinguished at the bar for near four years." [1] Wirt himself, relying upon the statements of several survivors of Patrick Henry, speaks of his lingering "in the background for three years," and of "the profits of his practice" as being so inadequate for the supply of even "the necessaries of life," that "for the first two or three years" he was living with his family in dependence upon his father-in-law. [2] Fortunately, however, we are not left in this case to grope our way toward the truth amid the ruins of the confused and decaying memories of old men. Since Wirt's time, there have come to light the fee-books of Patrick Henry, carefully and neatly kept by him from the beginning of his practice, and covering nearly his entire professional life down to old age. [3] The first entry in these books is for September, 1760; and from that date onward to the end of the year 1763, — by which time he had suddenly sprung into great professional prominence by his speech in "the Parsons' Cause," — he is found to have charged

---

[1] Judge Winston, MS.   [2] Wirt, 18, 19.

[3] These fee-books are now in the possession of Mr. William Wirt Henry, of Richmond.

fees in 1185 suits, besides many other fees for the preparation of legal papers out of court. From about the time of his speech in "the Parsons' Cause," as his fee-books show, his practice became enormous, and so continued to the end of his days, excepting when public duties or broken health compelled him to turn away clients. Thus it is apparent that, while the young lawyer did not attain anything more than local professional reputation until his speech against the parsons, he did acquire a very considerable practice almost immediately after his admission to the bar. Moreover, so far from his being a needy dependant on his father-in-law for the first two or three years, the same quiet records show that his practice enabled him, even during that early period, to assist his father-in-law by an important advance of money.

The fiction that Patrick Henry, during the first three or four years of his nominal career as a lawyer, was a briefless barrister, — earning his living at the bar of a tavern rather than at the bar of justice, — is the very least of those disparaging myths, which, through the frailty of human memory and the bitterness of partisan ill-will, have been permitted to settle upon his reputation. Certainly, no one would think it discreditable, or even surprising, if Patrick Henry, while still a very young lawyer, should have had little or no practice, provided only that, when the practice did come, the young lawyer had shown himself to have been a good one. It is precisely this honor which, during the past seventy years, has been denied him. Upon the evidence thus far most prominently before the public, one is compelled to conceive of him as having been destitute of nearly all the qualifications of a good lawyer, excepting those which give success with juries, particularly in criminal practice: he is represented as ignorant of the law, indolent, and grossly negligent of business, — with nothing, in fact, to give him the least success in the profession but an abnormal and quite unaccountable gift of persuasion through speech.

Referring to this period of his life, Wirt says:—

"Of the science of law he knew almost nothing; of the practical part he was so wholly ignorant that he was not only unable to draw a declaration or a plea, but incapable, it is said, of the most common or simple business of his profession, even of the mode of ordering a suit, giving a notice, or making a motion in court."[1]

This conception of Henry's professional character, to which Wirt seems to have come reluctantly, was founded, as is now evident, on the long-suppressed memorandum of Jefferson, who therein states that, after failing in merchandise, Patrick "turned his views to the law, for the acquisition or practice of which however, he was too lazy. Whenever the courts were closed for the winter session, he would make up a party of poor hunters of his neighborhood, would go off with them to the piny woods of

[1] Wirt, 18.

Fluvanna, and pass weeks in hunting deer, of which he was passionately fond, sleeping under a tent before a fire, wearing the same shirt the whole time, and covering all the dirt of his dress with a hunting-shirt. He never undertook to draw pleadings, if he could avoid it, or to manage that part of a cause, and very unwillingly engaged but as an assistant to speak in the cause. And the fee was an indispensable preliminary, observing to the applicant that he kept no accounts, never putting pen to paper, which was true." [1]

The last sentence of this passage, in which Jefferson declares that it was true that Henry "kept no accounts, never putting pen to paper," is, of course, now utterly set aside by the discovery of the precious fee-books; and these orderly and circumstantial records almost as completely annihilate the trustworthiness of all the rest of the passage. Let us consider, for example, Jefferson's statement that for the acquisition of the law, or for the practice of it, Henry was too lazy, and that much of the time between the sessions of the courts was passed by him in deer-hunting in the woods. Confining ourselves to the first three and a half years of his actual practice, in which, by the record, his practice was the smallest that he ever had, it is not easy for one to understand how a mere novice in the profession, and one so perfectly ignorant of its most rudimental forms, could have earned, during that brief period, the fees which he

[1] *Hist. Mag.* for 1867, 93.

charged in 1185 suits, and in the preparation of many legal papers out of court, and still have been seriously addicted to laziness. Indeed, if so much legal business could have been transacted within three years and a half, by a lawyer who, besides being young and incompetent, was also extremely lazy, and greatly preferred to go off to the woods and hunt for deer while his clients were left to hunt in vain for him, it becomes an interesting question just how much legal business we ought to expect to be done by a young lawyer who was not incompetent, was not lazy, and had no inordinate fondness for deer-hunting. It happens that young Thomas Jefferson himself was just such a lawyer. He began practice exactly seven years after Patrick Henry, and at precisely the same time of life, though under external circumstances far more favorable. As a proof of his uncommon zeal and success in the profession, his biographer, Randall, cites from Jefferson's fee-books the number of cases in which he was employed until he was finally drawn off from the law into political life. Oddly enough, for the first four years of his practice, the cases registered by Jefferson[1] number, in all, but 504. It should be mentioned that this number, as it includes only Jefferson's cases in the General Court, does not indicate all the business done by him during those first four years; and yet, even with this allowance, we are left standing rather helpless before the problem presented by

[1] Randall, *Life of Jefferson*, i. 47, 48.

the fact that this competent and diligent young lawyer — whom, forsooth, the rustling leaves of the forest could never for once entice from the rustle of the leaves of his law-books — did nevertheless transact, during his own first four years of practice, probably less than one half as much business as seems to have been done during a somewhat shorter space of time by our poor, ignorant, indolent, slovenly, client - shunning and forest-haunting Patrick.

But, if Jefferson's charge of professional indolence and neglect on the part of his early friend fares rather ill when tested by those minute and plodding records of his professional employments which were kept by Patrick Henry, a fate not much more prosperous overtakes Jefferson's other charge, — that of professional incompetence. It is more than intimated by Jefferson that, even had Patrick been disposed to engage in a general law practice, he did not know enough to do so successfully by reason of his ignorance of the most ordinary legal principles and legal forms. But the intellectual embarrassment which one experiences in trying to accept this view of Patrick Henry arises from the simple fact that these incorrigible fee-books show that it was precisely this general law practice that he did engage in, both in court and out of court; a practice only a small portion of which was criminal, the larger part of it consisting of the ordinary suits in country litigation; a practice which certainly involved the drawing of pleadings, and the preparation of many sorts of legal papers; a practice, moreover, which he seems to have acquired with extraordinary rapidity, and to have maintained with increasing success as long as he cared for it. These are items of history which are likely to burden the ordinary reader with no little perplexity, — a perplexity the elements of which are thus modestly stated by a living grandson of Patrick Henry: "How he acquired or retained a practice so large and continually increasing, so perfectly unfit for it as Mr. Jefferson represents him, I am at a loss to understand." [1]

As we go further in the study of this man's life, we shall have before us ample materials for dealing still further and still more definitely with the subject of his professional character, as that character itself became developed and matured. Meantime, however, the evidence already in view seems quite enough to enable us to form a tolerably clear notion of the sort of lawyer he was down to the end of 1763, which may be regarded as the period of his novitiate at the bar. It is perfectly evident that, at the time of his admission to the bar, he knew very little of the law, either in its principles or in its forms: he knew no more than could have been learned by a young man of genius in the course of four weeks in the study of Coke upon Littleton, and of the laws of Virginia. If, now, we are at liberty to suppose that his study of the

[1] William Wirt Henry, *Character and Public Career of Patrick Henry*, 3.

law then ceased, we may accept the view of his
professional incompetence held up by Jefferson;
but precisely that is what we are not at liberty to
suppose. All the evidence, fairly sifted, warrants
the belief that, on his return to Hanover with his
license to practice law, he used the next few months
in the further study of it; and that thenceforward,
just so fast as professional business came to his
hands, he tried to qualify himself to do that business, and to do it so well that his clients should
be inclined to come to him again in case of need.
Patrick Henry's is not the first case, neither is it
the last one, of a man coming to the bar miserably
unqualified for its duties, but afterward becoming
well qualified. We need not imagine, we do not
imagine, that he ever became a man of great learning in the law; but we do find it impossible to
believe that he continued to be a man of great
ignorance in it. The law, indeed, is the one profession on ear. h in which such success as he is
proved to have had, is impossible to such incompetence as he is said to have had. Moreover, in
trying to form a just idea of Patrick Henry, it is
never safe to forget that we have to do with a man
of genius, and that the ways by which a man of
genius reaches his results are necessarily his own,
— are often invisible, are always somewhat mysterious, to the rest of us. The genius of Patrick
Henry was powerful, intuitive, swift; by a glance
of the eye he could take in what an ordinary man
might spend hours in toiling for; his memory held

whatever was once committed to it; all his resources were at instant command; his faculty for
debate, his imagination, humor, tact, diction, elo-
cution, were rich and exquisite; he was also a man
of human and friendly ways, whom all men loved,
and whom all men wanted to help; and it would
not have been strange if he actually fitted himself
for the successful practice of such law business as
was then to be had in Virginia, and actually entered upon its successful practice with a quickness
the exact processes of which were unperceived even
by his nearest neighbors.

CHAPTER IV

A CELEBRATED CASE

THUS Patrick Henry had been for nearly four years in the practice of the law, with a vigor and a success quite extraordinary, when, late in the year 1763, he became concerned in a case so charged with popular interest, and so well suited to the display of his own marvellous genius as an advocate, as to make both him and his case immediately celebrated.

The side upon which he was retained happened to be the wrong side, — wrong both in law and in equity; having only this element of strength in it, namely, that by a combination of circumstances there were enlisted in its favor precisely those passions of the multitude which are the most selfish, the most blinding, and at the same time the most energetic. It only needed an advocate skilful enough to play effectively upon these passions, and a storm would be raised before which mere considerations of law and of equity would be swept out of sight.

In order to understand the real issue presented by "the Parsons' Cause," and consequently the essential weakness of the side to the service of which our young lawyer was now summoned, we shall need to turn about and take a brief tour into the earlier history of Virginia. In that colony, from the beginning, the Church of England was established by law, and was supported, like any other institution of the government, by revenues derived from taxation, — taxation levied in this case upon nearly all persons in the colony above the age of sixteen years. Moreover, those local subdivisions which, in the Northern colonies, were called towns, in Virginia were called parishes; and accordingly, in the latter, the usual local officers who manage the public business for each civil neighborhood were called, not selectmen or supervisors, as at the North, but vestrymen. Among the functions conferred by the law upon these local officers in Virginia was that of hiring the rector or minister, and of paying him his salary; and the same authority which gave to the vestry this power fixed likewise the precise amount of salary which they were to pay. Ever since the early days of the colony, this amount had been stated, not in money, which hardly existed there, but in tobacco, which was the staple of the colony. Sometimes the market value of tobacco would be very low, — so low that the portion paid to the minister would yield a sum quite insufficient for his support; and on such occasions, prior to 1692, the parishes had often kindly made up for such depreciation by voluntarily paying an extra quantity of tobacco.[1]

[1] Perry, *Hist. Coll.* i. 12.

After 1692, however, for reasons which need not now be detailed, this generous custom seems to have disappeared. For example, from 1709 to 1714, the price of tobacco was so low as to make its shipment to England, in many instances, a positive loss to its owner; while the sale of it on the spot was so disadvantageous as to reduce the minister's salary to about £25 a year, as reckoned in the depreciated paper currency of the colony. Of course, during those years, the distress of the clergy was very great; but, whatever it may have been, they were permitted to bear it, without any suggestion, either from the legislature or from the vestries, looking toward the least addition to the quantity of tobacco then to be paid them. On the other hand, from 1714 to 1720, the price of tobacco rose considerably above the average, and did something towards making up to the clergy the losses which they had recently incurred. Then, again, from 1720 to 1724, tobacco fell to the low price of the former period, and of course with the same results of unrelieved loss to the clergy.[1] Thus, however, in the process of time, there had become established, in the fiscal relations of each vestry to its minister, a rough but obvious system of fair play. When the price of tobacco was down, the parson was expected to suffer the loss; when the price of tobacco was up, he was allowed to enjoy the gain. Probably it did not then occur to any one that a majority of the good people of

---

[1] Perry, *Hist. Coll.* 316, 317.

Virginia could ever be brought to demand such a mutilation of justice as would be involved in depriving the parson of the occasional advantage of a very good market, and of making up for this by always leaving to him the undisturbed enjoyment of every occasional bad one. Yet it was just this mutilation of justice which, only a few years later, a majority of the good people of Virginia were actually brought to demand, and which, by the youthful genius of Patrick Henry, they were too well aided in effecting.

Returning now from our brief tour into a period of Virginian history just prior to that upon which we are at present engaged, we find ourselves arrived at the year 1748, in which year the legislature of Virginia, revising all previous regulations respecting the hiring and paying of the clergy, passed an act, directing that every parish minister should "receive an annual salary of 16,000 pounds of tobacco, . . . to be levied, assessed, collected, and paid" by the vestry. "And if the vestry of any parish" should "neglect or refuse to levy the tobacco due to the minister," they should "be liable to the action of the party grieved . . . for all damages which he . . . shall sustain by such refusal or neglect."[1] This act of the colonial legislature, having been duly approved by the king, became a law, and consequently was not liable to repeal or even to suspension except by the king's approval. Thus, at the period now reached, there

[1] Hening, *Statutes at Large*, vi. 88, 89.

was between every vestry and its minister a valid
contract for the annual payment, by the former to
the latter, of that particular quantity of tobacco,
— the clergy to take their chances as to the market
value of the product from year to year.

Thus matters ran on until 1755, when, by reason
of a diminished crop of tobacco, the legislature
passed an option law,[1] virtually suspending for
the next ten months the Act of 1748, and requiring the clergy, at the option of the vestries, to
receive their salaries for that year, not in tobacco,
but in the depreciated paper currency of the colony, at the rate of two pence for each pound of
tobacco due, — a price somewhat below the market
value of the article for that year. Most clearly
this act, which struck an arbitrary blow at the
validity of all contracts in Virginia, was one which
exceeded the constitutional authority of the legislature; since it suspended, without the royal approval, a law which had been regularly ratified by
the king. However, the operation of this act was
shrewdly limited to ten months, — a period just
long enough to accomplish its object, but too short
for the royal intervention against it to be of any
direct avail. Under these circumstances, the clergy
bore their losses for that year with some murmur-
ing indeed, but without any formal protest.[2]

Just three years afterward, in 1758, the legislature, with even less excuse than before, passed an

---

[1] *Ibid.* vi. 568, 569.
[2] Perry, *Hist. Coll.* i. 508 509.

act[1] similar to that of 1755, — its force, however, being limited to twelve months. The operation of this act, as affecting each parish minister, may be conveyed in very few words. In lieu of what was due him under the law for his year's services, namely, 16,000 pounds of tobacco, the market value of which for the year in question proved to be about £400 sterling, it compelled him to take, in the paper money of the colony, the sum of about £133. To make matters still worse, while the tobacco which was due him was an instant and an advantageous medium of exchange everywhere, and especially in England whence nearly all his merchant supplies were obtained, this paper money that was forced upon him was a depreciated currency even within the colony, and absolutely worthless outside of it; so that the poor parson, who could never demand his salary for any year until six full months after its close, would have proffered to him, at the end, perhaps, of another six months, just one third of the nominal sum due him, and that in a species of money of no value at all except in Virginia, and even in Virginia of a purchasing value not exceeding that of £20 sterling in England.[2]

Nor, in justification of such a measure, could it be truthfully said that there was at that time in the colony any general "dearth and scarcity,"[3] or

[1] Hening, *Statutes at Large*, vii. 240, 241.
[2] Perry, *Hist. Coll.* i. 467, 468.
[3] As was alleged in Richard Bland's *Letter to the Clergy*, 17.

any such public distress of any sort as might over-
rule the ordinary maxims of justice, and excuse,
in the name of humanity, a merely technical violation of law.   As a matter of fact, the only "dearth
and scarcity" in Virginia that year was "confined
to one or two counties on James River, and that
entirely owing to their own fault;"[1] wherever
there was any failure of the tobacco crop, it was
due to the killing of the plants so early in the
spring, that such land did not need to lie uncultivated, and in most cases was planted "in corn and
pease, which always turned to good account;"[2]
and although, for the whole colony, the crop of
tobacco "was short in quantity," yet "in cash
value it proved to be the best crop that Virginia
had ever had" since the settlement of the colony.[3]
Finally, it was by no means the welfare of the
poor that "was the object, or the effect, of the
law;" but it was "the rich planters" who, first
selling their tobacco at about fifty shillings the
hundred, and then paying to the clergy and others
their tobacco debts at the rate of sixteen shillings
the hundred, were "the chief gainers" by the act.[4]

Such, then, in all its fresh and unadorned ras-
cality, was the famous "option law," or "two-
penny act," of 1758: an act firmly opposed, on its
first appearance in the legislature, by a noble

---

[1] Perry, *Hist. Coll.* i. 467.
[2] *Ibid.* i. 466.
[3] *Ibid.* i. 465, 466.
[4] Meade, *Old Families of Virginia*, i. 223.

minority of honorable men; an act clearly indicating among a portion of the people of Virginia a survival of the old robber instincts of our Norse ancestors; an act having there the sort of frantic popularity that all laws are likely to have which give a dishonest advantage to the debtor class, — and in Virginia, unfortunately, on the subject of salaries due to the clergy, nearly all persons above sixteen years of age belonged to that class.[1]

At the time when this act was before the legislature for consideration, the clergy applied for a hearing, but were refused. Upon its passage by the two houses, the clergy applied to the acting governor, hoping to obtain his disapproval of the act; but his reply was an unblushing avowal of

[1] In the account here given of these Virginia "option laws," I have been obliged, by lack of space, to give somewhat curtly the bald results of rather careful studies which I have made upon the question in all accessible documents of the period; and I have not been at liberty to state many things, on both sides of the question, which would be necessary to a complete discussion of the subject. For instance, among the motives to be mentioned for the popularity of laws whose chief effects were to diminish the pay of the established clergy, should be considered those connected with a growing dissent from the established church in Virginia, and particularly with the very human dislike which even churchmen might have to paying in the form of a compulsory tax what they would have cheerfully paid in the form of a voluntary contribution. Perhaps the best modern defense of these laws is by A. H. Everett, in his *Life of Henry*, 230–233; but his statements seem to be founded on imperfect information. Wirt, publishing his opinion under the responsibility of his great professional and official position, affirms that on the whole question, "the clergy had much the best of the argument." *Life of Henry*, 22.

his determination to pursue any course, right or wrong, which would bring him popular favor. They then sent one of their own number to England, for the purpose of soliciting the royal disallowance of the act. After a full hearing of both sides, the privy council gave it as their opinion that the clergy of Virginia had their "certain remedy at law;" Lord Hardwicke, in particular, declaring that "there was no occasion to dispute about the authority by which the act was passed; for that no court in the judicature whatever could look upon it to be law, by reason of its manifest injustice alone." [1] Accordingly, the royal disallowance was granted. Upon the arrival in Virginia of these tidings, several of the clergy began suits against their respective vestries, for the purpose of compelling them to pay the amounts then legally due upon their salaries for the year 1758.

Of these suits, the first to come to trial was that of the Rev. Thomas Warrington, in the County Court of Elizabeth City. In that case, "a jury of his own parishioners found for him considerable damages, allowing on their oaths that there was above twice as much justly due to him as the act had granted;" [2] but "the court hindered him from immediately coming at the damages, by judging the act to be law, in which it is thought they were influenced more by the fear of giving offense to their superiors, than by their own opinion of the

[1] Perry, *Hist. Coll.* i. 510.
[2] *Ibid.* i. 513, 514.

reasonableness of the act, — they privately professing that they thought the parson ought to have his right." [1]

Soon afterward came to trial, in the court of King William County, the suit of the Rev. Alexander White, rector of St. David's parish. In this case, the court, instead of either sustaining or rejecting the disallowed act, simply shirked their responsibility, "refused to meddle in the matter, and insisted on leaving the whole affair to the jury;" who being thus freed from all judicial control, straightway rendered a verdict of neat and comprehensive lawlessness: "We bring in for the defendant." [2]

It was at this stage of affairs that the court of Hanover County reached the case of the Rev. James Maury, rector of Fredericksville parish, Louisa; and the court, having before it the evidence of the royal disallowance of the Act of 1758, squarely "adjudged the act to be no law." Of course, under this decision, but one result seemed possible. As the court had thus rejected the validity of the act whereby the vestry had withheld from their parson two thirds of his salary for the year 1758, it only remained to summon a special jury on a writ of inquiry to determine the damages thus sustained by the parson; and as this was a very simple question of arithmetic, the counsel for the defendants expressed his desire to withdraw from the case.

[1] *Ibid.* i. 496, 497.
[2] Perr~ *Hist. Coll.* i. 497.

Such was the situation, when these defendants,
having been assured by their counsel that all further struggle would be hopeless, turned for help
to the enterprising young lawyer who, in that very
place, had been for the previous three and a half
years pushing his way to notice in his profession.
To him, accordingly, they brought their cause, —
a desperate cause, truly, — a cause already lost
and abandoned by veteran and eminent counsel.
Undoubtedly, by the ethics of his profession, Patrick Henry was bound to accept the retainer that
was thus tendered him; and, undoubtedly, by the
organization of his own mind, having once accepted
that retainer, he was likely to devote to the cause
no tepid or half-hearted service.

The decision of the court, which has been referred to, was rendered at its November session.
On the first day of the session in December, the
order was executed for summoning a select jury
"to examine whether the plaintiff had sustained
any damages, and what." [1] Obviously, in the determination of these two questions, much would
depend on the personal composition of the jury;
and it is apparent that this matter was diligently
attended to by the sheriff. His plan seems to
have been to secure a good, honest jury of twelve
adult male persons, but without having among
them a single one of those over-scrupulous and
intractable people who, in Virginia, at that time,
were still technically described as gentlemen.

[1] Maury, *Mem. of a Huguenot Family*, 419.

With what delicacy and efficiency he managed this part of the business was thus described shortly afterward by the plaintiff, of course a deeply interested eye-witness: —

" The sheriff went into a public room full of gentlemen, and told his errand. One excused himself. . . as having already given his opinion in a similar case. On this, . . . he immediately left the room, without summoning any one person there. He afterwards met another gentleman . . . on the green, and, on saying he was not fit to serve, being a church warden, he took upon himself to excuse him, too, and, as far as I can learn made no further attempts to summon gentlemen. . . . Hence he went among the vulgar herd. After he had selected and set down upon his list about eight or ten of these, I met him with it in his hand, and on looking over it, observed to him that they were not such jurors as the court had directed him to get, — being people of whom I had never heard before, except one whom, I told him, he knew to be a party in the cause. . . . Yet this man's name was not erased. He was even called in court, and had he not excused himself, would probably have been admitted. For I cannot recollect that the court expressed either surprise or dislike that a more proper jury had not been summoned. Nay, though I objected against them, yet, as Patrick Henry, one of the defendants' lawyers, insisted they were honest men, and, therefore, unexceptionable, they were immediately called to the book and sworn." [1]

Having thus secured a jury that must have been reasonably satisfactory to the defendants, the hear-

[1] Maury, *Mem. of a Huguenot Family*, 419, 420.

ing began. Two gentlemen, being the largest pur-
chasers of tobacco in the county, were then sworn
as witnesses to prove the market price of the article in 1759. By their testimony it was established
that the price was then more than three times as
much as had been estimated in the payment of
paper money actually made to the plaintiff in that
year. Upon this state of facts, "the lawyers on
both sides" proceeded to display "the force and
weight of the evidence;" after which the case was
given to the jury. "In less than five minutes,"
they "brought in a verdict for the plaintiff, — one
penny damages." [1]

Just how the jury were induced, in the face of
the previous judgment of that very court, to render this astounding verdict, has been described in
two narratives: one by William Wirt, written
about fifty years after the event; the other by the
injured plaintiff himself, the Rev. James Maury,
written exactly twelve days after the event. Few
things touching the life of Patrick Henry can be
more notable or more instructive than the contrast
presented by these two narratives.

On reaching the scene of action, on the 1st of
December, Patrick Henry "found," says Wirt, —

"on the courtyard such a concourse as would have ap-
palled any other man in his situation. They were not people of the county merely who were there, but visitors from
all the counties to a considerable distance around. The
decision upon the demurrer had produced a violent fer-

[1] *Ibid.* 420.

ment among the people, and equal exultation on the part of the clergy, who attended the court in a large body, either to look down opposition, or to enjoy the final triumph of this hard fought contest, which they now considered as perfectly secure. . . . Soon after the opening of the court the cause was called. . . . The array before Mr. Henry's eyes was now most fearful. On the bench sat more than twenty clergymen, the most learned men in the colony. . . . The courthouse was crowded with an overwhelming multitude, and surrounded with an immense and anxious throng, who, not finding room to enter, were endeavoring to listen without in the deepest attention. But there was something still more awfully disconcerting than all this; for in the chair of the presiding magistrate sat no other person than his own father. Mr. Lyons opened the cause very briefly. . . . And now came on the first trial of Patrick Henry's strength. No one had ever heard him speak, [1] and curiosity was on tiptoe. He rose very awkwardly, and faltered much in his exordium. The people hung their heads at so unpromising a commencement; the clergy were observed to exchange sly looks with each other; and his father is described as having almost sunk with confusion, from his seat. But these feelings were of short duration, and soon gave place to others of a very different character. For now were those wonderful faculties which he possessed, for the first time developed; and now was first witnessed that mysterious and almost supernatural transformation of appearance, which the fire of his own eloquence never failed to work in him. For as his mind rolled along, and began to

[1] This cannot be true except in the sense that he had never before spoken to such an assemblage or in any great cause.

glow from its own action, all the exuviæ of the clown
seemed to shed themselves spontaneously. His attitude,
by degrees, became erect and lofty. The spirit of his
genius awakened all his features. His countenance
shone with a nobleness and grandeur which it had never
before exhibited. There was a lightning in his eyes
which seemed to rive the spectator. His action became
graceful, bold, and commanding; and in the tones of
his voice, but more especially in his emphasis, there was
a peculiar charm, a magic, of which any one who ever
heard him will speak as soon as he is named, but of
which no one can give any adequate description. They
can only say that it struck upon the ear and upon the
heart, in a manner which language cannot tell. Add to
all these, his wonder-working fancy, and the peculiar
phraseology in which he clothed its images: for he
painted to the heart with a force that almost petrified it.
In the language of those who heard him on this occasion, ' he made their blood run cold, and their hair to
rise on end.'

" It will not be difficult for any one who ever heard
this most extraordinary man, to believe the whole account of this transaction which is given by his surviving
hearers; and from their account, the court house of
Hanover County must have exhibited, on this occasion,
a scene as picturesque as has been ever witnessed in
real life. They say that the people, whose countenance
had fallen as he arose, had heard but a very few sentences before they began to look up; then to look at
each other with surprise, as if doubting the evidence
of their own senses; then, attracted by some strong gesture, struck by some majestic attitude, fascinated by the
spell of his eye, the charm of his emphasis, and the

varied and commanding expression of his countenance, they could look away no more. In less than twenty minutes, they might be seen in every part of the house, on every bench, in every window, stooping forward from their stands, in death-like silence; their features fixed in amazement and awe; all their senses listening and riveted upon the speaker, as if to catch the least strain of some heavenly visitant. The mockery of the clergy was soon turned into alarm; their triumph into confusion and despair; and at one burst of his rapid and overwhelming invective, they fled from the house in precipitation and terror. As for the father, such was his surprise, such his amazement, such his rapture, that, forgetting where he was, and the character which he was filling, tears of ecstasy streamed down his cheeks, without the power or inclination to repress them.

"The jury seem to have been so completely bewildered, that they lost sight not only of the Act of 1748, but that of 1758 also; for, thoughtless even of the admitted right of the plaintiff, they had scarcely left the bar, when they returned with a verdict of one penny damages. A motion was made for a new trial; but the court, too, had now lost the equipoise of their judgment, and overruled the motion by an unanimous vote. The verdict and judgment overruling the motion were followed by redoubled acclamations, from within and without the house. The people, who had with difficulty kept their hands off their champion from the moment of closing his harangue, no sooner saw the fate of the cause finally sealed, than they seized him at the bar; and in spite of his own exertions, and the continued cry of order from the sheriffs and the court, they bore him out of the courthouse, and raising him on their shoul-

ders, carried him about the yard, in a kind of election-
eering triumph." [1]

At the time when Wirt wrote this rhapsody, he
was unable, as he tells us, to procure from any
quarter a rational account of the line of argument
taken by Patrick Henry, or even of any other than
a single topic alluded to by him in the course of
his speech, — they who heard the speech saying
"that when it was over, they felt as if they had
just awaked from some ecstatic dream, of which
they were unable to recall or connect the particulars." [2]

There was present in that assemblage, however,
at least one person who listened to the young orator
without falling into an ecstatic dream, and whose
senses were so well preserved to him through it all
that he was able, a few days afterward, while the
whole occasion was fresh in his memory, to place
upon record a clear and connected version of the
wonder-working speech. This version is to be
found in a letter written by the plaintiff on the
12th of December, 1763, and has been brought to
light only within recent years.

After giving, for the benefit of the learned
counsel by whom the cause was to be managed, on
appeal, in the general court, a lucid and rather
critical account of the whole proceeding, Maury
adds: —

"One occurrence more, though not essential to the

[1] Wirt, 23–27.   [2] Ibid. 29.

cause, I can't help mentioning. . . . Mr. Henry, mentioned above (who had been called in by the defendants, as we suspected, to do what I some time ago told you of), after Mr. Lyons had opened the cause, rose and harangued the jury for near an hour. This harangue turned upon points as much out of his own depth, and that of the jury, as they were foreign from the purpose, — which it would be impertinent to mention here. However, after he had discussed those points, he labored to prove 'that the Act of 1758 had every characteristic of a good law ; that it was a law of general utility, and could not, consistently with what he called the original compact between the king and people . . . be annulled.' Hence he inferred, 'that a king, by disallowing acts of this salutary nature, from being the father of his people, degenerated into a tyrant, and forfeits all right to his subjects' obedience.' He further urged 'that the only use of an established church and clergy in society, is to enforce obedience to civil sanctions, and the observance of those which are called duties of imperfect obligation ; that when a clergy ceases to answer these ends, the community have no further need of their ministry, and may justly strip them of their appointments ; that the clergy of Virginia, in this particular instance of their refusing to acquiesce in the law in question, had been so far from answering, that they had most notoriously counteracted, those great ends of their institution ; that, therefore, instead of useful members of the state, they ought to be considered as enemies of the community ; and that, in the case now before them, Mr. Maury, instead of countenance, and protection, and damages, very justly deserved to be punished with signal severity.' And then he perorates to the following purpose, 'that excepting they (the jury) were disposed to rivet the chains of bondage on their own necks, he hoped they would not let slip the opportunity which now offered, of making such an example of him as might, hereafter, be a warning to himself and his brethren, not to have the temerity, for the future, to dispute the validity of such laws, authenticated by the only authority which, in his conception, could give force to laws for the government of this colony, — the authority of a legal representative of a council, and of a kind and benevolent and patriot governor.' You'll observe I do not pretend to remember his words, but take this to have been the sum and substance of this part of his labored oration. When he came to that part of it where he undertook to assert 'that a king, by annulling or disallowing acts of so salutary a nature, from being the father of his people, degenerated into a tyrant, and forfeits all right to his subjects' obedience,' the more sober part of the audience were struck with horror. Mr. Lyons called out aloud, and with an honest warmth, to the Bench, 'that the gentleman had spoken treason,' and expressed his astonishment, 'that their worships could hear it without emotion, or any mark of dissatisfaction.' At the same instant, too, amongst some gentlemen in the crowd behind me, was a confused murmur of 'treason, treason!' Yet Mr. Henry went on in the same treasonable and licentious strain, without interruption from the Bench, nay, even without receiving the least exterior notice of their disapprobation. One of the jury, too, was so highly pleased with these doctrines, that, as I was afterwards told, he every now and then gave the traitorous declaimer a nod of approbation. After the court was adjourned, he apologized to me for what he had said, alleging that his sole view in engaging in the cause, and in saying what he had, was to render himself popular. You see, then, it is so clear a point in this person's opinion that the ready road to popularity here is to trample under foot the interests of religion, the rights of the church, and the prerogatives of the crown."[1]

[1] Maury, *Mem. of a Huguenot Family*, 418–424, where the entire letter is given in print for the first time.

CHAPTER V

FIRST TRIUMPHS AT THE CAPITAL

IT is not in the least strange that the noble-minded clergyman, who was the plaintiff in the famous cause of the Virginia parsons, should have been deeply offended by the fierce and victorious eloquence of the young advocate on the opposite side, and should have let fall, with reference to him, some bitter words. Yet it could only be in a moment of anger that any one who knew him could ever have said of Patrick Henry that he was disposed "to trample under foot the interests of religion," or that he had any ill-will toward the church or its ministers. It is very likely that, in the many irritations growing out of a civil establishment of the church in his native colony, he may have shared in feelings that were not uncommon even among devout churchmen there; but in spite of this, then and always, to the very end of his life, his most sacred convictions and his tenderest affections seem to have been on the side of the institutions and ministers of Christianity, and even of Christianity in its historic form. Accordingly, both before and after his great speech, he tried to indicate to the good men whose legal

claims it had become his professional duty to resist,
that such resistance must not be taken by them as
implying on his part any personal unkindness. To
his uncle and namesake, the Reverend Patrick
Henry, who was even then a plaintiff in a similar
suit, and whom he had affectionately persuaded
not to remain at the courthouse to hear the coming speech against the pecuniary demands of himself and his order, he said "that the clergy had
not thought him worthy of being retained on their
side," and that "he knew of no moral principle
by which he was bound to refuse a fee from their
adversaries." [1] So, too, the conciliatory words,
which, after the trial, he tried to speak to the indignant plaintiff, and which the latter has reported
in the blunt form corresponding to his own angry
interpretation of them, after all may have borne
the better meaning given to them by Bishop Meade,
who says that Patrick Henry, in his apology to
Maury, "pleaded as an excuse for his course, that
he was a young lawyer, a candidate for practice
and reputation, and therefore must make the best
of his cause." [2]

These genial efforts at pacification are of rather
more than casual significance: they are indications
of character. They mark a distinct quality of the
man's nature, of which he continued to give evidence during the rest of his life, — a certain sweetness of spirit, which never deserted him through

[1] Wirt, 24.
[2] Meade, *Old Families and Churches of Va.* i. 220.

all the stern conflicts of his career. He was always a good fighter: never a good hater. He had the brain and the temperament of an advocate; his imagination and his heart always kindled hotly to the side that he had espoused, and with his imagination and his heart always went all the rest of the man; in his advocacy of any cause that he had thus made his own, he hesitated at no weapon either of offence or of defence; he struck hard blows — he spoke hard words — and he usually triumphed; and yet, even in the paroxysms of the combat, and still more so when the combat was over, he showed how possible it is to be a redoubtable antagonist without having a particle of malice.

Then, too, from this first great scene in his public life, there comes down to us another incident that has its own story to tell. In all the roar of talk within and about the courthouse, after the trial was over, one "Mr. Cootes, merchant of James River," was heard to say that "he would have given a considerable sum out of his own pocket rather than his friend Patrick should have been guilty of a crime but little, if any thing, inferior to that which brought Simon Lord Lovat to the block," — adding that Patrick's speech had "exceeded the most seditious and inflammatory harangues of the Tribunes of Old Rome."[1] Here, then, thus early in his career, even in this sorrowful and alarmed criticism on the supposed error of

[1] Maury, *Mem. of a Huguenot Fam.* 423.

his speech, we find a token of that loving interest in him and in his personal fate, which even in those days began to possess the heartstrings of many a Virginian all about the land, and which thenceforward steadily broadened and deepened into a sort of popular idolization of him. The mysterious hold which Patrick Henry came to have upon the people of Virginia is an historic fact, to be recognized, even if not accounted for. He was to make enemies in abundance, as will appear; he was to stir up against himself the alarm of many thoughtful and conservative minds, the deadly hatred of many an old leader in colonial politics, the deadly envy of many a younger aspirant to public influence; he was to go on ruffling the plumage and upsetting the combinations of all sorts of good citizens, who, from time to time, in making their reckonings without him, kept finding that they had reckoned without their host. But for all that, the willingness of this worthy Mr. Cootes of James River to part with his money, if need be, rather than his friend Patrick should go far wrong, seems to be one token of the beginning of that deep and swelling passion of love for him that never abated among the mass of the people of Virginia so long as Patrick lived, and perhaps has never abated since.

It is not hard to imagine the impulse which so astonishing a forensic success must have given to the professional and political career of the young advocate. Not only was he immediately retained

by the defendants in all the other suits of the same
kind then instituted in the courts of the colony,
but, as his fee-books show, from that hour his legal
practice of every sort received an enormous increase.   Moreover, the people of Virginia, always
a warm-hearted people, were then, to a degree
almost inconceivable at the North, sensitive to
oratory, and admirers of eloquent men.   The first
test by which they commonly ascertained the fitness of a man for public office, concerned his ability to make a speech; and it cannot be doubted
that from the moment of Patrick Henry's amazing
harangue in the "Parsons' Cause," — a piece of
oratory altogether surpassing anything ever before
heard in Virginia, — the eyes of men began to
fasten upon him as destined to some splendid and
great part in political life.

During the earlier years of his career, Williamsburg was the capital of the colony, — the official
residence of its governor, the place of assemblage
for its legislature and its highest courts, and, at
certain seasons of the year, the scene of no little
vice-regal and provincial magnificence.

Thither our Patrick had gone in 1760 to get
permission to be a lawyer.   Thither he now goes
once more, in 1764, to give some proof of his quality in the profession to which he had been reluctantly admitted, and to win for himself the first of
a long series of triumphs at the colonial capital,
— triumphs which gave food for wondering talk
to all his contemporaries, and long lingered in the

memories of old men.   Soon after the assembling
of the legislature, in the fall of 1764, the committee on privileges and elections had before them the
case of James Littlepage, who had taken his seat
as member for the county of Hanover, but whose
right to the seat was contested, on a charge of
bribery and corruption, by Nathaniel West Dandridge.   For a day or two before the hearing of
the case, the members of the house had "observed
an ill-dressed young man sauntering in the lobby,"
apparently a stranger to everybody, moving "awkwardly about . . . with a countenance of abstrac-
tion and total unconcern as to what was passing
around him;" but who, when the 'committee convened to consider the case of Dandridge against
Littlepage, at once took his place as counsel for
the former.   The members of the committee, either
not catching his name or not recalling the association attaching to it from the scene at Hanover
Court House nearly a twelvemonth before, were
so affected by his rustic and ungainly appearance
that they treated him with neglect and even with
discourtesy; until, when his turn came to argue
the cause of his client, he poured forth such a torrent of eloquence, and exhibited with so much
force and splendor the sacredness of the suffrage
and the importance of protecting it, that the inci-
vility and contempt of the committee were turned
into admiration.[1]   Nevertheless, it appears from
the journals of the House that, whatever may have

[1] Wirt, 39-41.

been the admiration of the committee for the eloquence of Mr. Dandridge's advocate, they did not award the seat to Mr. Dandridge.

Such was Patrick Henry's first contact with the legislature of Virginia,—a body of which he was soon to become a member, and over which, in spite of the social prestige, the talents, and the envious opposition of its old leaders, he was promptly to gain an ascendancy that constituted him, almost literally, the dictator of its proceedings, so long as he chose to hold a place in it. On the present occasion, having finished the somewhat obscure business that had brought him before the committee, it is probable that he instantly disappeared from the scene, not to return to it until the following spring, when he came back to transact business with the House itself. For, early in May, 1765, a vacancy having occurred in the representation for the county of Louisa, Patrick Henry, though not then a resident in that county, was elected as its member. The first entry to be met with in the journals, indicating his presence in the House, is that of his appointment, on the 20th of May, as an additional member of the committee for courts of justice. Between that date and the 1st of June, when the House was angrily dissolved by the governor, this young and very rural member contrived to do two or three quite notable things — things, in fact, so notable that they conveyed to the people of Virginia the tidings of the advent among them of a great political leader, gave an historic impulse to the series of measures which ended in the disruption of the British Empire, and set his own name a ringing through the world, — not without lively imputations of treason, and comforting assurances that he was destined to be hanged.

The first of these notable things is one which incidentally throws a rather painful glare on the corruptions of political life in our old and belauded colonial days.   The speaker of the House of Burgesses at that time was John Robinson, a man of great estate, foremost among all the landed aristocracy of Virginia.   He had then been speaker for about twenty-five years; for a long time, also, he had been treasurer of the colony; and in the latter capacity he had been accustomed for many years to lend the public money, on his own private account, to his personal and political friends, and particularly to those of them who were members of the House.   This profligate business had continued so long that Robinson had finally become a defaulter to an enormous amount; and in order to avert the shame and ruin of an exposure, he and his particular friends, just before the arrival of Patrick Henry, had invented a very pretty device, to be called a "public loan office," — "from which monies might be lent on public account, and on good landed security, to individuals," and by which, as was expected, the debts due to Robinson on the loans which he had been granting might be "transferred to the public, and his deficit thus

completely covered." [1]   Accordingly, the scheme
was brought forward under nearly every possible
advantage of influential support.   It was presented
to the House and to the public as a measure eminently wise and beneficial.   It was supported in
the House by many powerful and honorable members who had not the remotest suspicion of the
corrupt purpose lying at the bottom of it.   Apparently it was on the point of adoption when, from
among the members belonging to the upper counties, there arose this raw youth, who had only just
taken his seat, and who, without any information
respecting the secret intent of the measure, and
equally without any disposition to let the older
and statelier members do his thinking for him,
simply attacked it, as a scheme to be condemned
on general principles.   From the door of the lobby
that day there stood peering into the Assembly
Thomas Jefferson, then a law student at Williamsburg, who thus had the good luck to witness the
début of his old comrade.   "He laid open with so
much energy the spirit of favoritism on which the
proposition was founded, and the abuses to which
it would lead, that it was crushed in its birth." [2]
He "attacked the scheme . . . in that style of
bold, grand, and overwhelming eloquence for which
he became so justly celebrated afterwards.   He
carried with him all the members of the upper
counties, and left a minority composed merely of

[1] Mem. by Jefferson, in *Hist. Mag.* for 1867, 91.
[2] Jefferson's *Works*, vi. 365.

the aristocracy of the country. From this time his popularity swelled apace; and Robinson dying four years after, his deficit was brought to light, and discovered the true object of the proposition."[1]

But a subject far greater than John Robinson's project for a loan office was then beginning to weigh on men's minds. Already were visible far off on the edge of the sky, the first filmy threads of a storm-cloud that was to grow big and angry as the years went by, and was to accompany a political tempest under which the British Empire would be torn asunder, and the whole structure of American colonial society wrenched from its foundations. Just one year before the time now reached, news had been received in Virginia that the British ministry had announced in parliament their purpose to introduce, at the next session, an act for laying certain stamp duties on the American colonies. Accordingly, in response to these tidings, the House of Burgesses, in the autumn of 1764, had taken the earliest opportunity to send a respectful message to the government of England, declaring that the proposed act would be deemed by the loyal and affectionate people of Virginia as an alarming violation of their ancient constitutional rights. This message had been elaborately drawn up, in the form of an address to the king, a memorial to the House of Lords, and a remonstrance to the Commons;[2] the writers being a committee com-

---

[1] Mem. by Jefferson, in *Hist. Mag.* for 1867, 91.

[2] These documents are given in full in the Appendix to Wirt's *Life of Henry*, as Note A.

posed of gentlemen prominent in the legislature, and of high social standing in the colony, including Landon Carter, Richard Henry Lee, George Wythe, Edmund Pendleton, Benjamin Harrison, Richard Bland, and even Peyton Randolph, the king's attorney-general.

Meantime, to this appeal no direct answer had been returned; instead of which, however, was received by the House of Burgesses, in May, 1765, about the time of Patrick Henry's accession to that body, a copy of the Stamp Act itself. What was to be done about it? What was to be done by Virginia? What was to be done by her sister colonies? Of course, by the passage of the Stamp Act, the whole question of colonial procedure on the subject had been changed. While the act was, even in England, merely a theme for consideration, and while the colonies were virtually under invitation to send thither their views upon the subject, it was perfectly proper for colonial pamphleteers and for colonial legislatures to express, in every civilized form, their objections to it. But all this was now over. The Stamp Act had been discussed; the discussion was ended; the act had been decided on; it had become a law. Criticism upon it now, especially by a legislative body, was a very different matter from what criticism upon it had been, even by the same body, a few months before. Then, the loyal legislature of Virginia had fittingly spoken out, concerning the contemplated act, its manly words of disapproval and of protest; but now that the contemplated act had become an adopted act — had become the law of the land — could that same legislature again speak even those same words, without thereby becoming disloyal, — without venturing a little too near the verge of sedition, — without putting itself into an attitude, at least, of incipient nullification respecting a law of the general government?

It is perfectly evident that by all the old leaders of the House at that moment, — by Peyton Randolph, and Pendleton, and Wythe, and Bland, and the rest of them, — this question was answered in the negative. Indeed, it could be answered in no other way. Such being the case, it followed that, for Virginia and for all her sister colonies, an entirely new state of things had arisen. A most serious problem confronted them, — a problem involving, in fact, incalculable interests. On the subject of immediate concern, they had endeavored, freely and rightfully, to influence legislation, while that legislation was in process; but now that this legislation was accomplished, what were they to do? Were they to submit to it quietly, trusting to further negotiations for ultimate relief, or were they to reject it outright, and try to obstruct its execution? Clearly, here was a very great problem, a problem for statesmanship, — the best statesmanship anywhere to be had. Clearly this was a time, at any rate, for wise and experienced men to come to the front; a time, not for rash counsels, nor for spasmodic and isolated action on the part of any one colony, but for deliberate and united action on the part of all the colonies; a time in which all must move forward, or none. But, thus far, no colony had been heard from: there had not been time. Let Virginia wait a little. Let her make no mistake; let her not push forward into any ill-considered and dangerous measure; let her wait, at least, for some signal of thought or of purpose from her sister colonies. In the meanwhile, let her old and tried leaders continue to lead.

Such, apparently, was the state of opinion in the House of Burgesses when, on the 29th of May, a motion was made and carried, "that the House resolve itself into a committee of the whole House, immediately to consider the steps necessary to be taken in consequence of the resolutions of the House of Commons of Great Britain, relative to the charging certain stamp duties in the colonies and plantations in America." [1] On thus going into committee of the whole, to deliberate on the most difficult and appalling question that, up to that time, had ever come before an American legislature, the members may very naturally have turned in expectation to those veteran politicians and to those able constitutional lawyers who, for many years, had been accustomed to guide their deliberations, and who, especially in the last session, had taken charge of this very question of the Stamp Act. It will not be hard for us to imagine the

[1] *Jour. Va. House of Burgesses.*

disgust, the anger, possibly even the alarm, with which many may have beheld the floor now taken, not by Peyton Randolph, nor Richard Bland, nor George Wythe, nor Edmund Pendleton, but by this new and very unabashed member for the county of Louisa, — this rustic and clownish youth of the terrible tongue, — this eloquent but presumptuous stripling, who was absolutely without training or experience in statesmanship, and was the merest novice even in the forms of the House.

For what precise purpose the new member had thus ventured to take the floor, was known at the moment of his rising by only two other members, — George Johnston, the member for Fairfax, and John Fleming, the member for Cumberland. But the measureless audacity of his purpose, as being nothing less than that of assuming the leadership of the House, and of dictating the policy of Virginia in this stupendous crisis of its fate, was instantly revealed to all, as he moved a series of resolutions, which he proceeded to read from the blank leaf of an old law book, and which, probably, were as follows : —

" *Whereas*, the honorable House of Commons in England have of late drawn into question how far the General Assembly of this colony hath power to enact laws for laying of taxes and imposing duties, payable by the people of this, his majesty's most ancient colony : for settling and ascertaining the same to all future times, the House of Burgesses of this present General Assembly have come to the following resolves : —

" 1. *Resolved*, That the first adventurers and settlers of this, his majesty's colony and dominion, brought with them and transmitted to their posterity, and all other his majesty's subjects, since inhabiting in this, his majesty's said colony, all the privileges, franchises, and immunities that have at any time been held, enjoyed, and possessed, by the people of Great Britain.

" 2. *Resolved*, That by two royal charters, granted by king James the First, the colonists aforesaid are declared entitled to all the privileges, liberties, and immunities of denizens and natural born subjects, to all intents and purposes, as if they had been abiding and born within the realm of England.

" 3. *Resolved*, That the taxation of the people by themselves or by persons chosen by themselves to represent them, who can only know what taxes the people are able to bear, and the easiest mode of raising them, and are equally affected by such taxes themselves, is the distinguishing characteristic of British freedom, and without which the ancient constitution cannot subsist.

" 4. *Resolved*, That his majesty's liege people of this most ancient colony have uninterruptedly enjoyed the right of being thus governed by their own Assembly in the article of their taxes and internal police, and that the same hath never been forfeited, or any other way given up, but hath been constantly recognized by the kings and people of Great Britain.

" 5. *Resolved*, therefore, That the General Assembly of this colony have the only and sole exclusive right and power to lay taxes and impositions upon the inhabitants of this colony; and that every attempt to vest such power in any person or persons whatsoever, other than the General Assembly aforesaid, has a manifest tendency to destroy British as well as American freedom.

"6. *Resolved,* That his majesty's liege people, the inhabitants of this colony, are not bound to yield obedience to any law or ordinance whatever, designed to impose any taxation whatsoever upon them, other than the laws or ordinances of the General Assembly aforesaid.

"7. *Resolved,* That any person who shall, by speaking or writing, assert or maintain that any person or persons, other than the General Assembly of this colony, have any right or power to impose or lay any taxation on the people here, shall be deemed an enemy to his majesty's colony." [1]

No reader will find it hard to accept Jefferson's statement that the debate on these resolutions was "most bloody." "They were opposed by Randolph, Bland, Pendleton, Nicholas, Wythe, and all the old members, whose influence in the House had till then been unbroken." [2] There was every reason, whether of public policy or of private feeling, why the old party leaders in the House should now bestir themselves, and combine, and put forth

[1] Of this famous series of resolutions, the first five are here given precisely as they are given in Patrick Henry's own certified copy still existing in manuscript, and in the possession of Mr. W. W. Henry; but as that copy evidently contains only that portion of the series which was reported from the committee of the whole, and was adopted by the House, I have here printed also what I believe to have been the preamble, and the last two resolutions in the series as first drawn and introduced by Patrick Henry. For this portion of the series, I depend on the copy printed in the *Boston Gazette,* for July 1, 1765, and reprinted in R. Frothingham, *Rise of the Republic,* 180 note. In Wirt's *Life of Henry,* 56–59, is a transcript of the first five resolutions as given in Henry's handwriting: but it is inaccurate in two places.

[2] Mem. by Jefferson, in *Hist. Mag.* for 1867, 91.

all their powers in debate, to check, and if possible to rout and extinguish, this self-conceited but most dangerous young man. "Many threats were uttered, and much abuse cast on me," said Patrick himself, long afterward. Logic, learning, eloquence, denunciation, derision, intimidation, were poured from all sides of the House upon the head of the presumptuous intruder; but alone, or almost alone, he confronted and defeated all his assailants. "Torrents of sublime eloquence from Mr. Henry, backed by the solid reasoning of Johnston, prevailed."[1]

It was sometime in the course of this tremendous fight, extending through the 29th and 30th of May, that the incident occurred which has long been familiar among the anecdotes of the Revolution, and which may be here recalled as a reminiscence not only of his own consummate mastery of the situation, but of a most dramatic scene in an epoch-making debate. Reaching the climax of a passage of fearful invective, on the injustice and the impolicy of the Stamp Act, he said in tones of thrilling solemnity, "Cæsar had his Brutus; Charles the First, his Cromwell; and George the Third ['Treason,' shouted the speaker. 'Treason,' 'treason,' rose from all sides of the room. The orator paused in stately defiance till these rude exclamations were ended, and then, rearing

---

[1] Mem. by Jefferson, in *Hist. Mag.* for 1867, 91. Henry was aided in this debate by Robert Munford, also, and by John Fleming: W. W. Henry, *Life, Corr. and Speeches of P. Henry,* i. 82n.

himself with a look and bearing of still prouder and fiercer determination, he so closed the sentence as to baffle his accusers, without in the least flinching from his own position,] — and George the Third may profit by their example. If this be treason, make the most of it."[1]

Of this memorable struggle nearly all other details have perished with the men who took part in it. After the House, in committee of the whole, had, on the 29th of May, spent sufficient time in the discussion, "Mr. Speaker resumed the chair," says the Journal, "and Mr. Attorney reported that the said committee had had the said matter under consideration, and had come to several resolutions thereon, which he was ready to deliver in at the table. Ordered that the said report be received to-morrow." It is probable that on the morrow the battle was renewed with even greater fierceness than before. The Journal pro-

[1] For this splendid anecdote we are indebted to Judge John Tyler, who, then a youth of eighteen, listened to the speech as he stood in the lobby by the side of Jefferson. Edmund Randolph, in his *History of Virginia*, still in manuscript, has a somewhat different version of the language of the orator, as follows: "'Cæsar had his Brutus, Charles the First, his Cromwell, and George the Third' — 'Treason, Sir,' exclaimed the Speaker; to which Mr. Henry instantly replied, 'and George the Third, may he never have either.'" The version furnished by John Tyler is, of course, the more effective and characteristic; and as Tyler actually heard the speech, and as, moreover, his account is confirmed by Jefferson who also heard it, his account can hardly be set aside by that of Randolph who did not hear it, and was indeed but a boy of twelve at the time it was made. L. G. Tyler, *Letters and Times of the Tylers*, i. 56; Wirt, 65.

ceeds: "May 30. Mr. Attorney, from the committee of the whole House, reported according to order, that the committee had considered the steps necessary to be taken in consequence of the resolutions of the House of Commons of Great Britain, relative to the charging certain stamp duties in the colonies and plantations in America, and that they had come to several resolutions thereon, which he read in his place and then delivered at the table; when they were again twice read, and agreed to by the House, with some amendments." Then were passed by the House, probably, the first five resolutions as offered by Henry in the committee, but "passed," as he himself afterward wrote, "by a very small majority, perhaps of one or two only."

Upon this final discomfiture of the old leaders, one of their number, Peyton Randolph, swept angrily out of the house, and brushing past young Thomas Jefferson, who was standing in the door of the lobby, he swore, with a great oath, that he "would have given five hundred guineas for a single vote."[1] On the afternoon of that day, Patrick Henry, knowing that the session was practically ended, and that his own work in it was done, started for his home. He was seen "passing along Duke of Gloucester Street, . . . wearing buckskin breeches, his saddle bags on his arm, leading a lean horse, and chatting with Paul Carrington, who walked by his side."[2]

[1] Mem. by Jefferson, *Hist. Mag.* for 1867, 91.
[2] Campbell, *Hist. Va.* 542.

That was on the 30th of May. The next morning, the terrible Patrick being at last quite out of the way, those veteran lawyers and politicians of the House, who had found this young protagonist, alone too much for them all put together, made bold to undo the worst part of the work he had done the day before; they expunged the fifth resolution. In that mutilated form, without the preamble, and with the last three of the original resolutions omitted, the first four then remained on the journal of the House as the final expression of its official opinion. Meantime, on the wings of the wind, and on the eager tongues of men, had been borne, past recall, far northward and far southward, the fiery unchastised words of nearly the entire series, to kindle in all the colonies a great flame of dauntless purpose;[1] while Patrick

[1] The subject of the Virginia resolutions presents several difficulties which I have not thought it best to discuss in the text, where I have given merely the results of my own rather careful and repeated study of the question. In brief, my conclusion is this : That the series as given above, consisting of a preamble and seven resolutions, is the series as originally prepared by Patrick Henry, and introduced by him on Wednesday, May 29, in the committee of the whole, and probably passed by the committee on that day ; that at once, without waiting for the action of the House upon the subject, copies of the series got abroad, and were soon published in the newspapers of the several colonies, as though actually adopted by the House ; that on Thursday, May 30, the series was cut down in the House by rejection of the preamble and the resolutions 6 and 7, and by the adoption of only the first five as given above ; that on the day after that, when Patrick Henry had gone home, the House still further cut down the series by expunging the resolution which is above numbered as 5 : and that, many

himself, perhaps then only half conscious of the
fateful work he had just been doing, travelled
homeward along the dusty highway, at once the
jolliest, the most popular, and the least pretentious
man in all Virginia, certainly its greatest orator,
possibly even its greatest statesman.

years afterwards, when Patrick Henry came to prepare a copy for
transmission to posterity, he gave the resolutions just as they stood
when adopted by the House on May 30, and not as they stood
when originally introduced by him in committee of the whole on
the day before, nor as they stood when mutilated by the cowardly
act of the House on the day after. It will be noticed, therefore,
that the so-called resolutions of Virginia, which were actually
published and known to the colonies in 1765, and which did so
much to fire their hearts, were not the resolutions as adopted by
the House, but were the resolutions as first introduced, and probably passed, in committee of the whole; and that even this copy of
them was inaccurately given, since it lacked the resolution numbered above as 3, probably owing to an error in the first hurried
transcription of them. Those who care to study the subject further will find the materials in *Prior Documents*, 6, 7; Marshall,
Life of Washington, i. note iv.; Frothingham, *Rise of the Republic*, 180 note; Gordon, *Hist. Am. Rev.*, i. 129–139; *Works of Jefferson*, vi. 366, 367; Wirt, *Life of Henry*, 56–63; Everett, *Life
of Henry*, 265–273, with important note by Jared Sparks in Appendix, 391–398. It may be mentioned that the narrative given
in Burk, *Hist. Va.*, iii. 305–310, is untrustworthy.

CHAPTER VI

CONSEQUENCES

SELDOM has a celebrated man shown more indifference to the preservation of the records and credentials of his career than did Patrick Henry. While some of his famous associates in the Revolution diligently kept both the letters they received, and copies of the letters they wrote, and made, for the benefit of posterity, careful memoranda concerning the events of their lives, Patrick Henry did none of these things. Whatever letters he wrote, he wrote at a dash, and then parted with them utterly; whatever letters were written to him, were invariably handed over by him to the comfortable custody of luck; and as to the correct historic perpetuation of his doings, he seems almost to have exhausted his interest in each one of them so soon as he had accomplished it, and to have been quite content to leave to other people all responsibility for its being remembered correctly, or even remembered at all.

To this statement, however, a single exception has to be made. It relates to the great affair described in the latter part of the previous chapter.

Of course, it was perceived at the time that

the passing of the Virginia resolutions against the Stamp Act was a great affair; but just how great an affair it was, neither Patrick Henry nor any other mortal man could tell until years had gone by, and had unfolded the vast sequence of world-resounding events, in which that affair was proved to be a necessary factor. It deserves to be particularly mentioned that, of all the achievements of his life, the only one which he has taken the pains to give any account of is his authorship of the Virginia resolutions, and his successful championship of them. With reference to this achievement, the account he gave of it was rendered with so much solemnity and impressiveness as to indicate that, in the final survey of his career, he regarded this as the one most important thing he ever did. But before we cite the words in which he thus indicated this judgment, it will be well for us to glance briefly at the train of historic incidents which now set forth the striking connection between that act of Patrick Henry and the early development of that intrepid policy which culminated in American independence.

It was on the 29th of May, 1765, as will be remembered, that Patrick Henry moved in the committee of the whole the adoption of his series of resolutions against the Stamp Act; and before the sun went down that day, the entire series, as is probable, was adopted by the committee. On the following day, the essential portion of the series was adopted, likewise, by the House. But what was the contemporary significance of these resolutions? As the news of them swept from colony to colony, why did they so stir men's hearts to excitement, and even to alarm? It was not that the language of those resolutions was more radical or more trenchant than had been the language already used on the same subject, over and over again, in the discussions of the preceding twelve months. It was that, in the recent change of the political situation, the significance of that language had changed. Prior to the time referred to, whatever had been said on the subject, in any of the colonies, had been said for the purpose of dissuading the government from passing the Stamp Act. But the government had now passed the Stamp Act; and, accordingly, these resolutions must have been meant for a very different purpose. They were a virtual declaration of resistance to the Stamp Act; a declaration of resistance made, not by an individual writer, nor by a newspaper, but by the legislature of a great colony; and, moreover, they were the very first declaration of resistance which was so made.[1]

This it is which gives us the contemporary key to their significance, and to the vast excitement produced by them, and to the enormous influence they had upon the trembling purposes of the colonists at that precise moment. Hence it was, as a sagacious writer of that period has told us, that

[1] See this view supported by Wirt, in his life by Kennedy, ii. 73.

merely upon the adoption of these resolves by the committee of the whole, men recognized their momentous bearing, and could not be restrained from giving publicity to them, without waiting for their final adoption by the House. "A manuscript of the unrevised resolves," says William Gordon, "soon reached Philadelphia, having been sent off immediately upon their passing, that the earliest information of what had been done might be obtained by the Sons of Liberty. . . . At New York the resolves were handed about with great privacy: they were accounted so treasonable, that the possessors of them declined printing them in that city." But a copy of them having been procured with much difficulty by an Irish gentleman resident in Connecticut, "he carried them to New England, where they were published and circulated far and wide in the newspapers, without any reserve, and proved eventually the occasion of those disorders which afterward broke out in the colonies. . . . The Virginia resolutions gave a spring to all the disgusted; and they began to adopt different measures."[1]

But while the tidings of these resolutions were thus moving toward New England, and before they had arrived there, the assembly of the great colony of Massachusetts had begun to take action. Indeed, it had first met on the very day on which Patrick Henry had introduced his resolutions into the committee of the whole at Williamsburg. On

[1] Gordon, *Hist. of Am. Rev.* i. 131.

the 8th of June, it had resolved upon a circular letter concerning the Stamp Act, addressed to all the sister colonies, and proposing that all should send delegates to a congress to be held at New York, on the first Tuesday of the following October, to deal with the perils and duties of the situation. This circular letter at once started upon its tour.

The first reception of it, however, was discouraging. From the speaker of the New Jersey assembly came the reply that the members of that body were "unanimously against uniting on the present occasion;" and for several weeks thereafter, "no movement appeared in favor of the great and wise measure of convening a congress." At last, however, the project of Massachusetts began to feel the accelerating force of a mighty impetus. The Virginia resolutions, being at last divulged throughout the land, "had a marked effect on public opinion." They were "heralded as the voice of a colony . . . The fame of the resolves spread as they were circulated in the journals. . . . The Virginia action, like an alarum, roused the patriots to pass similar resolves."[1] On the 8th of July, "The Boston Gazette" uttered this most significant sentence: "The people of Virginia have spoken very sensibly, and the frozen politicians of a more northern government say they have spoken treason."[2] On the same day, in that

[1] Frothingham, *Rise of the Republic*, 178–181.
[2] Cited in Frothingham, 181.

same town of Boston, an aged lawyer and patriot[1]
lay upon his death bed; and in his admiration for
the Virginians on account of these resolves, he exclaimed, "They are men; they are noble spirits."[2]
On the 13th of August, the people of Providence
instructed their representatives in the legislature
to vote in favor of the congress, and to procure
the passage of a series of resolutions in which
were incorporated those of Virginia.[3] On the 15th
of August, from Boston, Governor Bernard wrote
home to the ministry: "Two or three months ago,
I thought that this people would submit to the
Stamp Act. Murmurs were indeed continually
heard; but they seemed to be such as would die
away. But the publishing of the Virginia resolves
proved an alarm bell to the disaffected."[4] On
the 23d of September, General Gage, the commander of the British forces in America, wrote
from New York to Secretary Conway that the
Virginia resolves had given "the signal for a
general outcry over the continent."[5] And finally,
in the autumn of 1774, an able loyalist writer,
looking back over the political history of the colonies from the year of the Stamp Act, singled out
the Virginia resolves as the baleful cause of all
the troubles that had then come upon the land.
"After it was known," said he, "that the Stamp

[1] Oxenbridge Thacher.
[2] *Works of John Adams*, x. 287.
[3] Frothingham, 181.
[4] Cited by Sparks, in Everett, *Life of Henry*, 396.
[5] Frothingham, *Rise of the Republic*, 181.

Act was passed, some resolves of the House of Burgesses in Virginia, denying the right of Parliament to tax the colonies, made their appearance. We read them with wonder; they savored of independence; they flattered the human passions; the reasoning was specious; we wished it conclusive. The transition to believing it so was easy; and we, and almost all America, followed their example, in resolving that Parliament had no such right."[1]

All these facts, and many more that might be produced, seem to point to the Virginia resolutions of 1765 as having come at a great primary crisis of the Revolution, — a crisis of mental confusion and hesitation, — and as having then uttered, with trumpet voice, the very word that was fitted to the hour, and that gave to men's minds clearness of vision, and to their hearts a settled purpose. It must have been in the light of such facts as these that Patrick Henry, in his old age, reviewing his own wonderful career, determined to make a sort of testamentary statement concerning his relation to that single transaction, — so vitally connected with the greatest epoch in American history.

Among the papers left by him at his death was one significantly placed by the side of his will, carefully sealed, and bearing this superscription: "Inclosed are the resolutions of the Virginia Assembly in 1765, concerning the Stamp Act. Let my executors open this paper." On opening the

[1] Daniel Leonard, in *Novanglus and Massachusettensis*, 147, 148.

document, his executors found on one side of the
sheet the first five resolutions in the famous series
introduced by him; and on the other side, these
weighty words: —

The within resolutions passed the House of Burgesses
in May, 1765. They formed the first opposition to the
Stamp Act, and the scheme of taxing America by the
British parliament. All the colonies, either through fear,
or want of opportunity to form an opposition, or from
influence of some kind or other, had remained silent. I
had been for the first time elected a Burgess a few days
before; was young, inexperienced, unacquainted with
the forms of the House, and the members that composed
it. Finding the men of weight averse to opposition, and
the commencement of the tax at hand, and that no person was likely to step forth, I determined to venture;
and alone, unadvised, and unassisted, on a blank leaf of
an old law book, wrote the within.[1] Upon offering them

[1] As the historic importance of the Virginia resolutions became
more and more apparent, a disposition was manifested to deny to
Patrick Henry the honor of having written them. As early as
1790, Madison, between whom and Henry there was nearly always
a sharp hostility, significantly asked Edmund Pendleton to tell him
"where the resolutions proposed by Mr. Henry really originated."
Letters and Other Writings of Madison, i. 515. Edmund Randolph
is said to have asserted that they were written by William Fleming; a statement of which Jefferson remarked, "It is to me in-
comprehensible." *Works*, vi. 484. But to Jefferson's own testimony on the same subject, I would apply the same remark. In
his Memorandum, he says without hesitation that the resolutions
"were drawn up by George Johnston, a lawyer of the Northern
Neck, a very able, logical, and correct speaker." *Hist. Mag.* for
1867, 91. But in another paper, written at about the same time,
Jefferson said: "I can readily enough believe these resolutions
were written by Mr. Henry himself. They bear the stamp of his

to the House, violent debates ensued. Many threats were uttered, and much abuse cast on me by the party for submission. After a long and warm contest, the resolutions passed by a very small majority, perhaps of one or two only. The alarm spread throughout America with astonishing quickness, and the ministerial party were overwhelmed. The great point of resistance to British taxation was universally established in the colonies. This brought on the war, which finally separated the two countries, and gave independence to ours.

Whether this will prove a blessing or a curse, will depend upon the use our people make of the blessings which a gracious God hath bestowed on us. If they are wise, they will be great and happy. If they are of a contrary character, they will be miserable. Righteousness alone can exalt them as a nation.

Reader! whoever thou art, remember this; and in thy sphere practice virtue thyself, and encourage it in others. P. HENRY.[1]

But while this renowned act in Patrick Henry's life had consequences so notable in their bearing on great national and international movements, it is interesting to observe, also, its immediate effects on his own personal position in the world, and on

mind, strong, without precision. That they were written by Johnston, who seconded them, was only the rumor of the day, and very possibly unfounded." *Works*, vi. 484. In the face of all this tissue of rumor, guesswork, and self-contradiction, the deliberate statement of Patrick Henry himself that he wrote the five resolutions referred to by him, and that he wrote them "alone, unadvised, and unassisted," must close the discussion.

[1] Verified from the original manuscript, now in possession of Mr. W. W. Henry.

the development of his career. We can hardly be surprised to find, on the one hand, that his act gave deep offence to one very considerable class of persons in Virginia, — the official representatives of the English government, and their natural allies, those thoughtful and conscientious colonists who, by temperament and conviction, were inclined to lay a heavy accent on the principle of civil authority and order. Of course, as the official head of this not ignoble class, stood Francis Fauquier, the lieutenant-governor of the colony; and his letter to the lords of trade, written from Williamsburg a few days after the close of the session, contains a striking narrative of this stormy proceeding, and an almost amusing touch of official undervaluation of Patrick Henry: "In the course of the debate, I have heard that very indecent language was used by a Mr. Henry, a young lawyer, who had not been above a month a member of the House, and who carried all the young members with him."[1] But a far more specific and intense expression of antipathy came, a few weeks later, from the Reverend William Robinson, the colonial commissary of the Bishop of London. Writing, on the 12th of August, to his metropolitan, he gave an account of Patrick Henry's very offensive management of the cause against the parsons, before becoming a member of the House of Burgesses; and then added: —

---

[1] Cited by Sparks, in Everett, *Life of Henry*, 302.

" He has since been chosen a representative for one of the counties, in which character he has lately distinguished himself in the House of Burgesses on occasion of the arrival of an act of Parliament for stamp duties, while the Assembly was sitting. He blazed out in a violent speech against the authority of Parliament and the king, comparing his majesty to a Tarquin, a Cæsar, and a Charles the First, and not sparing insinuations that he wished another Cromwell would arise. He made a motion for several outrageous resolves, some of which passed and were again erased as soon as his back was turned. . . . Mr. Henry, the hero of whom I have been writing, is gone quietly into the upper parts of the country to recommend himself to his constituents by spreading treason and enforcing firm resolutions against the authority of the British Parliament." [1]

Such was Patrick Henry's introduction to the upper spheres of English society, — spheres in which his name was to become still better known as time rolled on, and for conduct not likely to efface the impression of this bitter beginning.

As to his reputation in the colonies outside of Virginia, doubtless the progress of it, during this period, was slow and dim; for the celebrity acquired by the resolutions of 1765 attached to the colony rather than to the person. Moreover, the boundaries of each colony, in those days, were in most cases the boundaries likewise of the personal reputations it cherished. It was not until Patrick Henry came forward, in the Congress of 1774,

[1] Perry, *Hist. Coll.* i. 514, 515.

upon an arena that may be called national, that his name gathered about it the splendor of a national fame. Yet, even before 1774, in the rather dull and ungossiping newspapers of that time, and in the letters and diaries of its public men, may be discovered an occasional allusion showing that already his name had broken over the borders of Virginia, had traveled even so far as to New England, and that in Boston itself he was a person whom people were beginning to talk about. For example, in his Diary for the 22d of July, 1770, John Adams speaks of meeting some gentlemen from Virginia, and of going out to Cambridge with them. One of them is mentioned by name as having this distinction, — that he "is an intimate friend of Mr. Patrick Henry, the first mover of the Virginia resolves in 1765."[1] Thus, even so early, the incipient revolutionist in New England had got his thoughts on his brilliant political kinsman in Virginia.

But it was chiefly within the limits of his own splendid and gallant colony, and among an eager and impressionable people whose habitual hatred of all restraints turned into undying love for this dashing champion of natural liberty, that Patrick Henry was now instantly crowned with his crown of sovereignty. By his resolutions against the Stamp Act, as Jefferson testifies, "Mr. Henry took the lead out of the hands of those who had heretofore guided the proceedings of the House,

---

[1] *Works of John Adams*, ii. 249.

that is to say, of Pendleton, Wythe, Bland, Randolph, and Nicholas."[1] Wirt does not put the case too strongly when he declares, that "after this debate there was no longer a question among the body of the people, as to Mr. Henry's being the first statesman and orator in Virginia. Those, indeed, whose ranks he had scattered, and whom he had thrown into the shade, still tried to brand him with the names of declaimer and demagogue. But this was obviously the effect of envy and mortified pride. . . . From the period of which we have been speaking, Mr. Henry became the idol of the people of Virginia."[2]

[1] *Works of Jefferson*, vi. 368.
[2] *Life of Henry*, 66.

CHAPTER VII

STEADY WORK

FROM the close of Patrick Henry's first term in the Virginia House of Burgesses, in the spring of 1765, to the opening of his first term in the Continental Congress, in the fall of 1774, there stretches a period of about nine years, which, for the purposes of our present study, may be rapidly glanced at and passed by.

In general, it may be described as a period during which he had settled down to steady work, both as a lawyer and as a politician. The first five years of his professional life had witnessed his advance, as we have seen, by strides which only genius can make, from great obscurity to great distinction; his advance from a condition of universal failure to one of success so universal that his career may be said to have become within that brief period solidly established. At the bar, upon the hustings, in the legislature, as a master of policies, as a leader of men, he had already proved himself to be, of his kind, without a peer in all the colony of Virginia, — a colony which was then the prolific mother of great men. With him, therefore, the period of training and of tentative struggle had passed: the period now entered upon was one of recognized mastership and of assured performance, along lines certified by victories that came gayly, and apparently at his slightest call.

We note, at the beginning of this period, an event indicating substantial prosperity in his life: he acquires the visible dignity of a country-seat. Down to the end of 1763, and probably even to the summer of 1765, he had continued to live in the neighborhood of Hanover Court House. After coming back from his first term of service in the House of Burgesses, where he had sat as member for the county of Louisa, he removed his residence into that county, and established himself there upon an estate called Roundabout, purchased by him of his father. In 1768 he returned to Hanover, and in 1771 he bought a place in that county called Scotch Town, which continued to be his seat until shortly after the Declaration of Independence, when, having become governor of the new State of Virginia, he took up his residence at Williamsburg, in the palace long occupied by the official representatives of royalty.

For the practice of his profession, the earlier portion of this period was perhaps not altogether unfavorable. The political questions then in debate were, indeed, exciting, but they had not quite reached the ultimate issue, and did not yet demand from him the complete surrender of his life. Those years seem to have been marked by great professional activity on his part, and by considerable

growth in his reputation, even for the higher and
more difficult work of the law. Of course, as the
vast controversy between the colonists and Great
Britain grew in violence, all controversies between
one colonist and another began to seem petty, and
to be postponed; even the courts ceased to meet
with much regularity, and finally ceased to meet at
all; while Patrick Henry himself, forsaking his
private concerns, became entirely absorbed in the
concerns of the public.

The fluctuations in his engagements as a lawyer,
during all these years, may be traced·with some
certainty by the entries in his fee-books.   For the
year 1765, he charges fees in 547 cases; for 1766,
in 114 cases; for 1767, in 554 cases; for 1768, in
354 cases. With the next year there begins a
great falling off in the number of his cases; and
the decline continues till 1774, when, in the con-
vulsions of the time, his practice stops altogether.
Thus, for 1769, there are registered 132 cases;
for 1770, 94 cases; for 1771, 102 cases; for 1772,
43 cases; for 1773, 7 cases; and for 1774, none.[1]

The character of the professional work done by
him during this period deserves a moment's consideration.   Prior to 1769, he had limited himself
to practice in the courts of the several counties.
In that year he began to practice in the general
court, — the highest court in the colony, — where
of course were tried the most important and difficult causes, and where thenceforward he had

[1] MS.

constantly to encounter the most learned and
acute lawyers at the bar, including such men as
Pendleton, Wythe, Blair, Mercer, John Randolph,
Thompson Mason, Thomas Jefferson, and Robert
C. Nicholas.[1]

There could never have been any doubt of his
supreme competency to deal with such criminal
causes as he had to manage in that court or in any
other; and with respect to the conduct of other
than criminal causes, all purely contemporaneous
evidence, now to be had, implies that he had not
ventured to present himself before the higher tribunals of the land until he had qualified himself
to bear his part there with success and honor.
Thus, the instance may be mentioned of his appearing in the Court of Admiralty, "in behalf of
a Spanish captain, whose vessel and cargo had
been libeled. A gentleman who was present, and
who was very well qualified to judge, was heard to
declare, after the trial was over, that he never
heard a more eloquent or argumentative speech in
his life; that Mr. Henry was on that occasion
greatly superior to Mr. Pendleton, Mr. Mason, or
any other counsel who spoke to the subject; and
that he was astonished how Mr. Henry could have
acquired such a knowledge of the maritime law, to
which it was believed he had never before turned
his attention."[2] Moreover, in 1771, just two
years from the time when Patrick Henry began
practice in the General Court, Robert C. Nicholas,

[1] Wirt, 70, 71.   [2] Wirt, 71, 72.

then a veteran member of the profession, "who had enjoyed the first practice at the bar," had occasion to retire, and began looking about among the younger men for some competent lawyer to whom he might safely intrust the unfinished business of his clients. He first offered his practice to Thomas Jefferson, who, however, was compelled to decline it. Afterward, he offered it to Patrick Henry, who accepted it; and accordingly, by public advertisement, Nicholas informed his clients that he had committed to Patrick Henry the further protection of their interests,[1] — a perfectly conclusive proof, it should seem, of the real respect in which Patrick Henry's qualifications as a lawyer were then held, not only by the public but by the profession. Certainly such evidence as this can hardly be set aside by the supposed recollections of one old gentleman, of broken memory and unbroken resentment, who long afterward tried to convince Wirt that, even at the period now in question, Patrick Henry was "wofully deficient as a lawyer," was unable to contend with his associates "on a mere question of law," and was "so little acquainted with the fundamental principles of his profession . . . as not to be able to see the remote bearings of the reported cases."[2] The expressions here quoted are, apparently, Wirt's own paraphrase of the statements which were made to him by Jefferson, and which, in many of their

[1] Randall, *Life of Jefferson*, i. 49; Wirt, 77.
[2] Wirt, 71.

details, can now be proved, on documentary evidence, to be the work of a hand that had forgot, not indeed its cunning, but at any rate its accuracy.

As to the political history of Patrick Henry during this period, it may be easily described. The doctrine on which he had planted himself by his resolutions in 1765, namely, that the parliamentary taxation of unrepresented colonies is unconstitutional, became the avowed doctrine of Virginia, and of all her sister colonies; and nearly all the men who, in the House of Burgesses, had, for reasons of propriety, or of expediency, or of personal feeling, opposed the passage of his resolutions, soon took pains to make it known to their constituents that their opposition had not been to the principle which those resolutions expressed. Thenceforward, among the leaders in Virginian politics, there was no real disagreement on the fundamental question; only such disagreement touching methods as must always occur between spirits who are cautious and spirits who are bold. Chief among the former were Pendleton, Wythe, Bland, Peyton Randolph, and Nicholas. In the van of the latter always stood Patrick Henry, and with him Jefferson, Richard Henry Lee, the Pages, and George Mason. But between the two groups, after all, was surprising harmony, which is thus explained by one who in all that business had a great part and who never was a laggard:—

" Sensible, however, of the importance of unanimity

among our constituents, although we often wished to have gone faster, we slackened our pace, that our less ardent colleagues might keep up with us ; and they, on their part, differing nothing from us in principle, quickened their gait somewhat beyond that which their prudence might of itself have advised, and thus consolidated the phalanx which breasted the power of Britain. By this harmony of the bold with the cautious, we advanced with our constituents in undivided mass, and with fewer examples of separation than, perhaps, existed in any other part of the union." [1]

All deprecated a quarrel with Great Britain; all deprecated as a boundless calamity the possible issue of independence; all desired to remain in loyal, free, and honorable connection with the British empire; and against the impending danger of an assault upon the freedom, and consequently the honor, of this connection, all stood on guard.

One result, however, of this practical unanimity among the leaders in Virginia was the absence, during all this period, of those impassioned and dramatic conflicts in debate, which would have called forth historic exhibitions of Patrick Henry's eloquence and of his gifts for conduct and command. He had a leading part in all the counsels of the time; he was sent to every session of the House of Burgesses; he was at the front in all local committees and conventions; he was made a member of the first Committee of Correspondence; and all these incidents in this portion of his life

[1] Jefferson's *Works*, vi. 368.

culminated in his mission as one of the deputies from Virginia to the first Continental Congress.

Without here going into the familiar story of the occasion and purposes of the Congress of 1774, we may briefly indicate Patrick Henry's relation to the events in Virginia which immediately preceded his appointment to that renowned assemblage. On the 24th of May, 1774, the House of Burgesses, having received the alarming news of the passage of the Boston Port Bill, designated the day on which that bill was to take effect — the first day of June — "as a day of fasting, humiliation, and prayer, devoutly to implore the Divine interposition for averting the heavy calamity which threatens destruction to our civil rights, and the evils of civil war; to give us one heart and one mind firmly to oppose, by all just and proper means, every injury to American rights; and that the minds of his majesty and his parliament may be inspired from above with wisdom, moderation, and justice, to remove from the loyal people of America all cause of danger, from a continued pursuit of measures pregnant with their ruin." [1] Two days afterward, the governor, Lord Dunmore, .having summoned the House to the council chamber, made to them this little speech: —

" Mr. Speaker and gentlemen of the House of Burgesses, I have in my hand a paper published by order of your House, conceived in such terms as reflect highly upon his majesty and the Parliament of Great Britain,

[1] 4 *Am. Arch.* i. 350.

which makes it necessary for me to dissolve you, and you are dissolved accordingly." [1]

At ten o'clock on the following day, May 27, the members of the late House met by agreement at the Raleigh Tavern, and there promptly passed a nobly-worded resolution, deploring the policy pursued by Parliament and suggesting the establishment of an annual congress of all the colonies, "to deliberate on those general measures which the united interests of America may from time to time require." [2]

During the anxious days and nights immediately preceding the dissolution of the House, its prominent members held many private conferences with respect to the course to be pursued by Virginia. In all these conferences, as we are told, "Patrick Henry was the leader;" [3] and a very able man, George Mason, who was just then a visitor at Williamsburg, and was admitted to the consultations of the chiefs, wrote at the time concerning him: "He is by far the most powerful speaker I ever heard. . . . But his eloquence is the smallest part of his merit. He is, in my opinion, the first man upon this continent, as well in abilities as public virtues." [4]

---

[1] Campbell, *Hist. Va.* 573.

[2] 4 *Am. Arch.* i. 350, 351. The narrative of these events as given by Wirt and by Campbell has several errors. They seem to have been misled by Jefferson, who, in his account of the business (*Works*, i. 122, 123), is, if possible, rather more inaccurate than usual.

[3] Campbell, *Hist. Va.* 573.

[4] Mason to Martin Cockburn, *Va. Hist. Reg.* iii. 27-29.

In response to a recommendation made by leading members of the recent House of Burgesses, a convention of delegates from the several counties of Virginia assembled at Williamsburg, on August 1, 1774, to deal with the needs of the hour, and especially to appoint deputies to the proposed congress at Philadelphia. The spirit in which this convention transacted its business is sufficiently shown in the opening paragraphs of the letter of instructions which it gave to the deputies whom it sent to the congress: —

"The unhappy disputes between Great Britain and her American colonies, which began about the third year of the reign of his present majesty, and since, continually increasing, have proceeded to lengths so dangerous and alarming as to excite just apprehensions in the minds of his majesty's faithful subjects of this colony that they are in danger of being deprived of their natural, ancient, constitutional, and chartered rights, have compelled them to take the same into their most serious consideration; and being deprived of their usual and accustomed mode of making known their grievances, have appointed us their representatives, to consider what is proper to be done in this dangerous crisis of American affairs.

" It being our opinion that the united wisdom of North America should be collected in a general congress of all the colonies, we have appointed the honorable Peyton Randolph, Esquire, Richard Henry Lee, George Washington, Patrick Henry, Richard Bland, Benjamin Harrison, and Edmund Pendleton, Esquires, deputies to represent this colony in the said congress, to be held at

Philadelphia on the first Monday in September next. And that they may be the better informed of our sentiments touching the conduct we wish them to observe on this important occasion, we desire that they will express, in the first place, our faith and true allegiance to his majesty King George the Third, our lawful and rightful sovereign; and that we are determined, with our lives and fortunes, to support him in the legal exercise of all his just rights and prerogatives; and however misrepresented, we sincerely approve of a constitutional connection with Great Britain, and wish most ardently a return of that intercourse of affection and commercial connection that formerly united both countries; which can only be effected by a removal of those causes of discontent which have of late unhappily divided us. . . . The power assumed by the British Parliament to bind America by their statutes, in all cases whatsoever, is unconstitutional, and the source of these unhappy differences." [1]

The convention at Williamsburg, of which, of course, Patrick Henry was a member, seems to have adjourned on Saturday, the 6th of August. Between that date and the time for his departure to attend the congress at Philadelphia, we may imagine him as busily engaged in arranging his affairs for a long absence from home, and even then as not getting ready to begin the long journey until many of his associates had nearly reached the end of it.

[1] The full text of this letter of instructions is given in 4 *Am. Arch.* i. 689, 690. With this should be compared note C. in Jefferson's *Works*, i. 122-142.

CHAPTER VIII

IN THE FIRST CONTINENTAL CONGRESS

On the morning of Tuesday, the 30th of August, Patrick Henry arrived on horseback at Mt. Vernon, the home of his friend and colleague, George Washington; and having remained there that day and night, he set out for Philadelphia on the following morning, in the company of Washington and of Edmund Pendleton. From the jottings in Washington's diary,[1] we can so far trace the progress of this trio of illustrious horsemen, as to ascertain that on Sunday, the 4th of September, they "breakfasted at Christiana Ferry; dined at Chester;" and reached Philadelphia for supper — thus arriving in town barely in time to be present at the first meeting of the Congress on the morning of the 5th.

John Adams had taken pains to get upon the ground nearly a week earlier; and carefully gathering all possible information concerning his future associates, few of whom he had then ever seen, he wrote in his diary that the Virginians were said to "speak in raptures about Richard Henry Lee

[1] *Washington's Writings*, ii. 503.

and Patrick Henry, one the Cicero, and the other the Demosthenes, of the age."[1]

Not far from the same time, also, a keen-witted Virginian, Roger Atkinson, at his home near Petersburg, was writing to a friend about the men who had gone to represent Virginia in the great Congress; and this letter of his, though not meant for posterity, has some neat, off-hand portraits which posterity may, nevertheless, be glad to look at. Peyton Randolph is "a venerable man . . . an honest man; has knowledge, temper, experience, judgment, — above all, integrity; a true Roman spirit." Richard Bland is "a wary, old, experienced veteran at the bar and in the senate; has something of the look of old musty parchments, which he handleth and studieth much. He formerly wrote a treatise against the Quakers on water-baptism." Washington "is a soldier, — a warrior; he is a modest man; sensible; speaks little; in action cool, like a bishop at his prayers." Pendleton "is an humble and religious man, and must be exalted. He is a smooth-tongued speaker, and, though not so old, may be compared to old Nestor, —

> ' Experienced Nestor, in persuasion skilled,
> Words sweet as honey from his lips distilled.' "

But Patrick Henry "is a real half-Quaker, — your brother's man, — moderate and mild, and in religious matters a saint; but the very devil in politics; a son of thunder. He will shake the

[1] *Works of John Adams*, ii. 357.

Senate. Some years ago he had liked to have talked treason into the House."[1]

Few of the members of this Congress had ever met before; and if all had arrived upon the scene as late as did these three members from Virginia, there might have been some difficulty, through a lack of previous consultation and acquaintance, in organizing the Congress on the day appointed, and in entering at once upon its business. In fact, however, more than a week before the time for the first meeting, the delegates had begun to make their appearance in Philadelphia; thenceforward with each day the arrivals continued; by Thursday, the 1st of September, twenty-five delegates, nearly one half of the entire body elected, were in town;[2] and probably, during all that week, no day and no night had passed without many an informal conference respecting the business before them, and the best way of doing it.

Concerning these memorable men of the first Continental Congress, it must be confessed that as the mists of a hundred years of glorifying oratory and of semi-poetic history have settled down upon them, they are now enveloped in a light which seems to distend their forms to proportions almost superhuman, and to cast upon their faces a gravity that hardly belongs to this world; and it may, perhaps, help us to bring them and their work somewhat nearer to the plane of natural human

[1] Meade, *Old Churches and Families of Va.* i. 220, 221.
[2] *Works of John Adams*, ii. 361.

life and motive, and into a light that is as the light of reality, if, turning to the daily memoranda made at the time by one of their number, we can see how merrily, after all, nay, with what flowing feasts, with what convivial communings, passed those days and nights of preparation for the difficult business they were about to take in hand.

For example, on Monday, the 29th of August, when the four members of the Massachusetts delegation had arrived within five miles of the city, they were met by an escort of gentlemen, partly residents of Philadelphia, and partly delegates from other colonies, who had come out in carriages to greet them.

"We were introduced," writes John Adams, "to all these gentlemen, and most cordially welcomed to Philadelphia. We then rode into town, and dirty, dusty, and fatigued as we were, we could not resist the importunity to go to the tavern, the most genteel one in America. There we were introduced to a number of other gentlemen of the city, . . . and to Mr. Lynch and Mr. Gadsden, of South Carolina. Here we had a fresh welcome to the city of Philadelphia; and after some time spent in conversation, a curtain was drawn, and in the other half of the chamber a supper appeared as elegant as ever was laid upon a table. About eleven o'clock we retired.

"30, Tuesday. Walked a little about town; visited the market, the State House, the Carpenters' Hall, where the Congress is to sit, etc.; then called at Mr. Mifflin's, a grand, spacious, and elegant house. Here we had much conversation with Mr. Charles Thomson, who is . . . the Sam Adams of Philadelphia, the life of the cause of liberty, they say. A Friend, Collins, came to see us, and invited us to dine on Thursday. We returned to our lodgings, and Mr. Lynch, Mr. Gadsden, Mr. Middleton, and young Mr. Rutledge came to visit us.

"31, Wednesday. Breakfasted at Mr. Bayard's, of Philadelphia, with Mr. Sprout, a Presbyterian minister. Made a visit to Governor Ward of Rhode Island, at his lodgings. There we were introduced to several gentlemen. Mr. Dickinson, the Farmer of Pennsylvania, came in his coach with four beautiful horses to Mr. Ward's lodgings, to see us. . . . We dined with Mr. Lynch, his lady and daughter, at their lodgings, . . . and a very agreeable dinner and afternoon we had, notwithstanding the violent heat. We were all vastly pleased with Mr. Lynch. He is a solid, firm, judicious man.

"September 1, Thursday. This day we breakfasted at Mr. Mifflin's. Mr. C. Thomson came in, and soon after Dr. Smith, the famous Dr. Smith, the provost of the college. . . . We then went to return visits to the gentlemen who had visited us. We visited a Mr. Cadwallader, a gentleman of large fortune, a grand and elegant house and furniture. We then visited Mr. Powell, another splendid seat. We then visited the gentlemen from South Carolina, and, about twelve, were introduced to Mr. Galloway, the speaker of the House in Pennsylvania. We dined at Friend Collins' . . . with Governor Hopkins, Governor Ward, Mr. Galloway, Mr. Rhoades, etc. In the evening all the gentlemen of the Congress who were arrived in town, met at Smith's, the new city tavern, and spent the evening together. Twenty-five members were come. Virginia, North Carolina, Maryland, and the city of New York were not arrived.

"2, Friday. Dined at Mr. Thomas Mifflin's with Mr. Lynch, Mr. Middleton, and the two Rutledges with their ladies. . . . We were very sociable and happy. After coffee we went to the tavern, where we were introduced to Peyton Randolph, Esquire, speaker of Virginia, Colonel Harrison, Richard Henry Lee, Esquire, and Colonel Bland. . . . These gentlemen from Virginia appear to be the most spirited and consistent of any. Harrison said he would have come on foot rather than not come. Bland said he would have gone, upon this occasion, if it had been to Jericho.

"3, Saturday. Breakfasted at Dr. Shippen's; Dr. Witherspoon was there. Col. R. H. Lee lodges there; he is a masterly man. . . . We went with Mr. William Barrell to his store, and drank punch, and ate dried smoked sprats with him; read the papers and our letters from Boston; dined with Mr. Joseph Reed, the lawyer; . . . spent the evening at Mr. Mifflin's, with Lee and Harrison from Virginia, the two Rutledges, Dr. Witherspoon, Dr. Shippen, Dr. Steptoe, and another gentleman; an elegant supper, and we drank sentiments till eleven o'clock. Lee and Harrison were very high. Lee had dined with Mr. Dickinson, and drank Burgundy the whole afternoon." [1]

Accordingly, at 10 o'clock on Monday morning, the 5th of September, when the delegates assembled at their rendezvous, the city tavern, and marched together through the streets to Carpenters' Hall, for most of them the stiffness of a first introduction was already broken, and they could greet one another that morning with something of

[1] *Works of John Adams*, ii. 357-364.

the freedom and good fellowship of boon companions. Moreover, they were then ready to proceed to business under the advantage of having arranged beforehand an outline of what was first to be done. It had been discovered, apparently, that the first serious question which would meet them after their formal organization, was one relating to the method of voting in the Congress, namely, whether each deputy should have a vote, or only each colony; and if the latter, whether the vote of each colony should be proportioned to its population and property.

Having arrived at the hall, and inspected it, and agreed that it would serve the purpose, the delegates helped themselves to seats. Then Mr. Lynch of South Carolina arose, and nominated Mr. Peyton Randolph of Virginia for president. This nomination having been unanimously adopted, Mr. Lynch likewise proposed Mr. Charles Thomson for secretary, which was carried without opposition; but as Mr. Thomson was not a delegate, and of course was not then present, the doorkeeper was instructed to go out and find him, and say to him that his immediate attendance was desired by the Congress.

Next came the production and inspection of credentials. The roll indicated that of the fifty-two delegates appointed, forty-four were already upon the ground, — constituting an assemblage of representative Americans, which, for dignity of character and for intellectual eminence, was undoubtedly the most imposing that the colonies had ever seen. In that room that day were such men as John Sullivan, John and Samuel Adams, Stephen Hopkins, Roger Sherman, James Duane, John Jay, Philip and William Livingston, Joseph Galloway, Thomas Mifflin, Cæsar Rodney, Thomas McKean, George Read, Samuel Chase, John and Edward Rutledge, Christopher Gadsden, Henry Middleton, Edmund Pendleton, George Washington, and Patrick Henry.

Having thus got through with the mere routine of organization, which must have taken a considerable time, James Duane, of New York, moved the appointment of a committee "to prepare regulations for this Congress." To this several gentlemen objected; whereupon John Adams, thinking that Duane's purpose might have been misunderstood, "asked leave of the president to request of the gentleman from New York an explanation, and that he would point out some particular regulations which he had in his mind." In reply to this request, Duane "mentioned particularly the method of voting, whether it should be by colonies, or by the poll, or by interests."[1] Thus Duane laid his finger on perhaps the most sensitive nerve in that assemblage; but as he sat down, the discussion of the subject which he had mentioned was interrupted by a rather curious incident. This was the return of the doorkeeper, having under his escort Mr. Charles Thomson. The latter walked

[1] *Works of John Adams*, ii. 365.

up the aisle, and standing opposite to the president, said, with a bow, that he awaited his pleasure. The president replied: "Congress desire the favor of you, sir, to take their minutes." Without a word, only bowing his acquiescence, the secretary took his seat at his desk, and began those modest but invaluable services from which he did not cease until the Congress of the Confederation was merged into that of the Union.

The discussion, into which this incident had fallen as a momentary episode, was then resumed. "After a short silence," says the man who was thus inducted into office, "Patrick Henry arose to speak. I did not then know him. He was dressed in a suit of parson's gray, and from his appearance I took him for a Presbyterian clergyman, used to haranguing the people. He observed that we were here met in a time and on an occasion of great difficulty and distress; that our public circumstances were like those of a man in deep embarrassment and trouble, who had called his friends together to devise what was best to be done for his relief; — one would propose one thing, and another a different one, whilst perhaps a third would think of something better suited to his unhappy circumstances, which he would embrace, and think no more of the rejected schemes with which he would have nothing to do." [1]

[1] *Am. Quarterly Review*, i. 30, whence it is quoted in *Works of John Adams*, iii. 29, 30, note. As regards the value of this testimony of Charles Thomson, we should note that it is something

Such is the rather meagre account, as given by one ear-witness, of Patrick Henry's first speech in the Congress of 1774. From another ear-witness, we have another account, likewise very meagre, but giving, probably, a somewhat more adequate idea of the drift and point of what he said:—

"Mr. Henry then arose, and said this was the first general congress which had ever happened; that no former congress could be a precedent; that we should have occasion for more general congresses, and therefore that a precedent ought to be established now; that it would be a great injustice if a little colony should have the same weight in the councils of America as a great one; and therefore he was for a committee."[1]

The notable thing about both these accounts is that they agree in showing Patrick Henry's first speech in Congress to have been not, as has been represented, an impassioned portrayal of "general grievances," but a plain and quiet handling of a mere "detail of business." In the discussion he was followed by John Sullivan, who merely observed that "a little colony had its all at stake as well as a great one." The floor was then taken by John Adams, who seems to have made a searching and vigorous argument, — exhibiting the great difficulties attending any possible conclusion to which they might come respecting the method of

alleged to have been said by him at the age of ninety, in a conversation with a friend, and by the latter reported to the author of the article above cited in the *Am. Quart. Rev.*

[1] *Works of John Adams*, ii. 365.

voting. At the end of his speech, apparently, the House adjourned, to resume the consideration of the subject on the following day.[1]

Accordingly, on Tuesday morning the discussion was continued, and at far greater length than on the previous day; the first speaker being Patrick Henry himself, who seems now to have gone into the subject far more broadly, and with much greater intensity of thought, than in his first speech.

"'Government,' said he, 'is dissolved. Fleets and armies and the present state of things show that government is dissolved. Where are your landmarks, your boundaries of colonies? We are in a state of nature, sir. I did propose that a scale should be laid down; that part of North America which was once Massachusetts Bay, and that part which was once Virginia, ought to be considered as having a weight. Will not people complain, — "Ten thousand Virginians have not outweighed one thousand others?"

"'I will submit, however; I am determined to submit, if I am overruled.

"'A worthy gentleman near me [John Adams] seemed to admit the necessity of obtaining a more adequate representation.

[1] It seems to me that the second paragraph on page 366 of volume ii. of the *Works of John Adams* must be taken as his memorandum of his own speech; and that what follows on that page, as well as on page 367, and the first half of page 368, is erroneously understood by the editor as belonging to the first day's debate. It must have been an outline of the second day's debate. This is proved partly by the fact that it mentions Lee as taking part in the debate; but according to the journal, Lee did not appear in Congress until the second day. 4 *Am. Arch.* i. 898.

"'I hope future ages will quote our proceedings with applause. It is one of the great duties of the democratical part of the constitution to keep itself pure. It is known in my province that some other colonies are not so numerous or rich as they are. I am for giving all the satisfaction in my power.

"'The distinctions between Virginians, Pennsylvanians, New Yorkers, and New Englanders are no more. I am not a Virginian, but an American.

"'Slaves are to be thrown out of the question; and if the freemen can be represented according to their numbers, I am satisfied.'

"The subject was then debated at length by Lynch, Rutledge, Ward, Richard Henry Lee, Gadsden, Bland, and Pendleton, when Patrick Henry again rose: —

"'I agree that authentic accounts cannot be had, if by authenticity is meant attestations of officers of the crown. I go upon the supposition that government is at an end. All distinctions are thrown down. All America is thrown into one mass. We must aim at the minutiæ of rectitude.'"

Patrick Henry was then followed by John Jay, who seems to have closed the debate, and whose allusion to what his immediate predecessor had said gives us some hint of the variations in Revolutionary opinion then prevailing among the members, as well as of the advanced position always taken by Patrick Henry: —

"'Could I suppose that we came to frame an American constitution, instead of endeavoring to correct the faults in an old one, I can't yet think that all government is at an end. The measure of arbitrary power is not full;

and I think it must run over, before we undertake to frame a new constitution. To the virtue, spirit, and abilities of Virginia we owe much. I should always, therefore, from inclination as well as justice, be for giving Virginia its full weight. I am not clear that we ought not to be bound by a majority, though ever so small; but I only mentioned it as a matter of danger worthy of consideration.' " [1]

Of this entire debate, the most significant issue is indicated by the following passage from the journal for Tuesday, the 6th of September: —

" *Resolved*, that in determining questions in this Congress, each colony or province shall have one vote; the Congress not being possessed of, or at present able to procure, proper materials for ascertaining the importance of each colony." [2]

So far as it is now possible to ascertain it, such was Patrick Henry's part in the first discussion held by the first Continental Congress, — a discussion occupying parts of two days, and relating purely to methods of procedure by that body, and not to the matters of grievance between the colonies and Great Britain. We have a right to infer something as to the quality of the first impression made upon his associates by Patrick Henry in consequence of his three speeches in this discussion, from the fact that when, at the close of it, an order was taken for the appointment of two grand committees, one "to state the rights of the colo-

[1] *Works of John Adams*, ii. 366-368.
[2] 4 *Am. Arch.* i. 898, 899.

nies," the other "to examine and report the several statutes which affect the trade and manufactures of the colonies," Patrick Henry was chosen to represent Virginia on the latter committee,[1] — a position not likely to have been selected for a man who, however eloquent he may have seemed, had not also shown business-like and lawyer-like qualities.

The Congress kept steadily at work from Monday, the 5th of September, to Wednesday, the 26th of October, — just seven weeks and two days. Though not a legislative body, it resembled all legislative bodies then in existence, in the fact that it sat with closed doors, and that it gave to the public only such results as it chose to give. Upon the difficult and exciting subjects which came before it, there were, very likely, many splendid passages of debate; and we cannot doubt that in all these discussions Patrick Henry took his usually conspicuous and powerful share. Yet no official record was kept of what was said by any member; and it is only from the hurried private memoranda of two of his colleagues that we are able to learn anything more respecting Patrick Henry's participation in the debates of those seven weeks.

For example, just two weeks after the opening of this Congress, one of its most critical members, Silas Deane of Connecticut, in a letter to his wife, gave some capital sketches of his more prominent

[1] 4 *Am. Arch.* i. 899.

associates there, especially those from the South,
— as Randolph, Harrison, Washington, Pendleton, Richard Henry Lee, and Patrick Henry.
The latter he describes as "a lawyer, and the
completest speaker I ever heard. If his future
speeches are equal to the small samples he has
hitherto given us, they will be worth preserving;
but in a letter I can give you no idea of the music
of his voice, or the high-wrought yet natural elegance of his style and manner."[1]

It was on the 28th of September that Joseph
Galloway brought forward his celebrated plan for
a permanent reconciliation between Great Britain
and her colonies. This was simply a scheme for
what we should now call home rule, on a basis of
colonial confederation, with an American parliament to be elected every three years by the legislatures of the several colonies, and with a gover-
nor-general to be appointed by the crown. The
plan came very near to adoption.[2] The member
who introduced it was a man of great ability and
great influence; it was supported by James Duane
and John Jay; it was pronounced by Edward Rutledge to be "almost a perfect plan;" and in the
final trial it was lost only by a vote of six colonies
to five. Could it have been adopted, the disruption of the British empire would certainly have
been averted for that epoch, and, as an act of vio-

---

[1] *Conn. Hist. Soc. Coll.* ii. 181.

[2] The text of Galloway's plan is given in 4 *Am. Arch.* i. 905,
906.

lence and of unkindness, would perhaps have been
averted forever; while the thirteen English colonies would have remained English colonies, without ceasing to be free.

The plan, however, was distrusted and resisted,
with stern and implacable hostility, by the more
radical members of the Congress, particularly by
those from Massachusetts and Virginia; and an
outline of what Patrick Henry said in his assault
upon it, delivered on the very day on which it was
introduced, is thus given by John Adams: —

"The original constitution of the colonies was founded
on the broadest and most generous base. The regulation of our trade was compensation enough for all the
protection we ever experienced from her.

"We shall liberate our constituents from a corrupt
House of Commons, but throw them into the arms of an
American legislature, that may be bribed by that nation
which avows, in the face of the world, that bribery is a
part of her system of government.

"Before we are obliged to pay taxes as they do, let
us be as free as they; let us have our trade open with
all the world.

"We are not to consent by the representatives of
representatives.

"I am inclined to think the present measures lead to
war." [1]

The only other trace to be discovered of Patrick
Henry's activity in the debates of this Congress
belongs to the day just before the one on which

[1] *Works of John Adams*, ii. 390.

Galloway's plan was introduced. The subject then under discussion was the measure for non-importation and non-exportation. On considerations of forbearance, Henry tried to have the date for the application of this measure postponed from November to December, saying, characteristically, "We don't mean to hurt even our rascals, if we have any." [1]

Probably the most notable work done by this Congress was its preparation of those masterly state papers in which it interpreted and affirmed the constitutional attitude of the colonies, and which, when laid upon the table of the House of Lords, drew forth the splendid encomium of Chatham. [2] In many respects the most important, and certainly the most difficult, of these state papers, was the address to the king. The motion for such an address was made on the 1st of October. On the same day the preparation of it was entrusted to a very able committee, consisting of Richard Henry Lee, John Adams, Thomas Johnson, Patrick Henry, and John Rutledge; and on the 21st of October the committee was strengthened by the accession of John Dickinson, who had entered the Congress but four days before. [3] Precisely what part Patrick Henry took in the preparation of this address is not now known; but there is no evidence whatever for the assertion [4] that the first draft,

---

[1] *Works of John Adams*, ii. 385.
[2] Hansard, *Parl. Hist.* xviii. 155, 156 note, 157.
[3] 4 *Am. Arch.* i. 906, 907, 927.
[4] Wirt, 109.

which, when submitted to Congress, proved to be unsatisfactory, was the work of Patrick Henry. That draft, as is now abundantly proved, was prepared by the chairman of the committee, Richard Henry Lee, but after full instructions from Congress and from the committee itself.[1] In its final form, the address was largely moulded by the expert and gentle hand of John Dickinson.[2] No one can doubt, however, that even though Patrick Henry may have contributed nothing to the literary execution of this fine address, he was not inactive in its construction,[3] and that he was not likely to have suggested any abatement from its free and manly spirit.

The only other committee on which he is known to have served during this Congress was one to which his name was added on the 19th of September, — "the committee appointed to state the rights of the colonies,"[4] an object, certainly, far better suited to the peculiarities of his talents and of his temper than that of the committee for the conciliation of a king.

Of course, the one gift in which Patrick Henry excelled all other men of his time and neighborhood was the gift of eloquence; and it is not to be

---

[1] *Works of John Adams*, x. 79; ii. 396, note; Lee's *Life of R. H. Lee*, i. 116–118, 270–272.

[2] *Political Writings*, ii. 19–29.

[3] Thus John Adams, on 11th October, writes: "Spent the evening with Mr. Henry at his lodgings consulting about a petition to the king." *Works*, ii. 396.

[4] 4 *Am. Arch.* i. 904.

doubted that in many other forms of effort, involving, for example, plain sense, practical experience, and knowledge of details, he was often equaled, and perhaps even surpassed, by men who had not a particle of his genius for oratory. This fact, the analogue of which is common in the history of all men of genius, seems to be the basis of an anecdote which, possibly, is authentic, and which, at any rate, has been handed down by one who was always a devoted friend[1] of the great orator. It is said that, after Henry and Lee had made their first speeches, Samuel Chase of Maryland was so impressed by their superiority that he walked over to the seat of one of his colleagues and said: "We might as well go home; we are not able to legislate with these men." But some days afterward, perhaps in the midst of the work of the committee on the statutes affecting trade and commerce, the same member was able to relieve himself by the remark: "Well, after all, I find these are but men, and, in mere matters of business, but very common men."[2]

It seems hardly right to pass from these studies upon the first Continental Congress, and upon Patrick Henry's part in it, without some reference to Wirt's treatment of the subject in a book which has now been, for nearly three quarters of a century, the chief source of public information con-

---

[1] Judge John Tyler, in Wirt, 109, note.

[2] For another form of this tradition, see Curtis's *Life of Webster*, i. 588.

cerning Patrick Henry. There is perhaps no other portion of this book which is less worthy of respect.[1] It is not only unhistoric in nearly all the very few alleged facts of the narrative, but it does great injustice to Patrick Henry by representing him virtually as a mere declaimer, as an ill-instructed though most impressive rhapsodist in debate, and as without any claim to the character of a serious statesman, or even of a man of affairs; while, by the somewhat grandiose and melodramatic tone of some portion of the narrative, it is singularly out of harmony with the real tone of that famous assemblage, — an assemblage of Anglo-Saxon lawyers, politicians, and men of business, who were probably about as practical and sober-minded a company as had been got together for any manly undertaking since that of Runnymede.

Wirt begins by convening his Congress one day too soon, namely, on the 4th of September, which was Sunday; and he represents the members as "personally strangers" to one another, and as sitting, after their preliminary organization, in a "long and deep silence," the members meanwhile looking around upon each other with a sort of helpless anxiety, "every individual" being reluctant "to open a business so fearfully momentous." But

"in the midst of this deep and death-like silence, and just when it was beginning to become painfully embar-

[1] Pages 105–113.

rassing, Mr. Henry arose slowly, as if borne down by the weight of the subject. After faltering, according to his habit, through a most impressive exordium, in which he merely echoed back the consciousness of every other heart in deploring his inability to do justice to the occasion, he launched gradually into a recital of the colonial wrongs. Rising, as he advanced, with the grandeur of his subject, and glowing at length with all the majesty and expectation of the occasion, his speech seemed more than that of mortal man. Even those who had heard him in all his glory in the House of Burgesses of Virginia were astonished at the manner in which his talents seemed to swell and expand themselves to fill the vaster theatre in which he was now placed. There was no rant, no rhapsody, no labor of the understanding, no straining of the voice, no confusion of the utterance. His countenance was erect, his eye steady, his action noble, his enunciation clear and firm, his mind poised on its centre, his views of his subject comprehensive and great, and his imagination coruscating with a magnificence and a variety which struck even that assembly with amazement and awe. He sat down amidst murmurs of astonishment and applause; and, as he had been before proclaimed the greatest orator of Virginia, he was now on every hand admitted to be the first orator of America." [1]

This great speech from Patrick Henry, which certainly was not made on that occasion, and probably was never made at all, Wirt causes to be followed by a great speech from Richard Henry Lee, although the journal could have informed him that

[1] Wirt, 105, 106.

Lee was not even in the House on that day.
Moreover, he makes Patrick Henry to be the
author of the unfortunate first draft of the address
to the king, — a document which was written by
another man; and on this fiction he founds two
or three pages of lamentation and of homily with
reference to Patrick Henry's inability to express
himself in writing, in consequence of "his early
neglect of literature." Finally, he thinks it due "to
historic truth to record that the superior powers"
of Patrick Henry "were manifested only in debate;" and that, although he and Richard Henry
Lee "took the undisputed lead in the Assembly,"
"during the first days of the session, while general
grievances were the topic," yet they were both
"completely thrown into the shade" "when called
down from the heights of declamation to that
severer test of intellectual excellence, the details
of business," — the writer here seeming to forget
that "general grievances" were not the topic
"during the first days of the session," and that
the very speeches by which these two men are said
to have made their mark there, were speeches on
mere rules of the House relating to methods of
procedure.[1]

Since the death of Wirt, and the publication of
the biography of him by Kennedy, it has been
possible for us to ascertain just how the genial
author of "The Life and Character of Patrick

[1] The exact rules under debate during those first two days are
given in 4 *Am. Arch.* i. 898, 899.

Henry " came to be so gravely misled in this part of his book. "The whole passage relative to the first Congress" appears to have been composed from data furnished by Jefferson, who, however, was not a member of that Congress; and in the original manuscript the very words of Jefferson were surrounded with quotation marks, and were attributed to him by name. When, however, that great man, who loved not to send out calumnies into the world with his own name attached to them, came to inspect this portion of Wirt's manuscript, he was moved by his usual prudence to write such a letter as drew from Wirt the following consolatory assurance: —

"Your repose shall never be endangered by any act of mine, if I can help it. Immediately on the receipt of your last letter, and before the manuscript had met any other eye, I wrote over again the whole passage relative to the first Congress, omitting the marks of quotation, and removing your name altogether from the communication." [1]

The final adjournment of the first Continental Congress, it will be remembered, did not occur until its members had spent together more than seven weeks of the closest intellectual intimacy. Surely, no mere declaimer however enchanting, no sublime babbler on the rights of man, no political charlatan strutting about for the display of his preternatural gift of articulate wind, could have grappled in keen debate, for all those weeks, on

[1] Kennedy, *Mem. of Wirt*, i. 364.

the greatest of earthly subjects, with fifty of the ablest men in America, without exposing to their view all his own intellectual poverty, and without losing the very last shred of their intellectual respect for him. Whatever may have been the impression formed of Patrick Henry as a mere orator by his associates in that Congress, nothing can be plainer than that those men carried with them to their homes that report of him as a man of extraordinary intelligence, integrity, and power, which was the basis of his subsequent fame for many years among the American people. Long afterward, John Adams, who formed his estimate of Patrick Henry chiefly from what he saw of him in that Congress, and who was never much addicted to bestowing eulogiums on any man but John Adams, wrote to Jefferson that "in the Congress of 1774 there was not one member, except Patrick Henry, who appeared . . . sensible of the precipice, or rather the pinnacle, on which we stood, and had candor and courage enough to acknowledge it."[1] To Wirt likewise, a few years later, the same hard critic of men testified that Patrick Henry always impressed him as a person "of deep reflection, keen sagacity, clear foresight, daring enterprise, inflexible intrepidity, and untainted integrity, with an ardent zeal for the liberties, the honor, and felicity of his country and his species."[2]

Of the parting interview between these two men, at the close of that first period of thorough

---

[1] *Works of John Adams*, x. 78.   [2] *Ibid*. x. 277.

personal acquaintance, there remains from the hand of one of them a graphic account that reveals to us something of the conscious kinship which seems ever afterward to have bound together their robust and impetuous natures.

"When Congress," says John Adams, "had finished their business, as they thought, in the autumn of 1774, I had with Mr. Henry, before we took leave of each other, some familiar conversation, in which I expressed a full conviction that our resolves, declarations of rights, enumeration of wrongs, petitions, remonstrances, and addresses, associations, and non-importation agreements, however they might be expected by the people in America, and however necessary to cement the union of the colonies, would be but waste paper in England. Mr. Henry said they might make some impression among the people of England, but agreed with me that they would be totally lost upon the government. I had but just received a short and hasty letter, written to me by Major Hawley, of Northampton, containing 'a few broken hints,' as he called them, of what he thought was proper to be done, and concluding [1] with these words: 'After all, we must fight.' This letter I read to Mr. Henry, who listened with great attention; and as soon as I had pronounced the words, 'After all, we must fight,' he raised his head, and with an energy and vehemence that I can never forget, broke out with: 'By God, I am of that man's mind!'" [2]

[1] As a matter of fact, the letter from Hawley began with these words, instead of "concluding" with them.

[2] *Works of John Adams*, x. 277, 278.

This anecdote, it may be mentioned, contains the only instance on record, for any period of Patrick Henry's life, implying his use of what at first may seem a profane oath. John Adams, upon whose very fallible memory in old age the story rests, declares that he did not at the time regard Patrick Henry's words as an oath, but rather as a solemn asseveration, affirmed religiously, upon a very great occasion. At any rate, that asseveration proved to be a prophecy; for from it there then leaped a flame that lighted up for an instant the next inevitable stage in the evolution of events, — the tragic and bloody outcome of all these wary lucubrations and devices of the assembled political wizards of America.

It is interesting to note that, at the very time when the Congress at Philadelphia was busy with its stern work, the people of Virginia were grappling with the peril of an Indian war assailing them from beyond their western mountains. There has recently been brought to light a letter written at Hanover, on the 15th of October, 1774, by the aged mother of Patrick Henry, to a friend living far out towards the exposed district; and this letter is a touching memorial both of the general anxiety over the two concurrent events, and of the motherly pride and piety of the writer: —

"My son Patrick has been gone to Philadelphia near seven weeks. The affairs of Congress are kept with great secrecy, nobody being allowed to be present. I assure you we have our lowland troubles and fears with respect to Great Britain. Perhaps our good God may bring good to us out of these many evils which threaten us, not only from the mountains but from the seas." [1]

[1] Peyton, *History of Augusta County.* 345, where will be found the entire letter.

CHAPTER IX

"AFTER ALL, WE MUST FIGHT"

WE now approach that brilliant passage in the life of Patrick Henry when, in the presence of the second revolutionary convention of Virginia, he proclaimed the futility of all further efforts for peace, and the instant necessity of preparing for war.

The speech which he is said to have made on that occasion has been committed to memory and declaimed by several generations of American schoolboys, and is now perhaps familiarly known to a larger number of the American people than any other considerable bit of secular prose in our language. The old church at Richmond, in which he made this marvelous speech, is in our time visited every year, as a patriotic shrine, by thousands of pilgrims, who seek curiously the very spot upon the floor where the orator is believed to have stood when he uttered those words of flame. It is chiefly the tradition of that one speech which to-day keeps alive, in millions of American homes, the name of Patrick Henry, and which lifts him, in the popular faith, almost to the rank of some mythical hero of romance.

In reality, that speech, and the resolutions in support of which that speech was made, constituted Patrick Henry's individual declaration of war against Great Britain. But the question is: To what extent, if any, was he therein original, or even in advance of his fellow-countrymen, and particularly of his associates in the Virginia convention?

It is essential to a just understanding of the history of that crisis in revolutionary thought, and it is of very high importance, likewise, to the historic position of Patrick Henry, that no mistake be committed here; especially that he be not made the victim of a disastrous reaction from any over-statement [1] respecting the precise nature and extent of the service then rendered by him to the cause of the Revolution.

We need, therefore, to glance for a moment at the period between October, 1774, and March, 1775, with the purpose of tracing therein the more important tokens of the growth of the popular conviction that a war with Great Britain had become inevitable, and was to be immediately prepared for by the several colonies, — two propositions which form the substance of all that Patrick Henry said on the great occasion now before us.

As early as the 21st of October, 1774, the first Continental Congress, after having suggested all

[1] For an example of such overstatement, see Wirt, 114–123. See, also, the damaging comments thereon by Rives, *Life of Madison*, i. 63, 64.

possible methods for averting war, made this solemn declaration to the people of the colonies: "We think ourselves bound in duty to observe to you that the schemes agitated against these colonies have been so conducted as to render it prudent that you should extend your views to mournful events, and be in all respects prepared for every emergency."[1]　Just six days later, John Dickinson, a most conservative and peace-loving member of that Congress, wrote to an American friend in England: "I wish for peace ardently; but must say, delightful as it is, it will come more grateful by being unexpected.　The first act of violence on the part of administration in America, or the attempt to reinforce General Gage this winter or next year, will put the whole continent in arms, from Nova Scotia to Georgia."[2]　On the following day, the same prudent statesman wrote to another American friend, also in England: "The most peaceful provinces are now animated; and a civil war is unavoidable, unless there be a quick change of British measures."[3]　On the 29th of October, the eccentric Charles Lee, who was keenly watching the symptoms of colonial discontent and resistance, wrote from Philadelphia to an English nobleman: "Virginia, Rhode Island, and Carolina are forming corps.　Massachusetts Bay has long had a sufficient number instructed to become instructive of the rest.　Even this Quakering province is

[1] 4 *Am. Arch.* i. 928.　　　　[2] 4 *Ibid.* i. 947.
[3] *Ibid.*

following the example. . . . In short, unless the
banditti at Westminster speedily undo everything
they have done, their royal paymaster will hear of
reviews and manœuvres not quite so entertaining
as those he is presented with in Hyde Park and
Wimbledon Common."[1] On the 1st of November, a gentleman in Maryland wrote to a kinsman
in Glasgow: "The province of Virginia is raising
one company in every county. . . . This province
has taken the hint, and has begun to raise men in
every county also; and to the northward they have
large bodies, capable of acquitting themselves with
honor in the field."[2] At about the same time,
the General Assembly of Connecticut ordered that
every town should at once supply itself with "dou-
ble the quantity of powder, balls, and flints" that
had been hitherto required by law.[3] On the 5th
of November, the officers of the Virginia troops
accompanying Lord Dunmore on his campaign
against the Indians held a meeting at Fort Gower,
on the Ohio River, and passed this resolution:
"That we will exert every power within us for the
defence of American liberty, and for the support
of her just rights and privileges, not in any pre-
cipitate, riotous, or tumultuous manner, but when
regularly called forth by the unanimous voice of
our countrymen."[4] Not far from the same time,
the people of Rhode Island carried off to Providence from the batteries at Newport forty-four

[1] 4 *Am. Arch.* i. 949, 950.   [2] *Ibid.* i. 953.
[3] *Ibid.* 858.   [4] *Ibid.* i. 963.

pieces of cannon; and the governor frankly told
the commander of a British naval force near at
hand that they had done this in order to prevent
these cannon from falling into his hands, and with
the purpose of using them against "any power that
might offer to molest the colony." [1] Early in
December, the Provincial Convention of Maryland
recommended that all persons between sixteen and
fifty years of age should form themselves into military companies, and "be in readiness to act on any
emergency," — with a sort of grim humor prefa-
cing their recommendation by this exquisite morsel
of argumentative irony: —

" *Resolved* unanimously, that a well-regulated militia,
composed of the gentlemen freeholders and other freemen, is the natural strength and only stable security of
a free government; and that such militia will relieve
our mother country from any expense in our protection
and defence, will obviate the pretence of a necessity for
taxing us on that account, and render it unnecessary to
keep any standing army — ever dangerous to liberty —
in this province." [2]

The shrewdness of this courteous political thrust
on the part of the convention of Maryland seems
to have been so heartily relished by others that it
was thenceforward used again and again by similar
conventions elsewhere; and in fact, for the next
few months, these sentences became almost the
stereotyped formula by which revolutionary assem-
blages justified the arming and drilling of the mi-

[1] Hildreth, iii. 52. [2] 4 *Am. Arch.* i. 1032.

litia, — as, for example, that of Newcastle County, Delaware,[1] on the 21st of December; that of Fairfax County, Virginia,[2] on the 17th of January, 1775; and that of Augusta County, Virginia,[3] on the 22d of February.

In the mean time Lord Dunmore was not blind to all these military preparations in Virginia; and so early as the 24th of December, 1774, he had written to the Earl of Dartmouth: "Every county, besides, is now arming a company of men, whom they call an independent company, for the avowed purpose of protecting their committees, and to be employed against government, if occasion require."[4] Moreover, this alarming fact of military preparation, which Lord Dunmore had thus reported concerning Virginia, could have been reported with equal truth concerning nearly every other colony. In the early part of January, 1775, the Assembly of Connecticut gave order that the entire militia of that colony should be mustered every week.[5] In the latter part of January, the provincial convention of Pennsylvania, though representing a colony of Quakers, boldly proclaimed that, if the administration "should determine by force to effect a submission to the late arbitrary acts of the British Parliament," it would "resist such force, and at every hazard . . . defend the rights and liberties of America."[6] On the 15th

[1] 4 *Am. Arch.* i. 1022.
[2] *Ibid.* i. 1145.
[3] *Ibid.* i. 1254.
[4] *Ibid.* i. 1062.
[5] *Ibid.* i. 1139.
[6] *Ibid.* i. 1171.

of February, the Provincial Congress of Massachusetts urged the people to "spare neither time, pains, nor expense, at so critical a juncture, in perfecting themselves forthwith in military discipline."[1]

When, therefore, so late as Monday, the 20th of March, 1775, the second revolutionary convention of Virginia assembled at Richmond, its members were well aware that one of the chief measures to come before them for consideration must be that of recognizing the local military preparations among their own constituents, and of placing them all under some common organization and control. Accordingly, on Thursday, the 23d of March, after three days had been given to necessary preliminary subjects, the inevitable subject of military preparations was reached. Then it was that Patrick Henry took the floor and moved the adoption of the following resolutions, supporting his motion, undoubtedly, with a speech: —

"*Resolved*, That a well-regulated militia, composed of gentlemen and yeomen, is the natural strength and only security of a free government; that such a militia in this colony would forever render it unnecessary for the mother country to keep among us for the purpose of our defence any standing army of mercenary forces, always subversive of the quiet and dangerous to the liberties of the people, and would obviate the pretext of taxing us for their support.

"*Resolved*, That the establishment of such a militia

[1] 4 *Am. Arch.* i. 1340.

is at this time peculiarly necessary, by the state of our laws for the protection and defence of the country, some of which have already expired, and others will shortly do so; and that the known remissness of government in calling us together in a legislative capacity, renders it too insecure, in this time of danger and distress, to rely that opportunity will be given of renewing them in general assembly, or making any provision to secure our inestimable rights and liberties from those further violations with which they are threatened.

"*Resolved, therefore,* That this colony be immediately put into a posture of defence; and that . . . be a committee to prepare a plan for the embodying, arming, and disciplining such a number of men as may be sufficient for that purpose." [1]

No one' who reads these resolutions in the light of the facts just given, can find in them anything by which to account for the opposition which they are known to have met with in that assemblage. For that assemblage, it must be remembered, was not the Virginia legislature: it was a mere convention, and a revolutionary convention at that, gathered in spite of the objections of Lord Dunmore, representing simply the deliberate purpose of those Virginians who meant not finally to submit to unjust laws; some of its members, likewise, being under express instructions from their constituents to take measures for the immediate and adequate military organization of the colony. Not a man, probably, was sent to that convention, not a man

[1] 4 *Am. Arch.* ii. 167, 168.

surely would have gone to it, who was not in substantial sympathy with the prevailing revolutionary
spirit.

Of course, even they who were in sympathy with
that spirit might have objected to Patrick Henry's
resolutions, had those resolutions been marked by
any startling novelty in doctrine, or by anything
extreme or violent in expression. But, plainly,
they were neither extreme nor violent; they were
not even novel. They contained nothing essential
which had not been approved, in almost the same
words, more than three months before, by similar
conventions in Maryland and in Delaware; which
had not been approved, in almost the same words,
many weeks before, by county conventions in Virginia, — in one instance, by a county convention
presided over by Washington himself; which had
not been approved, in other language, either weeks
or months before, by Massachusetts, Rhode Island,
Connecticut, Pennsylvania, and other colonies;
which was not sanctioned by the plainest prudence
on the part of all persons who intended to make
any further stand whatsoever against the encroachments of Parliament. It is safe to say that no
man who had within him enough of the revolutionary spirit to have prompted his attendance at a
revolutionary convention could have objected to
any essential item in Patrick Henry's resolutions.

Why, then, were they objected to? Why was
their immediate passage resisted? The official
journal of the convention throws no light upon the

question: it records merely the adoption of the resolutions, and is entirely silent respecting any discussion that they may have provoked. Thirty years afterward, however, St. George Tucker, who, though not a member of this convention, had yet as a visitor watched its proceedings that day, gave from memory some account of them; and to him we are indebted for the names of the principal men who stood out against Patrick Henry's motion. "This produced," he says, "an animated debate, in which Colonel Richard Bland, Mr. Nicholas, the treasurer, and I think Colonel Harrison, of Berkeley, and Mr. Pendleton, were opposed to the resolution, as conceiving it to be premature;"[1] all these men being prudent politicians, indeed, but all fully committed to the cause of the Revolution.

At first, this testimony may seem to leave us as much in the dark as before; and yet all who are familiar with the politics of Virginia at that period will see in this cluster of names some clew to the secret of their opposition. It was an opposition to Patrick Henry himself, and as far as possible to any measure of which he should be the leading champion. Yet even this is not enough. Whatever may have been their private motives in resisting a measure advocated by Patrick Henry, they must still have had some reason which they would be willing to assign. St. George Tucker tells us that they conceived his resolutions to be "prema-

[1] MS.

ture." But in themselves his resolutions, so far
from being premature, were rather tardy; they
lagged weeks and even months behind many of the
best counties in Virginia· itself, as well as behind
those other colonies to which in political feeling
Virginia was always most nearly akin.

The only possible explanation of the case seems
to be found, not in the resolutions themselves, but
in the special interpretation put upon them by
Patrick Henry in the speech which, according to
parliamentary usage, he seems to have made in
moving their adoption. What was that interpretation? In the true answer to that question, no
doubt, lies the secret of the resistance which his
motion encountered. For, down to that day, no
public body in America, and no public man, had
openly spoken of a war with Great Britain in any
more decisive way than as a thing highly probable,
indeed, but still not inevitable. At last Patrick
Henry spoke of it, and he wanted to induce the
convention of Virginia to speak of it, as a thing
inevitable. Others had said, "The war must come,
and will come, — unless certain things are done."
Patrick Henry, brushing away every prefix or suffix
of uncertainty, every half-despairing "if," every
fragile and pathetic "unless," exclaimed, in the
hearing of all men: "Why talk of things being
now done which can avert the war? Such things
will not be done. The war is coming: it has come
already." Accordingly, other conventions in the
colonies, in adopting similar resolutions, had merely

announced the probability of war. Patrick Henry
would have this convention, by adopting his resolutions, virtually declare war itself.

In this alone, it is apparent, consisted the real
priority and offensiveness of Patrick Henry's position as a revolutionary statesman on the 23d of
March, 1775. In this alone were his resolutions
"premature." The very men who opposed them
because they were to be understood as closing the
door against the possibility of peace, would have
favored them had they only left that door open, or
even ajar. But Patrick Henry demanded of the
people of Virginia that they should treat all further talk of peace as mere prattle; that they should
seize the actual situation by a bold grasp of it in
front; that, looking upon the war as a fact, they
should instantly proceed to get ready for it. And
therein, once more, in revolutionary ideas, was
Patrick Henry one full step in advance of his contemporaries. Therein, once more, did he justify
the reluctant praise of Jefferson, who was a member of that convention, and who, nearly fifty years
afterward, said concerning Patrick Henry to a
great statesman from Massachusetts: "After all,
it must be allowed that he was our leader in the
measures of the Revolution in Virginia, and in that
respect more is due to him than to any other person. . . . He left all of us far behind." [1]

Such, at any rate, we have a right to suppose,
was the substantial issue presented by the resolu-

[1] Curtis, *Life of Webster*, i. 585.

tions of Patrick Henry, and by his introductory
speech in support of them; and upon this issue
the little group of politicians — able and patriotic
men, who always opposed his leadership — then
arrayed themselves against him, making the most,
doubtless, of everything favoring the possibility
and the desirableness of a peaceful adjustment of
the great dispute. But their opposition to him
only produced the usual result, — of arousing him
to an effort which simply overpowered and scattered
all further resistance. It was in review of their
whole quivering platoon of hopes and fears, of
doubts, cautions, and delays, that he then made
the speech which seems to have wrought astonishing effects upon those who heard it, and which,
though preserved in a most inadequate report, now
fills so great a space in the traditions of revolutionary eloquence : —

" ' No man, Mr. President, thinks more highly than I
do of the patriotism, as well as the abilities, of the very
honorable gentlemen who have just addressed the House.
But different men often see the same subject in different
lights ; and, therefore, I hope it will not be thought dis-
respectful to those gentlemen if, entertaining, as I do,
opinions of a character very opposite to theirs, I should
speak forth my sentiments freely, and without reserve.
This is no time for ceremony. The question before the
house is one of awful moment to this country. For my
own part, I consider it as nothing less than a question of
freedom or slavery. And in proportion to the magni-
tude of the subject ought to be the freedom of the de-

bate. It is only in this way that we can hope to arrive at truth, and fulfil the great responsibility which we hold to God and our country. Should I keep back my opinions at such a time, through fear of giving offence, I should consider myself as guilty of treason towards my country, and of an act of disloyalty towards the majesty of Heaven, which I revere above all earthly kings.

" 'Mr. President, it is natural to man to indulge in the illusions of Hope. We are apt to shut our eyes against a painful truth, and listen to the song of that siren till she transforms us into beasts. Is this the part of wise men, engaged in a great and arduous struggle for liberty? Are we disposed to be of the number of those who, having eyes, see not, and having ears, hear not, the things which so nearly concern their temporal salvation? For my part, whatever anguish of spirit it may cost, I am willing to know the whole truth; to know the worst, and to provide for it.

" 'I have but one lamp by which my feet are guided, and that is the lamp of experience. I know of no way of judging of the future but by the past. And, judging by the past, I wish to know what there has been in the conduct of the British ministry, for the last ten years, to justify those hopes with which gentlemen have been pleased to solace themselves and the House. Is it that insidious smile with which our petition has been lately received? Trust it not, sir; it will prove a snare to your feet. Suffer not yourselves to be betrayed with a kiss. Ask yourselves how this gracious reception of our petition comports with those warlike preparations which cover our waters and darken our land. Are fleets and armies necessary to a work of love and reconciliation? Have we shown ourselves so unwilling to be reconciled, that force must be called in to win back our love? Let us not deceive ourselves, sir. These are the implements of war and subjugation, — the last arguments to which kings resort.

"'I ask gentlemen, sir, what means this martial array, if its purpose be not to force us to submission? Can gentlemen assign any other possible motive for it? Has Great Britain any enemy in this quarter of the world, to call for all this accumulation of navies and armies? No, sir, she has none. They are meant for·us: they can be meant for no other. They are sent over to bind and rivet upon us those chains which the British ministry have been so long forging.

"'And what have we to oppose to them? Shall we try argument? Sir, we have been trying that for the last ten years. Have we anything new to offer upon the subject? Nothing. We have held the subject up in every light of which it is capable; but it has been all in vain. Shall we resort to entreaty, and humble supplication? What terms shall we find which have not been already exhausted?

"'Let us not, I beseech you, sir, deceive ourselves longer. Sir, we have done everything that could be done to avert the storm which is now coming on. We have petitioned; we have remonstrated; we have supplicated; we have prostrated ourselves before the throne, and have implored its interposition to arrest the tyrannical hands of the ministry and Parliament. Our petitions have been slighted; our remonstrances have produced additional violence and insult; our supplications have been disregarded; and we have been spurned with contempt from the foot of the throne.

"'In vain, after these things, may we indulge the fond

hope of peace and reconciliation. There is no longer any room for hope. If we wish to be free; if we mean to preserve inviolate those inestimable privileges for which we have been so long contending; if we mean not basely to abandon the noble struggle in which we have been so long engaged, and which we have pledged ourselves never to abandon until the glorious object of our contest shall be obtained, — we must fight! I repeat it, sir, — we must fight! An appeal to arms, and to the God of hosts, is all that is left us.' "

Up to this point in his address, the orator seems to have spoken with great deliberation and self-restraint. St. George Tucker, who was present, and who has left a written statement of his recollections both of the speech and of the scene, says: —

"It was on that occasion that I first felt a full impression of Mr. Henry's powers. In vain should I attempt to give any idea of his speech. He was calm and collected; touched upon the origin and progress of the dispute between Great Britain and the colonies, the various conciliatory measures adopted by the latter, and the uniformly increasing tone of violence and arrogance on the part of the former."

Then follows, in Tucker's narrative, the passage included in the last two paragraphs of the speech as given above, after which he adds: —

"Imagine to yourself this speech delivered with all the calm dignity of Cato of Utica; imagine to yourself the Roman senate assembled in the capitol when it was entered by the profane Gauls, who at first were awed by their presence as if they had entered an assembly of the gods; imagine that you heard that Cato addressing such a senate; imagine that you saw the handwriting on the wall of Belshazzar's palace; imagine you heard a voice as from heaven uttering the words, 'We must fight!' as the doom of fate, — and you may have some idea of the speaker, the assembly to whom he addressed himself, and the auditory of which I was one." [1]

But, by a comparison of this testimony of St. George Tucker with that of others who heard the speech, it is made evident that, as the orator then advanced toward the conclusion and real climax of his argument, he no longer maintained "the calm dignity of Cato of Utica," but that his manner gradually deepened into an intensity of passion and a dramatic power which were overwhelming. He thus continued: —

" 'They tell us, sir, that we are weak, — unable to cope with so formidable an adversary. But when shall we be stronger? Will it be the next week, or the next year? Will it be when we are totally disarmed, and when a British guard shall be stationed in every house? Shall we gather strength by irresolution and inaction? Shall we acquire the means of effectual resistance by lying supinely on our backs, and hugging the delusive phantom of Hope, until our enemies shall have bound us hand and foot?

" 'Sir, we are not weak, if we make a proper use of those means which the God of nature hath placed in our power. Three millions of people armed in the holy cause of liberty, and in such a country as that which we

[1] MS.

possess, are invincible by any force which our enemy can send against us.

"'Besides, sir, we shall not fight our battles alone. There is a just God who presides over the destinies of nations, and who will raise up friends to fight our battles for us. The battle, sir, is not to the strong alone: it is to the vigilant, the active, the brave. Besides, sir, we have no election. If we were base enough to desire it, it is now too late to retire from the contest. There is no retreat but in submission and slavery. Our chains are forged. Their clanking may be heard on the plains of Boston. The war is inevitable. And let it come! I repeat it, sir, let it come!

"'It is in vain, sir, to extenuate the matter. Gentlemen may cry peace, peace, but there is no peace. The war is actually begun. The next gale that sweeps from the north will bring to our ears the clash of resounding arms. Our brethren are already in the field. Why stand we here idle? What is it that gentlemen wish? what would they have? Is life so dear, or peace so sweet, as to be purchased at the price of chains and slavery? Forbid it, Almighty God! I know not what course others may take, but as for me, give me liberty, or give me death!'"

Of this tremendous speech there are in existence two traditional descriptions, neither of which is inconsistent with the testimony given by St. George Tucker. He, as a lawyer and a judge, seems to have retained the impression of that portion of the speech which was the more argumentative and unimpassioned: the two other reporters seem to have remembered especially its later and more emotional

passages. Our first traditional description was
obtained by Henry Stephens Randall from a
clergyman, who had it from an aged friend, also a
clergyman, who heard the speech itself : —

"Henry rose with an unearthly fire burning in his
eye. He commenced somewhat calmly, but the smo-
thered excitement began more and more to play upon his
features and thrill in the tones of his voice. The ten-
dons of his neck stood out white and rigid like whip-
cords. His voice rose louder and louder, until the walls
of the building, and all within them, seemed to shake
and rock in its tremendous vibrations. Finally, his pale
face and glaring eye became terrible to look upon. Men
leaned forward in their seats, with their heads strained
forward, their faces pale, and their eyes glaring like the
speaker's. His last exclamation, 'Give me liberty, or
give me death!' was like the shout of the leader which
turns back the rout of battle. The old man from whom
this tradition was derived added that, 'when the orator
sat down, he himself felt sick with excitement. Every
eye yet gazed entranced on Henry. It seemed as if a
word from him would have led to any wild explosion of
violence. Men looked beside themselves.'" [1]

The second traditional description of the speech
is here given from a manuscript [2] of Edward Fontaine, who obtained it in 1834 from John Roane,
who himself heard the speech. Roane told Fontaine that the orator's "voice, countenance, and
gestures gave an irresistible force to his words,

[1] Randall, *Life of Jefferson*, i. 101, 102.
[2] Now in the library of Cornell University.

which no description could make intelligible to one who had never seen him, nor heard him speak;" but, in order to convey some notion of the orator's manner, Roane described the delivery of the closing sentences of the speech:—

"You remember, sir, the conclusion of the speech, so often declaimed in various ways by school-boys,—'Is life so dear, or peace so sweet, as to be purchased at the price of chains and slavery? Forbid it, Almighty God! I know not what course others may take, but as for me, give me liberty, or give me death!' He gave each of these words a meaning which is not conveyed by the reading or delivery of them in the ordinary way. When he said, 'Is life so dear, or peace so sweet, as to be purchased at the price of chains and slavery?' he stood in the attitude of a condemned galley slave, loaded with fetters, awaiting his doom. His form was bowed; his wrists were crossed; his manacles were almost visible as he stood like an embodiment of helplessness and agony. After a solemn pause, he raised his eyes and chained hands towards heaven, and prayed, in words and tones which thrilled every heart, 'Forbid it, Almighty God!' He then turned towards the timid loyalists of the House, who were quaking with terror at the idea of the consequences of participating in proceedings which would be visited with the penalties of treason by the British crown; and he slowly bent his form yet nearer to the earth, and said, 'I know not what course others may take,' and he accompanied the words with his hands still crossed, while he seemed to be weighed down with additional chains. The man appeared transformed into an oppressed, heart-broken, and hopeless felon. After re-

maining in this posture of humiliation long enough to
impress the imagination with the condition of the colony
under the iron heel of military despotism, he arose
proudly, and exclaimed, 'but as for me,' — and the
words hissed through his clenched teeth, while his body
was thrown back, and every muscle and tendon was
strained against the fetters which bound him, and, with
his countenance distorted by agony and rage, he looked
for a moment like Laocoön in a death struggle with
coiling serpents; then the loud, clear, triumphant notes,
'Give me liberty,' electrified the assembly. It was not
a prayer, but a stern demand, which would submit to no
refusal or delay. The sound of his voice, as he spoke
these memorable words, was like that of a Spartan pæan
on the field of Platæa; and, as each syllable of the word
'liberty' echoed through the building, his fetters were
shivered; his arms were hurled apart; and the links of
his chains were scattered to the winds. When he spoke
the word 'liberty' with an emphasis never given it before, his hands were open, and his arms elevated and extended; his countenance was radiant; he stood erect and
defiant; while the sound of his voice and the sublimity of
his attitude made him appear a magnificent incarnation
of Freedom, and expressed all that can be acquired or
enjoyed by nations and individuals invincible and free.
After a momentary pause, only long enough to permit
the echo of the word 'liberty' to cease, he let his left
hand fall powerless to his side, and clenched his right
hand firmly, as if holding a dagger with the point aimed
at his breast. He stood like a Roman senator defying
Cæsar, while the unconquerable spirit of Cato of Utica
flashed from every feature; and he closed the grand
appeal with the solemn words, 'or give me death!' which

sounded with the awful cadence of a hero's dirge, fear-
less of death, and victorious in death; and he suited the
action to the word by a blow upon the left breast with
the right hand, which seemed to drive the dagger to the
patriot's heart." [1]

Before passing from this celebrated speech, it
is proper to say something respecting the authenticity of the version of it which has come down to
us, and which is now so universally known in
America. The speech is given in these pages substantially as it was given by Wirt in his "Life of
Henry." Wirt himself does not mention whence
he obtained his version; and all efforts to discover
that version as a whole, in any writing prior to
Wirt's book, have thus far been unsuccessful.
These facts have led even so genial a critic as
Grigsby to incline to the opinion that "much of
the speech published by Wirt is apocryphal." [2]
It would, indeed, be an odd thing, and a source
of no little disturbance to many minds, if such
should turn out to be the case, and if we should
have to conclude that an apocryphal speech written by Wirt, and attributed by him to Patrick
Henry fifteen years after the great orator's death,
had done more to perpetuate the renown of Patrick Henry's oratory than had been done by any
and all the words actually spoken by the orator
himself during his lifetime. On the other hand,
it should be said that Grigsby himself admits that
"the outline of the argument" and "some of its

[1] MS.   [2] *Va. Conv. of* 1776, 150, note.

expressions " are undoubtedly "authentic." That
this is so is apparent, likewise, from the written
recollections of St. George Tucker, wherein the
substance of the speech is given, besides one entire
passage in almost the exact language of the version by Wirt. Finally, John Roane, in 1834, in
his conversation with Edward Fontaine, is said
to have "verified the correctness of the speech as
it was written by Judge Tyler for Mr. Wirt." [1]
This, unfortunately, is the only intimation that
has anywhere been found attributing Wirt's version to the excellent authority of Judge John
Tyler. If the statement could be confirmed, it
would dispel every difficulty at once. But, even
though the statement should be set aside, enough
would still remain to justify us in thinking that
Wirt's version of the famous speech by no means
deserves to be called "apocryphal," in any such
sense as that word has when applied, for example,
to the speeches in Livy and in Thucydides, or in
Botta. In the first place, Wirt's version certainly
gives the substance of the speech as actually made
by Patrick Henry on the occasion named; and,
for the form of it, Wirt seems to have gathered
testimony from all available living witnesses, and
then, from such sentences or snatches of sentences
as these witnesses could remember, as well as from
his own conception of the orator's method of expression, to have constructed the version which he
has handed down to us. Even in that case, it is

[1] MS.

probably far more accurate and authentic than are most of the famous speeches attributed to public characters before reporters' galleries were opened, and before the art of reporting was brought to its present perfection.

Returning, now, from this long account of Patrick Henry's most celebrated speech, to the assemblage in which it was made, it remains to be mentioned that the resolutions, as offered by Patrick Henry, were carried; and that the committee, called for by those resolutions, to prepare a plan for "embodying, arming, and disciplining" the militia,[1] was at once appointed. Of this committee Patrick Henry was chairman; and with him were associated Richard Henry Lee, Nicholas, Harrison, Riddick, Washington, Stephen, Lewis, Christian, Pendleton, Jefferson, and Zane. On the following day, Friday, the 24th of March, the committee brought in its report, which was laid over for one day, and then, after some amendment, was unanimously adopted.

The convention did not close its labors until Monday, the 27th of March. The contemporaneous estimate of Patrick Henry, not merely as a leader in debate, but as a constitutional lawyer, and as a man of affairs, may be partly gathered from the fact of his connection with each of the two other important committees of this convention, — the committee "to inquire whether his majesty may of right advance the terms of granting lands

[1] 4 *Am. Arch.* ii. 168.

in this colony,"[1] on which his associates were the great lawyers, Bland, Jefferson, Nicholas, and Pendleton; and the committee "to prepare a plan for the encouragement of arts and manufactures in this colony,"[2] on which his associates were Nicholas, Bland, Mercer, Pendleton, Cary, Carter of Stafford, Harrison, Richard Henry Lee, Clapham, Washington, Holt, and Newton.

[1] 4 *Am. Arch.* ii. 1742.   [2] *Ibid.* 170.

CHAPTER X

THE RAPE OF THE GUNPOWDER

SEVERAL of the famous men of the Revolution, whose distinction is now exclusively that of civilians, are supposed to have cherished very decided military aspirations; to have been rather envious of the more vivid renown acquired by some of their political associates who left the senate for the field; and, indeed, to have made occasional efforts to secure for themselves the opportunity for glory in the same pungent and fascinating form. A notable example of this class of Revolutionary civilians with abortive military desires, is John Hancock. In June, 1775, when Congress had before it the task of selecting one who should be the military leader of the uprisen colonists, John Hancock, seated in the president's chair, gave unmistakable signs of thinking that the choice ought to fall upon himself. While John Adams was speaking in general terms of the military situation, involving, of course, the need of a commander-in-chief, Hancock heard him "with visible pleasure;" but when the orator came to point out Washington as the man best fitted for the leadership, "a sudden and striking change" came over the countenance of the president. "Mortification and resentment were expressed as forcibly as his face could exhibit them;"[1] and it is probable that, to the end of his days, he was never able entirely to forgive Washington for having carried off the martial glory that he had really believed to be within his own reach. But even John Adams, who so pitilessly unveiled the baffled military desires of Hancock, was perhaps not altogether unacquainted with similar emotions in his own soul. Fully three weeks prior to that notable scene in Congress, in a letter to his wife in which he was speaking of the amazing military spirit then running through the continent, and of the military appointments then held by several of his Philadelphia friends, he exclaimed in his impulsive way, "Oh that I were a soldier! I will be."[2] And on the very day on which he joined in the escort of the new generals, Washington, Lee, and Schuyler, on their first departure from Philadelphia for the American camp, he sent off to his wife a characteristic letter revealing something of the anguish with which he, a civilian, viewed the possibility of his being at a disadvantage with these military men in the race for glory: —

"The three generals were all mounted on horseback, accompanied by Major Mifflin, who is gone in the character of aide-de-camp. All the delegates from the Massachusetts, with their servants and carriages, attended. Many others of the delegates from the Congress; a large

[1] *Works of John Adams*, ii. 415–417.
[2] *Letters of John Adams to his Wife*, i. 40.

troop of light horse in their uniforms; many officers of militia, besides, in theirs; music playing, etc., etc. Such is the pride and pomp of war. I, poor creature, worn out with scribbling for my bread and my liberty, low in spirits and weak in health, must leave to others to wear the laurels which I have sown; others to eat the bread which I have earned." [1]

Of Patrick Henry, however, it may be said that his permanent fame as an orator and a statesman has almost effaced the memory of the fact that, in the first year of the war, he had considerable prominence as a soldier; that it was then believed by many, and very likely by himself, that, having done as much as any man to bring on the war, he was next to do as much as any man in the actual conduct of it, and was thus destined to add to a civil renown of almost unapproached brilliance, a similar renown for splendid talents in the field. At any rate, the "first overt act of war" in Virginia, as Jefferson testifies,[2] was committed by Patrick Henry. The first physical resistance to a royal governor, which in Massachusetts was made by the embattled farmers at Lexington and Concord, was made in Virginia almost as early, under the direction and inspiration of Patrick Henry's leadership. In the first organization of the Revolutionary army in Virginia, the chief command was given to Patrick Henry. Finally, that he never had the opportunity of proving in battle

[1] *Letters of John Adams to his Wife,* i. 47, 48.
[2] *Works of Jefferson,* i. 116.

whether or not he had military talents, and that, after some months of nominal command, he was driven by a series of official slights into an abandonment of his military career, may have been occasioned solely by a proper distrust of his military capacity on the part of the Virginia Committee of Safety, or it may have been due in some measure to the unslumbering jealousy of him which was at the time attributed to the leading members of that committee. The purpose of this chapter, and of the next, will be to present a rapid grouping of these incidents in his life, — incidents which now have the appearance of a mere episode, but which once seemed the possible beginnings of a deliberate and conspicuous military career.

Within the city of Williamsburg, at the period now spoken of, had long been kept the public storehouse for gunpowder and arms. In the dead of the night[1] preceding the 21st of April, 1775, — a little less than a month, therefore, after the convention of Virginia had proclaimed the inevitable approach of a war with Great Britain, — a detachment of marines from the armed schooner Magdalen, then lying in the James River, stealthily visited this storehouse, and, taking thence fifteen half-barrels of gunpowder,[2] carried them off in Lord Dunmore's wagon to Burwell's Ferry, and put them on board their vessel. Of course, the news of this exploit flew fast through the colony, and everywhere awoke alarm and exaspera-

[1] 4 *Am. Arch.* ii. 1227.   [2] *Ibid.* iii. 390.

tion. Soon some thousands of armed men made ready to march to the capital to demand the restoration of the gunpowder. On Tuesday, the 25th of April, the independent company of Fredericksburg notified their colonel, George Washington, that, with his approbation, they would be prepared to start for Williamsburg on the following Saturday, "properly accoutred as light-horsemen," and in conjunction with "any other bodies of armed men who" might be "willing to appear in support of the honor of Virginia."[1]

Similar messages were promptly sent to Washington from the independent companies of Prince William[2] and Albemarle counties.[3] On Wednesday, the 26th of April, the men in arms who had already arrived at Fredericksburg sent to the capital a swift messenger "to inquire whether the gunpowder had been replaced in the public magazine."[4] On Saturday, the 29th, — being the day already fixed for the march upon Williamsburg, — one hundred and two gentlemen, representing fourteen companies of light-horse, met in council at Fredericksburg, and, after considering a letter from the venerable Peyton Randolph which their messenger had brought back with him, particularly Randolph's assurance that the affair of the gunpowder was to be satisfactorily arranged, came to the resolution that they would proceed no further at that time; adding, however, this solemn decla-

[1] 4 *Am. Arch.* ii. 387.
[2] *Ibid.* ii. 395.
[3] *Ibid.* ii. 442, 443.
[4] *Ibid.* ii. 426.

ration: "We do now pledge ourselves to each other
to be in readiness, at a moment's warning, to reas-
semble, and by force of arms to defend the law,
the liberty, and rights of this or any sister colony
from unjust and wicked invasion." [1]

It is at this point that Patrick Henry comes
upon the scene. Thus far, during the trouble, he
appears to have been watching events from his
home in Hanover County. As soon, however, as
word was brought to him of the tame conclusion
thus reached by the assembled warriors at Fredericksburg, his soul took fire at the lamentable mistake which he thought they had made. To him it
seemed on every account the part of wisdom that
the blow, which would have to be "struck sooner
or later, should be struck at once, before an overwhelming force should enter the colony;" that the
spell by which the people were held in a sort of
superstitious awe of the governor should be broken;
"that the military resources of the country should
be developed;" that the people should be made to
"see and feel their strength by being brought out
together; that the revolution should be set in actual motion in the colony; that the martial prowess
of the country should be awakened, and the soldiery
animated by that proud and resolute confidence
which a successful enterprise in the commencement
of a contest never fails to inspire." [2]

[1] 4 *Am. Arch.* ii. 443.

[2] Patrick Henry's reasons were thus stated by him at the time
to Colonel Richard Morris and Captain George Dabney, and by
the latter were communicated to Wirt, 136, 137.

Accordingly, he resolved that, as the troops lately rendezvoused at Fredericksburg had forborne to strike this needful blow, he would endeavor to repair the mistake by striking it himself. At once, therefore, he despatched expresses to the officers and men of the independent company of his own county, "requesting them to meet him in arms at New Castle on the second of May, on business of the highest importance to American liberty."[1] He also summoned the county committee to meet him at the same time and place.

At the place and time appointed his neighbors were duly assembled; and when he had laid before them, in a speech of wonderful eloquence, his view of the situation, they instantly resolved to put themselves under his command, and to march at once to the capital, either to recover the gunpowder itself, or to make reprisals on the king's property sufficient to replace it. Without delay the march began, Captain Patrick Henry leading. By sunset of the following day, they had got as far as to Doncastle's Ordinary, about sixteen miles from Williamsburg, and there rested for the night. Meantime, the news that Patrick Henry was marching with armed men straight against Lord Dunmore, to demand the restoration of the gunpowder or payment for it, carried exhilaration or terror in all directions. On the one hand, many prudent and conservative gentlemen were horrified at his rashness, and sent messenger after messen-

[1] Wirt, 137, 138.

ger to beg him to stay his fearful proceeding, to turn about, and to go home.[1] On the other hand, as the word flew from county to county that Patrick Henry had taken up the people's cause in this vigorous fashion, five thousand men sprang to arms, and started across the country to join the ranks of his followers, and to lend a hand in case of need. At Williamsburg, the rumor of his approach brought on a scene of consternation. The wife and family of Lord Dunmore were hurried away to a place of safety. Further down the river, the commander of his majesty's ship Fowey was notified that "his excellency the Lord Dunmore, governor of Virginia," was "threatened with an attack at daybreak, . . . at his palace at Williamsburg;" and for his defence was speedily sent off a detachment of marines.[2] Before daybreak, however, the governor seems to have come to the prudent decision to avert, by a timely settlement with Patrick Henry, the impending attack; and accordingly, soon after daybreak, a messenger arrived at Doncastle's Ordinary, there to tender immediate satisfaction in money for the gunpowder that had been ravished away.[3] The troops, having already resumed their march, were halted; and soon a settlement of the trouble was effected, according to the terms of the following singular document: —

[1] Wirt, 141.   [2] 4 *Am. Arch.* ii. 504
[3] Cooke, *Virginia*, 432.

DONCASTLE'S ORDINARY, NEW KENT, May 4, 1775.

Received from the Honorable Richard Corbin, Esq., his majesty's receiver-general, £330, as a compensation for the gunpowder lately taken out of the public magazine by he governor's order; which money I promise to convey to the Virginia delegates at the General Congress, to be under their direction laid out in gunpowder for the colony's use, and to be stored as they shall direct, until the next colony convention or General Assembly; unless it shall be necessary, in the mean time, to use the same in defence of this colony. It is agreed, that in case the next convention shall determine that any part of the said money ought to be returned to his majesty's receiver-general, that the same shall be done accordingly.

PATRICK HENRY, JUNIOR.[1]

The chief object for which Patrick Henry and his soldiers had taken the trouble to come to that place having been thus suddenly accomplished, there was but one thing left for them to do before they should return to their homes. Robert Carter Nicholas, the treasurer of the colony, was at Williamsburg; and to him Patrick Henry at once despatched a letter informing him of the arrangement that had been made, and offering to him any protection that he might in consequence require: —

May 4, 1775.

SIR, — The affair of the powder is now settled, so as to produce satisfaction in me, and I earnestly wish to the colony in general. The people here have it in charge

[1] 4 *Am. Arch.* ii. 540.

from the Hanover committee, to tender their services to
you as a public officer, for the purpose of escorting the
public treasury to any place in this colony where the
money would be judged more safe than in the city of
Williamsburg. The reprisal now made by the Hanover
volunteers, though accomplished in a manner least liable
to the imputation of violent extremity, may possibly be
the cause of future injury to the treasury. If, therefore, you apprehend the least danger, a sufficient guard
is at your service. I beg the return of the bearer may
be instant, because the men wish to know their destina-
tion.

With great regard, I am, sir,
Your most humble servant,
PATRICK HENRY, JUNIOR.

To ROBERT CARTER NICHOLAS, Esq., Treasurer.[1]

Patrick Henry's desire for an immediate answer
from the respectable Mr. Nicholas was gratified,
although it came in the form of a dignified rebuff:
Mr. Nicholas "had no apprehension of the necessity or propriety of the proffered service." [2]

No direct communication seems to have been
had at that time with Lord Dunmore; but two
days afterward his lordship, having given to Patrick Henry ample time to withdraw to a more
agreeable distance, sent thundering after him this
portentous proclamation: —

Whereas I have been informed from undoubted authority that a certain Patrick Henry, of the county of
Hanover, and a number of deluded followers, have taken

---

[1] 4 *Am. Arch.* ii. 541.   [2] *Ibid.*

up arms, chosen their officers, and styling themselves an independent company, have marched out of their county, encamped, and put themselves in a posture of war, and have written and dispatched letters to divers parts of the country, exciting the people to join in these outrageous and rebellious practices, to the great terror of all his majesty's faithful subjects, and in open defiance of law and government; and have committed other acts of violence, particularly in extorting from his majesty's receiver-general the sum of three hundred and thirty pounds, under pretence of replacing the powder I thought proper to order from the magazine; whence it undeniably appears that there is no longer the least security for the life or property of any man: wherefore, I have thought proper, with the advice of his majesty's council, and in his majesty's name, to issue this my proclamation, strictly charging all persons, upon their allegiance, not to aid, abet, or give countenance to the said Patrick Henry, or any other persons concerned in such unwarrantable combinations, but on the contrary to oppose them and their designs by every means; which designs must, otherwise, inevitably involve the whole country in the most direful calamity, as they will call for the vengeance of offended majesty and the insulted laws to be exerted here, to vindicate the constitutional authority of government.

Given under my hand and the seal of the colony, at Williamsburg, this 6th day of May, 1775, and in the fifteenth year of his majesty's reign.

DUNMORE.

God save the king.[1]

[1] 4 *Am. Arch.* ii. 516.

Beyond question, there were in Virginia at that time many excellent gentlemen who still trusted that the dispute with Great Britain might be composed without bloodshed, and to whom Patrick Henry's conduct in this affair must have appeared foolhardy, presumptuous, and even criminal. The mass of the people of Virginia, however, did not incline to take that view of the subject. They had no faith any longer in timid counsels, in hesitating measures. They believed that their most important earthly rights were in danger. They longed for a leader with vigor, promptitude, courage, caring less for technical propriety than for justice, and not afraid to say so, by word or deed, to Lord Dunmore and to Lord Dunmore's master. Such a leader they thought they saw in Patrick Henry. Accordingly, even on his march homeward from Doncastle's Ordinary, the heart of Virginia began to go forth to him in expressions of love, of gratitude, and of homage, such as no American colonist perhaps had ever before received. Upon his return home, his own county greeted him with its official approval.[1] On the 8th of May, the county of Louisa sent him her thanks;[2] and on the following day, messages to the same effect were sent from the counties of Orange and Spottsylvania.[3] On the 19th of May, an address "to the inhabitants of Virginia," under the signature of "Brutus," saluted Patrick Henry as "his

---

[1] 4 *Am. Arch.* ii. 540, 541.　　　[2] *Ibid.* ii. 529.
[3] *Ibid.* ii. 539, 540.

country's and America's unalterable and unappalled great advocate and friend."[1]   On the 22d
of May, Prince William County declared its thanks
to be "justly due to Captain Patrick Henry, and
the gentlemen volunteers who attended him, for
their proper and spirited conduct."[2]   On the 26th
of May, Loudoun County declared its cordial
approval.[3]   On the 9th of June, the volunteer
company of Lancaster County resolved "that every
member of this company do return thanks to the
worthy Captain Patrick Henry and the volunteer
company of Hanover, for their spirited conduct on
a late expedition, and they are determined to protect him from any insult that may be offered him,
on that account, at the risk of life and fortune."[4]
On the 19th of June, resolutions of gratitude and
confidence were voted by the counties of Prince
Edward and of Frederick, the latter saying: —

"We should blush to be thus late in our commenda-
tions of, and thanks to, Patrick Henry, Esquire, for his
patriotic and spirited behavior in making reprisals for
the powder so unconstitutionally . . . taken from the
public magazine, could we have entertained a thought
that any part of the colony would have condemned a
measure calculated for the benefit of the whole; but as
we are informed this is the case, we beg leave . . .
to assure that gentleman that we did from the first, and
still do, most cordially approve and commend his conduct in that affair.   The good people of this county will

---

[1] 4 *Am. Arch.* ii. 641.   [2] *Ibid.* ii. 667.
[3] *Ibid.* ii. 710, 711.   [4] *Ibid.* ii. 938.

never fail to approve and support him to the utmost of their powers in every action derived from so rich a source as the love of his country. We heartily thank him for stepping forth to convince the tools of despotism that freeborn men are not to be intimidated, by any form of danger, to submit to the arbitrary acts of their rulers." [1]

On the 10th of July, the county of Fincastle prolonged the strain of public affection and applause by assuring Patrick Henry that it would support and justify him at the risk of life and fortune.[2]

In the mean time, the second Continental Congress had already convened at Philadelphia, beginning its work on the 10th of May. The journal mentions the presence, on that day, of all the delegates from Virginia, excepting Patrick Henry, who, of course, had been delayed in his preparations for the journey by the events which we have just described. Not until the 11th of May was he able to set out from his home; and he was then accompanied upon his journey, to a point beyond the borders of the colony, by a spontaneous escort of armed men, — a token, not only of the popular love for him, but of the popular anxiety lest Dunmore should take the occasion of an unprotected journey to put him under arrest. "Yesterday,"

---

[1] 4 *Am. Arch.* ii. 1024.

[2] *Ibid.* ii. 1620, 1621. For notable comments on Patrick Henry's "striking and lucky *coup de main*," see Rives, *Life of Madison*, i. 93, 94; *Works of Jefferson*, i. 116, 117; Charles Mackay, *Founders of the American Republic*, 232–234; 327.

says a document dated at Hanover, May the 12th, 1775, "Patrick Henry, one of the delegates for this colony, escorted by a number of respectable young gentlemen, volunteers from this and King William and Caroline counties, set out to attend the General Congress. They proceeded with him as far as Mrs. Hooe's ferry, on the Potomac, by whom they were most kindly and hospitably entertained, and also provided with boats and hands to cross the river; and after partaking of this lady's beneficence, the bulk of the company took their leave of Mr. Henry, saluting him with two platoons and repeated huzzas. A guard accompanied that worthy gentleman to the Maryland side, who saw him safely landed; and committing him to the gracious and wise Disposer of all human events, to guide and protect him whilst contending for a restitution of our dearest rights and liberties, they wished him a safe journey, and happy return to his family and friends." [1]

[1] 4 *Am. Arch.* ii. 541.

CHAPTER XI

IN CONGRESS AND IN CAMP

On Thursday, the 18th of May, Patrick Henry took his seat in the second Continental Congress; and he appears thenceforward to have continued in attendance until the very end of the session, which occurred on the 1st of August. From the official journal of this Congress, it is impossible to ascertain the full extent of any member's participation in its work. Its proceedings were transacted in secret; and only such results were announced to the public as, in the opinion of Congress, it was desirable that the public should know. Then, too, from the private correspondence and the diaries of its members but little help can be got. As affecting Patrick Henry, almost the only non-official testimony that has been found is that of Jefferson, who, however, did not enter this Congress until its session was half gone, and who, forty years afterward, wrote what he probably supposed to be his recollections concerning his old friend's deportment and influence in that body : —

"I found Mr. Henry to be a silent and almost unmeddling member in Congress. On the original opening of that body, while general grievances were the topic, he was in his element, and captivated all by his bold and splendid eloquence. But as soon as they came to specific matters, to sober reasoning and solid argumentation, he had the good sense to perceive that his declamation, however excellent in its proper place, had no weight at all in such an assembly as that, of cool-headed, reflecting, judicious men. He ceased, therefore, in a great measure, to take any part in the business. He seemed, indeed, very tired of the place, and wonderfully relieved when, by appointment of the Virginia convention to be colonel of their first regiment, he was permitted to leave Congress about the last of July." [1]

Perhaps the principal value of this testimony is to serve as an illustration of the extreme fragility of any man's memory respecting events long passed, even in his own experience. Thus, Jefferson here remembers how "wonderfully relieved" Patrick Henry was at being "permitted to leave Congress" on account of his appointment by the Virginia convention "to be colonel of their first regiment." But, from the official records of the time, it can now be shown that neither of the things which Jefferson thus remembers, ever had any existence in fact. In the first place, the journal of the Virginia convention [2] indicates that Patrick Henry's appointment as colonel could not have been the occasion of any such relief from congressional duties as Jefferson speaks of; for that appointment was not made until five days after Congress itself

[1] *Hist. Mag.* for Aug. 1867, 92.
[2] 4 *Am. Arch.* iii. 375.

had adjourned, when, of course, Patrick Henry and his fellow delegates, including Jefferson, were already far advanced on their journey back to Virginia. In the second place, the journal of Congress [1] indicates that Patrick Henry had no such relief from congressional duties, on any account, but was bearing his full share in its business, even in the plainest and most practical details, down to the very end of the session.

Any one who now recalls the tremendous events that were taking place in the land while the second Continental Congress was in session, and the immense questions of policy and of administration with which it had to deal, will find it hard to believe that its deliberations were out of the range of Patrick Henry's sympathies or capacities, or that he could have been the listless, speechless, and ineffective member depicted by the later pen of Jefferson. When that Congress first came together, the blood was as yet hardly dry on the grass in Lexington Common; on the very morning on which its session opened, the colonial troops burst into the stronghold at Ticonderoga; and when the session had lasted but six weeks, its members were conferring together over the ghastly news from Bunker Hill. The organization of some kind of national government for thirteen colonies precipitated into a state of war; the creation of a national army; the selection of a commander-in-chief, and of the officers to serve under him; the

[1] 4 *Am. Arch.* ii. 1902.

hurried fortification of coasts, harbors, cities; the supply of the troops with clothes, tents, weapons, ammunition, food, medicine; protection against the Indian tribes along the frontier of nearly every colony; the goodwill of the people of Canada, and of Jamaica; a solemn, final appeal to the king and to the people of England; an appeal to the people of Ireland; finally, a grave statement to all mankind of "the causes and necessity of their taking up arms," — these were among the weighty and soul-stirring matters which the second Continental Congress had to consider and to decide upon. For any man to say, forty years afterward, even though he say it with all the authority of the renown of Thomas Jefferson, that, in the presence of such questions, the spirit of Patrick Henry was dull or unconcerned, and that, in a Congress which had to deal with such questions, he was "a silent and almost unmeddling member," is to put a strain upon human confidence which it is unable to bear.

The formula by which the daily labors of this Congress are frequently described in its own journal is, that "Congress met according to adjournment, and, agreeable to the order of the day, again resolved itself into a committee of the whole to take into consideration the state of America; and after some time spent therein, the president resumed the chair, and Mr. Ward, from the committee, reported that they had proceeded in the business, but, not having completed it, desired him to move for leave to sit again."[1] And al-

[1] 4 *Am. Arch.* ii. 1834.

though, from the beginning to the end of the session, no mention is made of any word spoken in
debate by any member, we can yet glean, even
from that meagre record, enough to prove that
upon Patrick Henry was laid about as much labor
in the form of committee-work as upon any other
member of the House, — a fair test, it is believed,
of any man's zeal, industry, and influence in any
legislative body.

Further, it will be noted that the committee-
work to which he was thus assigned was often of
the homeliest and most prosaic kind, calling not
for declamatory gifts, but for common sense, dis-
crimination, experience, and knowledge of men
and things. He seems, also, to have had special
interest and authority in the several anxious phases
of the Indian question as presented by the exigen-
cies of that awful crisis, and to have been placed
on every committee that was appointed to deal
with any branch of the subject. Thus, on the
16th of June, he was placed with General Schuyler, James Duane, James Wilson, and Philip
Livingston, on a committee "to take into consideration the papers transmitted from the convention
of New York, relative to Indian affairs, and report what steps, in their opinion, are necessary to
be taken for securing and preserving the friendship of the Indian nations."[1] On the 19th of
June, he served with John Adams and Thomas
Lynch on a committee to inform Charles Lee of

[1] 4 *Am. Arch.* ii. 1849.

his appointment as second major-general; and when
Lee's answer imported that his situation and circumstances as a British officer required some further and very careful negotiations with Congress,
Patrick Henry was placed upon the special committee to which this delicate business was intrusted.[1]
On the 21st of June, the very day on which, according to the journal, "Mr. Thomas Jefferson
appeared as a delegate for the colony of Virginia,
and produced his credentials," his colleague, Patrick Henry, rose in his place and stated that Washington "had put into his hand sundry queries, to
which he desired the Congress would give an answer." These queries necessarily involved subjects
of serious concern to the cause for which they were
about to plunge into war, and would certainly require for their consideration "cool-headed, reflecting, and judicious men." The committee appointed
for the purpose consisted of Silas Deane, Patrick
Henry, John Rutledge, Samuel Adams, and Richard Henry Lee.[2] On the 10th of July, "Mr.
Alsop informed the Congress that he had an in-
voice of Indian goods, which a gentleman in this
town had delivered to him, and which the said
gentleman was willing to dispose of to the Congress." The committee "to examine the said in-
voice and report to the Congress" was composed
of Philip Livingston, Patrick Henry, and John
Alsop.[3] On the 12th of July, it was resolved to

[1] 4 *Am. Arch.* ii. 1850, 1851.   [2] *Ibid.* ii. 1852.
[3] *Ibid.* ii. 1878.

organize three departments for the management of Indian affairs, the commissioners to "have power to treat with the Indians in their respective departments, in the name and on behalf of the United Colonies, in order to preserve peace and friendship with the said Indians, and to prevent their taking any part in the present commotions." On the following day the commissioners for the middle department were elected, namely, Franklin, Patrick Henry, and James Wilson.[1] On the 17th of July, a committee was appointed to negotiate with the Indian missionary, the Rev. Samuel Kirkland, respecting his past and future services among the Six Nations, "in order to secure their friendship, and to continue them in a state of neutrality with respect to the present controversy between Great Britain and these colonies." This committee consisted of Thomas Cushing, Patrick Henry, and Silas Deane.[2] Finally, on the 31st of July, next to the last day of the session, a committee consisting of one member for each colony was appointed to serve in the recess of Congress, for the very practical and urgent purpose of inquiring "in all the colonies after virgin lead and leaden ore, and the best methods of collecting, smelting, and refining it;" also, after "the cheapest and easiest methods of making salt in these colonies." This was not a committee on which any man could be useful who had only "declamation" to contribute to its work; and the several colonies were repre-

[1] 4 *Am. Arch.* ii. 1879, 1883.   [2] *Ibid.* ii. 1884, 1885.

sented upon it by their most sagacious and their weightiest men, — as New Hampshire by Langdon, Massachusetts by John Adams, Rhode Island by Stephen Hopkins, Pennsylvania by Franklin, Delaware by Rodney, South Carolina by Gadsden, Virginia by Patrick Henry.[1]

On the day on which this committee was appointed, Patrick Henry wrote to Washington, then at the headquarters of the army near Boston, a letter which denoted on the part of the writer a perception, unusual at that time, of the gravity and duration of the struggle on which the colonies were just entering: —

PHILADELPHIA, July 31st, 1775.

SIR, — Give me leave to recommend the bearer, M[r] Frazer, to your notice and regard. He means to enter the American camp, and there to gain that experience, of which the general cause may be avail'd. It is my earnest wish that many Virginians might see service. It is not unlikely that in the fluctuation of things our country may have occasion for great military exertions. For this reason I have taken the liberty to trouble you with this and a few others of the same tendency. The public good which you, sir, have so eminently promoted, is my only motive. That you may enjoy the protection of Heaven and live long and happy is the ardent wish of,   Sir,

Y[r] mo. ob[t] hbl. serv.,

P. HENRY, JR.[2]

His Excellency, GENL. WASHINGTON.

[1] 4 *Am. Arch.* ii. 1902.   [2] MS.

On the following day Congress adjourned. As soon as possible after its adjournment, the Virginia delegates seem to have departed for home, to take their places in the convention then in session at Richmond; for the journal of that convention mentions that on Wednesday, August the 9th, "Patrick Henry, Edmund Pendleton, Benjamin Harrison, and Thomas Jefferson, Esquires, appeared in convention, and took their seats." [1] On the next day an incident occurred in the convention implying that Patrick Henry, during his absence in Congress, had been able to serve his colony by other gifts as well as by those of "bold and splendid eloquence:" it was resolved that "the powder purchased by Patrick Henry, Esquire, for the use of this colony, be immediately sent for." [2] On the day following that, the convention resolved unanimously that "the thanks of this convention are justly due to his excellency, George Washington, Esquire, Patrick Henry, and Edmund Pendleton, Esquires, three of the worthy delegates who represented this colony in the late Continental Congress, for their faithful discharge of that important trust; and this body are only induced to dispense with their future services of the like kind, by the appointment of the two former to other offices in the public service, incompatible with their attendance on this, and the infirm state of health of the latter." [3]

[1] 4 *Am. Arch.* iii. 377.   [2] *Ibid.* iii. 377, 378.
[3] *Ibid.* iii. 378.

Of course, the two appointments here referred to are of Washington as commander-in-chief of the forces of the United Colonies, and of Patrick Henry as commander-in-chief of the forces of Virginia, — the latter appointment having been made by the Virginia convention on the 5th of August. The commission, which passed the convention on the 28th of that month, constituted Patrick Henry "colonel of the first regiment of regulars, and commander-in-chief of all the forces to be raised for the protection and defence of this colony;" and while it required "all officers and soldiers, and every person whatsoever, in any way concerned, to be obedient" to him, "in all things touching the due execution of this commission," it also required him to be obedient to "all orders and instructions which, from time to time," he might "receive from the convention or Committee of Safety."[1] Accordingly, Patrick Henry's control of military proceedings in Virginia was, as it proved, nothing more than nominal: it was a supreme command on paper, tempered in actual experience by the incessant and distrustful interference of an ever-present body of civilians, who had all power over him.

A newspaper of Williamsburg for the 23d of September announces the arrival there, two days before, of "Patrick Henry, Esquire, commander-in-chief of the Virginia forces. He was met and escorted to town by the whole body of volunteers,

[1] 4 *Am. Arch.* iii. 393. See, also, his oath of office, *ibid.* iii. 411.

who paid him every mark of respect and distinction in their power."[1]   Thereupon he inspected the grounds about the city; and as a place suitable for the encampment, he fixed upon a site in the rear of the College of William and Mary.   Soon troops began to arrive in considerable numbers, and to prepare themselves for whatever service might be required of them.[2]   There was, however, a sad lack of arms and ammunition.   On the 15th of October, Pendleton, who was at the head of the Committee of Safety, gave this account of the situation in a letter to Richard Henry Lee, then in Congress at Philadelphia: —

"Had we arms and ammunition, it would give vigor to our measures. . . . Nine companies of regulars are here, and seem very clever men; others, we hear, are ready, and only wait to collect arms. Lord Dunmore's forces are only one hundred and sixty as yet, intrenched at Gosport, and supported by the ships drawn up before that and Norfolk."[3]

On the 30th of November, Lord Dunmore, who had been compelled by the smallness of his land force to take refuge upon his armed vessels off the coast, thus described the situation, in a letter to General Sir William Howe, then in command at Boston: —

"I must inform you that with our little corps, I think we have done wonders. We have taken and destroyed above four score pieces of ordnance, and, by landing in

[1] 4 *Am. Arch.* iii. 776.   [2] Wirt, 159.
[3] 4 *Am. Arch.* iii. 1067.

different parts of the country, we keep them in continual hot water. . . . Having heard that a thousand chosen men belonging to the rebels, great part of whom were riflemen, were on their march to attack us here, or to cut off our provisions, I determined to take possession of the pass at the Great Bridge, which secures us the greatest part of two counties to supply us with provisions. I accordingly ordered a stockade fort to be erected there, which was done in a few days; and I put an officer and twenty-five men to garrison it, with some volunteers and negroes, who have defended it against all the efforts of the rebels for these eight days. We have killed several of their men; and I make no doubt we shall now be able to maintain our ground there; but should we be obliged to abandon it, we have thrown up an intrenchment on the land side of Norfolk, which I hope they will never be able to force. Here we are, with only the small part of a regiment contending against the extensive colony of Virginia." [1]

But who were these "thousand chosen men belonging to the rebels," who, on their march to attack Lord Dunmore at Norfolk, had thus been held in check by his little fort at the Great Bridge? We are told by Dunmore himself that they were Virginia troops. But why was not Patrick Henry in immediate command of them? Why was Patrick Henry held back from this service, — the only active service then to be had in the field? And why was the direction of this important enterprise given to his subordinate, Colonel William Woodford, of the second regiment? There is abundant

[1] 4 *Am. Arch.* iii. 1713–1715.

evidence that Patrick Henry had eagerly desired
to conduct this expedition; that he had even soli-
cited the Committee of Safety to permit him to do
so; but that they, distrusting his military capacity, overruled his wishes, and gave this fine opportunity for military distinction to the officer next
below him in command.   Moreover, no sooner had
Colonel Woodford departed upon the service, than
he began to ignore altogether the commander-in-
chief, and to make his communications directly to
the Committee of Safety, — a course in which he
was virtually sustained by that body, on appeal
being made to them.   Furthermore, on the 9th of
December, Colonel Woodford won a brilliant victory over the enemy at the Great Bridge,[1] thus
apparently justifying to the public the wisdom of
the committee in assigning the work to him, and
also throwing still more into the background the
commander-in-chief, who was then chafing in camp
over his enforced retirement from this duty.   But
this was not the only cup of humiliation which
was pressed to his lips.   Not long afterward, there
arrived at the seat of war a few hundred North
Carolina troops, under command of Colonel Robert
Howe; and the latter, with the full consent of
Woodford, at once took command of their united
forces, and thenceforward addressed his official
letters solely to the convention of Virginia, or to
the Committee of Safety, paying not the slightest

[1] Graphic contemporary accounts of this battle may be found in
4 *Am. Arch.* iv. 224, 228, 229.

attention to the commander-in-chief.[1] Finally, on the 28th of December, Congress decided to raise in Virginia six battalions to be taken into continental pay;[2] and, by a subsequent vote, it likewise resolved to include within these six battalions the first and the second Virginia regiments already raised.[3] A commission was accordingly sent to Patrick Henry as colonel of the first Virginia battalion,[4] — an official intimation that the expected commission of a brigadier-general for Virginia was to be given to some one else.

On receiving this last affront, Patrick Henry determined to lay down his military appointments, which he did on the 28th of February, 1776, and at once prepared to leave the camp. As soon as this news got abroad among the troops, they all, according to a contemporary account,[5] "went into mourning, and, under arms, waited on him at his lodgings," when his officers presented to him an affectionate address: —

To PATRICK HENRY, JUNIOR, ESQUIRE:
Deeply impressed with a grateful sense of the obligations we lie under to you for the polite, humane, and tender treatment manifested to us throughout the whole of your conduct, while we have had the honor of being under your command, permit us to offer to you our sincere thanks, as the only tribute we have in our power to pay to your real merits. Notwithstanding your with-

[1] Wirt, 178.
[2] 4 *Am. Arch.* iii. 1962.
[3] *Ibid.* iv. 1669.
[4] *Ibid.* iv. 1517.
[5] *Ibid.* iv. 1515, 1516.

drawing yourself from service fills us with the most poignant sorrow, as it at once deprives us of our father and general, yet, as gentlemen, we are compelled to applaud your spirited resentment to the most glaring indignity. May your merit shine as conspicuous to the world in general as it hath done to us, and may Heaven shower its choicest blessings upon you.

WILLIAMSBURG, February 29, 1776.

His reply to this warm-hearted message was in the following words: —

GENTLEMEN, — I am extremely obliged to you for your approbation of my conduct. Your address does me the highest honor. This kind testimony of your regard to me would have been an ample reward for services much greater than I have had the power to perform. I return you, and each of you, gentlemen, my best acknowledgments for the spirit, alacrity, and zeal you have constantly shown in your several stations. I am unhappy to part with you. I leave the service, but I leave my heart with you. May God bless you, and give you success and safety, and make you the glorious instruments of saving our country.[1]

The grief and indignation thus exhibited by the officers who had served under Patrick Henry soon showed itself in a somewhat violent manner among the men. The "Virginia Gazette" for that time states that, "after the officers had received Colonel Henry's kind answer to their address, they insisted upon his dining with them at the Raleigh Tavern, before his departure; and after the dinner, a num-

[1] 4 *Am. Arch.* iv. 1516; also, Wirt, 180, 181.

ber of them proposed escorting him out of town,
but were prevented by some uneasiness getting
among the soldiery, who assembled in a tumultuous
manner and demanded their discharge, and declared their unwillingness to serve under any other
commander.   Upon which Colonel Henry found it
necessary to stay a night longer in town, which he
spent in visiting the several barracks; and used
every argument in his power with the soldiery to
lay aside their imprudent resolution, and to continue in the service, which he had quitted from
motives in which his honor alone was concerned."[1]
Moreover, several days after he had left the camp
altogether and had returned to his home, he was
followed by an address signed by ninety officers
belonging not only to his own regiment, but to
that of Colonel Woodford, — a document which
has no little value as presenting strongly one side
of contemporary military opinion respecting Patrick Henry's career as a soldier, and the treatment
to which he had been subjected.

SIR, — Deeply concerned for the good of our country, we sincerely lament the unhappy necessity of your
resignation, and with all the warmth of affection assure
you that, whatever may have given rise to the indignity
lately offered to you, we join with the general voice of
the people, and think it our duty to make this public
declaration of our high respect for your distinguished
merit.   To your vigilance and judgment, as a senator,
this United Continent bears ample testimony, while she

[1] 4 *Am. Arch.* iv. 1516.

prosecutes her steady opposition to those destructive ministerial measures which your eloquence first pointed out and taught to resent, and your resolution led forward to resist. To your extensive popularity the service, also, is greatly indebted for the expedition with which the troops were raised ; and while they were continued under your command, the firmness, candor, and politeness, which formed the complexion of your conduct towards them, obtained the signal approbation of the wise and virtuous, and will leave upon our minds the most grateful impression.

Although retired from the immediate concerns of war, we solicit the continuance of your kindly attention. We know your attachment to the best of causes ; we have the fullest confidence in your abilities, and in the rectitude of your views ; and, however willing the envious may be to undermine an established reputation, we trust the day will come when justice shall prevail, and thereby secure you an honorable and happy return to the glorious employment of conducting our councils and hazarding your life in the defence of your country.[1]

The public agitation over the alleged wrong which had thus been done to Patrick Henry during his brief military career, and which had brought that career to its abrupt and painful close, seems to have continued for a considerable time. Throughout the colony the blame was openly and bluntly laid upon the Committee of Safety, who, on account of envy, it was said, had tried "to bury in obscurity his martial talents." [2] On the other hand, the course pursued by that committee was

[1] 4 *Am. Arch.* iv. 1516, 1517.   [2] *Ibid.* iv. 1518.

ably defended by many, on the ground that Patrick Henry, with all his great gifts for civil life, really had no fitness for a leading military position. One writer asserted that even in the convention which had elected Patrick Henry as commander-in-chief, it was objected that "his studies had been directed to civil and not to military pursuits; that he was totally unacquainted with the art of war, and had no knowledge of military discipline; and that such a person was very unfit to be at the head of troops who were likely to be engaged with a well-disciplined army, commanded by experienced and able generals." [1] In the very middle of the period of his nominal military service, this opinion of his unfitness was still more strongly urged by the chairman of the Committee of Safety, who, on the 24th of December, 1775, said in a letter to Colonel Woodford: —

" Believe me, sir, the unlucky step of calling that gentleman from our councils, where he was useful, into the field, in an important station, the duties of which he must, in the nature of things, be an entire stranger to, has given me many an anxious and uneasy moment. In consequence of this mistaken step, which can't now be retracted or remedied, — for he has done nothing worthy of degradation, and must keep his rank, — we must be deprived of the service of some able officers, whose honor and former ranks will not suffer them to act under him in this juncture, when we so much need their services." [2]

This seems to have been, in substance, the impres-

[1] 4 *Am. Arch.* iv. 1519.   [2] Wirt, 175.

sion concerning Patrick Henry held at that time
by at least two friendly and most competent observers, who were then looking on from a distance,
and who, of course, were beyond the range of any
personal or partisan prejudice upon the subject.
Writing from Cambridge, on the 7th of March,
1776, before he had received the news of Henry's
resignation, Washington said to Joseph Reed, then
at Philadelphia: "I think my countrymen made
a capital mistake when they took Henry out of the
senate to place him in the field; and pity it is that
he does not see this, and remove every difficulty
by a voluntary resignation." [1]   On the 15th of that
month, Reed, in reply, gave to Washington this
bit of news: "We have some accounts from Virginia that Colonel Henry has resigned in disgust
at not being made a general officer; but it rather
gives satisfaction than otherwise, as his abilities
seem better calculated for the senate than the
field." [2]

Nevertheless, in all these contemporary judg-
ments upon the alleged military defects of Patrick
Henry, no reader can now fail to note an embarrassing lack of definiteness, and a tendency to infer
that, because that great man was so great in civil
life, as a matter of course, he could not be great,
also, in military life, — a proposition that could
be overthrown by numberless historical examples
to the contrary.   It would greatly aid us if we

[1] *Writings of Washington*, iii. 309.
[2] W. B. Reed, *Life of Joseph Reed*, i. 173.

could know precisely what, in actual experience, were the defects found in Patrick Henry as a military man, and precisely how these defects were exhibited by him in the camp at Williamsburg. In the writings of that period, no satisfaction upon this point seems thus far to have been obtained. There is, however, a piece of later testimony, derived by authentic tradition from a prominent member of the Virginia Committee of Safety, which really helps one to understand what may have been the exact difficulty with the military character of Patrick Henry, and just why, also, it could not be more plainly stated at the time. Clement Carrington, a son of Paul Carrington, told Hugh Blair Grigsby that the real ground of the action of the Committee of Safety "was the want of discipline in the regiment under the command of Colonel Henry. None doubted his courage, or his alacrity to hasten to the field; but it was plain that he did not seem to be conscious of the importance of strict discipline in the army, but regarded his soldiers as so many gentlemen who had met to defend their country, and exacted from them little more than the courtesy that was proper among equals. To have marched to the sea-board at that time with a regiment of such men, would have been to insure their destruction; and it was a thorough conviction of this truth that prompted the decision of the committee." [1]

Yet, even with this explanation, the truth re-

[1] Grigsby, *Va. Conv. of* 1776, 52, 53, note.

mains that Patrick Henry, as commander-in-chief of the Virginia forces, never was permitted to take command, or to see any real service in the field, or to look upon the face of an armed enemy, or to show, in the only way in which it could be shown, whether or not he had the gifts of a military leader in action. As an accomplished and noble-minded Virginian of our own time has said:—

"It may be doubted whether he possessed those qualities which make a wary partisan, and which are so often possessed in an eminent degree by uneducated men. Regular fighting there was none in the colony, until near the close of the war. . . . The most skilful partisan in the Virginia of that day, covered as it was with forests, cut up by streams, and beset by predatory bands, would have been the Indian warrior; and as a soldier approached that model, would he have possessed the proper tactics for the time. That Henry would not have made a better Indian fighter than Jay, or Livingston, or the Adamses, that he might not have made as dashing a partisan as Tarleton or Simcoe, his friends might readily afford to concede; but that he evinced, what neither Jay, nor Livingston, nor the Adamses did evince, a determined resolution to stake his reputation and his life on the issue of arms, and that he resigned his commission when the post of imminent danger was refused him, exhibit a lucid proof that, whatever may have been his ultimate fortune, he was not deficient in two grand elements of military success,—personal enterprise, and unquestioned courage."[1]

[1] Grigsby, *Va. Conv. of* 1776, 151, 152.

Patrick Henry making his Tarquin and Cæsar Speech

Charles Lee

CHAPTER XII

UPON this mortifying close of a military career which had opened with so much expectation and even *éclat*, Patrick Henry returned, early in March, 1776, to his home in the county of Hanover, — a home on which then rested the shadow of a great sorrow. In the midst of the public engagements and excitements which absorbed him during the previous year, his wife, Sarah, the wife of his youth, the mother of his six children, had passed away. His own subsequent release from public labor, however bitter in its occasion, must have brought to him a great solace in the few weeks of repose which he then had under his own roof, with the privilege of ministering to the happiness of his motherless children, and of enjoying once more their loving companionship and sympathy.

But in such a crisis of his country's fate, such a man as Patrick Henry could not be permitted long to remain in seclusion; and the promptness and the heartiness with which he was now summoned back into the service of the public as a civilian, after the recent humiliations of his military career, were accented, perhaps, on the part of his neighbors, by something of the fervor of intended compensation, if not of intended revenge. For, in the mean time, the American colonies had been swiftly advancing, along a path strewn with corpses and wet with blood, towards the doctrine that a total separation from the mother-country, — a thing hitherto contemplated by them only as a disaster and a crime, — might after all be neither, but on the contrary, the only resource left to them in their desperate struggle for political existence. This supreme question, it was plain, was to confront the very next Virginia convention, which was under appointment to meet early in the coming May. Almost at once, therefore, after his return home, Patrick Henry was elected by his native county to represent it in that convention.

On Monday morning, the 6th of May, the convention gathered at Williamsburg for its first meeting. On its roll of members we see many of those names which have become familiar to us in the progress of this history, — the names of those sturdy and well-trained leaders who guided Virginia during all that stormy period, — Pendleton, Cary, Mason, Nicholas, Bland, the Lees, Mann Page, Dudley Digges, Wythe, Edmund Randolph, and a few others. For the first time also, on such a roll, we meet the name of James Madison, an accomplished young political philosopher, then but four years from the inspiring instruction of President Witherspoon at Princeton. But while a few very able men had places in that convention, it was, at the time, by some observers thought to contain an unusually large number of incompetent persons. Three days after the opening of the session Landon Carter wrote to Washington: —

"I could have wished that ambition had not so visibly seized so much ignorance all over the colony, as it seems to have done ; for this present convention abounds with too many of the inexperienced creatures to navigate our bark on this dangerous coast ; so that I fear the few skilful pilots who have hitherto done tolerably well to keep her clear from destruction, will not be able to conduct her with common safety any longer." [1]

The earliest organization of the House was, on the part of the friends of Patrick Henry, made the occasion for a momentary flash of resentment against Edmund Pendleton, as the man who was believed by them to have been the guiding mind of the Committee of Safety in its long series of restraints upon the military activity of their chief. At the opening of the convention Pendleton was nominated for its president, — a most suitable nomination, and one which under ordinary circumstances would have been carried by acclamation. Thomas Johnson, however, a stanch follower of Patrick Henry, at once presented an opposing candidate; and although Pendleton was elected, he was not elected without a contest, or without this significant hint that the fires of indignation against

[1] 4 *Am. Arch.* vi. 390.

him were still burning in the hearts of a strong
party in that house and throughout the colony.

The convention lasted just two months lacking
a day; and in all the detail and drudgery of its
business, as the journal indicates, Patrick Henry
bore a very large part. In the course of the session, he seems to have served on perhaps a majority of all its committees. On the 6th of May, he
was made a member of the committee of privileges
and elections; on the 7th, of a committee "to
bring in an ordinance to encourage the making of
salt, saltpetre, and gunpowder;" on the 8th, of
the committee on "propositions and grievances;"
on the 21st, of a committee "to inquire for a
proper hospital for the reception and accommoda-
tion of the sick and wounded soldiers;" on the
22d, of a committee to inquire into the truth of
a complaint made by the Indians respecting encroachments on their lands; on the 23d, of a committee to bring in an ordinance for augmenting
the ninth regiment, for enlisting four troops of
horse, and for raising men for the defence of the
frontier counties; on the 4th of June, of a committee to inquire into the causes for the depreciation of paper money in the colony, and into the
rates at which goods are sold at the public store;
on the 14th of June, of a committee to prepare an
address to be sent by Virginia to the Shawanese
Indians; on the 15th of June, of a committee to
bring in amendments to the ordinance for prescrib-
ing a mode of punishment for the enemies of

America in this colony; and on the 22d of June, of a committee to prepare an ordinance "for enabling the present magistrates to continue the administration of justice, and for settling the general mode of proceedings in criminal and other cases." The journal also mentions his frequent activity in the House in the presentation of reports from some of these committees: for example, from the committee on propositions and grievances, on the 16th of May, on the 22d of May, and on the 15th of June. On the latter occasion, he made to the House three detailed reports on as many different topics.[1]

Of course, the question overshadowing all others in that convention was the question of independence. General Charles Lee, whose military duties just then detained him at Williamsburg, and who was intently watching the currents of political thought in all the colonies, assured Washington, in a letter written on the 10th of May, that "a noble spirit" possessed the convention; and that the members were "almost unanimous for independence," the only disagreement being "in their sentiments about the mode."[2] That Patrick Henry was in favor of independence hardly needs to be mentioned; yet it does need to be mentioned that he was among those who disagreed with some of his associates "about the mode." While he was as eager and as resolute for independence as

[1] The journal of this convention is in 4 *Am. Arch.* vi. 1509–1616.
[2] 4 *Am. Arch.* vi. 406.

any man, he doubted whether the time had then fully come for declaring independence. He thought that the declaration should be so timed as to secure, beyond all doubt, two great conditions of success, — first, the firm union of the colonies themselves, and secondly, the friendship of foreign powers, particularly of France and Spain. For these reàsons, he would have had independence delayed until a confederation of the colonies could be established by written articles, which, he probably supposed, would take but a few weeks; and also until American agents could have time to negotiate with the French and Spanish courts.

On the first day of the session, General Charles Lee, who was hot for an immediate declaration of independence, seems to have had a conversation upon the subject with Patrick Henry, during which the latter stated his reasons for some postponement of the measure. This led General Lee, on the following day, to write to Henry a letter which is really remarkable, some passages from which will help us the better to understand the public situation, as well as Patrick Henry's attitude towards it: —

WILLIAMSBURG, May 7, 1776.

DEAR SIR, — If I had not the highest opinion of your character and liberal way of thinking, I should not venture to address myself to you. And if I were not equally persuaded of the great weight and influence which the transcendent abilities you possess must naturally confer, I should not give myself the trouble of writing, nor you the trouble of reading this long letter. Since our conversation yesterday, my thoughts have been solely employed on the great question, whether independence ought or ought not to be immediately declared. Having weighed the argument on both sides, I am clearly of the opinion that we must, as we value the liberties of America, or even her existence, without a moment's delay declare for independence. . . . The objection you made yesterday, if I understood you rightly, to an immediate declaration, was by many degrees the most specious, indeed, it is the only tolerable, one that I have yet heard. You say, and with great justice, that we ought previously to have felt the pulse of France and Spain. I more than believe, I am almost confident, that it has been done. . . . But admitting that we are utter strangers to their sentiments on the subject, and that we run some risk of this declaration being coldly received by these powers, such is our situation that the risk must be ventured.

On one side there are the most probable chances of our success, founded on the certain advantages which must manifest themselves to French understandings by a treaty of alliance with America. . . . The superior commerce and marine force of England were evidently established on the monopoly of her American trade. The inferiority of France, in these two capital points, consequently had its source in the same origin. Any deduction from this monopoly must bring down her rival in proportion to this deduction. The French are and always have been sensible of these great truths. . . . But allowing that there can be no certainty, but mere chances, in our favor, I do insist upon it that these chances render it our duty to adopt the measure, as, by procrastination, our ruin is inevitable. Should it now

be determined to wait the result of a previous formal
negotiation with France, a whole year must pass over
our heads before we can be acquainted with the result.
In the mean time, we are to struggle through a campaign, without arms, ammunition, or any one necessary
of war. Disgrace and defeat will infallibly ensue; the
soldiers and officers will become so disappointed that
they will abandon their colors, and probably never be
persuaded to make another effort.

But there is another consideration still more cogent.
I can assure you that the spirit of the people cries out
for this declaration; the military, in particular, men
and officers, are outrageous on the subject; and a man
of your excellent discernment need not be told how
dangerous it would be, in our present circumstances, to
dally with the spirit, or disappoint the expectations, of
the bulk of the people. May not despair, anarchy, and
final submission be the bitter fruits? I am firmly persuaded that they will; and, in this persuasion, I most
devoutly pray that you may not merely recommend, but
positively lay injunctions on, your servants in Congress
to embrace a measure so necessary to our salvation.

> Yours, most sincerely,
> CHARLES LEE. [1]

Just eight days after that letter was written,
the Virginia convention took what may, at first
glance, seem to be the precise action therein described as necessary; and moreover, they did so
under the influence, in part, of Patrick Henry's

---

[1] 5 *Am. Arch.* i. 95–97. Campbell, in his *History of Virginia*,
645, 646, commits a rather absurd error in attributing this letter
to Thomas Nelson, Jr.

powerful advocacy of it.   On the 15th of May,
after considerable debate, one hundred and twelve
members being present, the convention unanimously resolved,

"That the delegates appointed to represent this colony
in General Congress be instructed to propose to that respectable body to declare the United Colonies free and
independent States, absolved from all allegiance to, or
dependence upon, the crown or Parliament of Great Britain; and that they give the assent of this colony to such
declaration, and to whatever measures may be thought
proper and necessary by the Congress for forming foreign
alliances and a confederation of the colonies, at such
time, and in the manner, as to them shall seem best:
provided, that the power of forming government for,
and the regulations of the internal concerns of, each
colony, be left to the respective colonial legislatures." [1]

On the testimony of Edmund Randolph, who
was a member of the convention, it is now known
that this momentous resolution "was drawn by
Pendleton, was offered in convention by Nelson,
and was advocated on the floor by Henry." [2]   Any
one who will carefully study it, however, will discover that this resolution was the result of a com-
promise; and especially, that it is so framed as to
meet Patrick Henry's views, at least to the extent
of avoiding the demand for an immediate declara-

[1] 4 *Am. Arch.* vi. 1524.
[2] Randolph's address at the funeral of Pendleton, in *Va. Gazette*
for 2 Nov. 1803, and cited by Grigsby, *Va. Conv. of* 1776, 203,
204.

tion, and of leaving it to Congress to determine
the time and manner of making it. Accordingly,
in letters of his, written five days afterward to his
most intimate friends in Congress, we see that his
mind was still full of anxiety about the two great
prerequisites, — a certified union among the colonies, and a friendly arrangement with France.
"Ere this reaches you," he wrote to Richard
Henry Lee, "our resolution for separating from
Britain will be handed you by Colonel Nelson.
Your sentiments as to the necessary progress of
this great affair correspond with mine. For may
not France, ignorant of the great advantages to
her commerce we intend to offer, and of the
permanency of that separation which is to take
place, be allured by the partition you mention?
To anticipate, therefore, the efforts of the enemy
by sending instantly American ambassadors to
France, seems to me absolutely necessary. Delay
may bring on us total ruin. But is not a confederacy of our States previously necessary?"[1]

On the same day, he wrote, also, a letter to
John Adams, in which he developed still more
vigorously his views as to the true order in which
the three great measures, — confederation, foreign
alliances, and independence, — should be dealt
with: —

"Before this reaches you, the resolution for finally
separating from Britain will be handed to Congress by

[1] *S. Lit. Messenger* for 1842; thence given in Campbell, *Hist.
Va.* 647, 648.

Colonel Nelson. I put up with it in the present form for the sake of unanimity. 'T is not quite so pointed as I could wish. Excuse me for telling you of what I think of immense importance; 't is to anticipate the enemy at the French court. The half of our continent offered to France, may induce her to aid our destruction, which she certainly has the power to accomplish. I know the free trade with all the States would be more beneficial to her than any territorial possessions she might acquire. But pressed, allured, as she will be, — but, above all, ignorant of the great thing we mean to offer, — may we not lose her? The consequence is dreadful. Excuse me again. The confederacy: — that must precede an open declaration of independency and foreign alliances. Would it not be sufficient to confine it, for the present, to the objects of offensive and defensive nature, and a guaranty of the respective colonial rights? If a minute arrangement of things is attempted, such as equal representation, etc., etc., you may split and divide; certainly will delay the French alliance, which with me is everything." [1]

In the mean time, however, many of the people of Virginia had received with enthusiastic approval the news of the great step taken by their convention on the 15th of May. Thus "on the day following," says the "Virginia Gazette," published at Williamsburg, "the troops in this city, with the train of artillery, were drawn up and went through their firings and various other military manœuvres, with the greatest exactness; a continental union flag was displayed upon the capitol;

[1] *Works of John Adams,* iv. 201.

and in the evening many of the inhabitants illu-
minated their houses."[1] Moreover, the great step
taken by the Virginia convention, on the day just
mentioned, committed that body to the duty of
taking at once certain other steps of supreme importance. They were about to cast off the government of Great Britain: it was necessary for them,
therefore, to provide some government to be put
in the place of it. Accordingly, in the very same
hour in which they instructed their delegates in
Congress to propose a declaration of independence,
they likewise resolved, "That a committee be appointed to prepare a declaration of rights, and
such a plan of government as will be most likely
to maintain peace and order in this colony, and
secure substantial and equal liberty to the people."[2]

Of this committee, Patrick Henry was a member; and with him were associated Archibald Cary,
Henry Lee, Nicholas, Edmund Randolph, Bland,
Dudley Digges, Paul Carrington, Mann Page,
Madison, George Mason, and others. The two
tasks before the committee — that of drafting a
statement of rights, and that of drafting a constitution for the new State of Virginia — must have
pressed heavily upon its leading members. In the
work of creating a new state government, Virginia was somewhat in advance of the other colonies; and for this reason, as well as on account of
its general preëminence among the colonies, the
course which it should take in this crisis was

[1] 4 *Am. Arch.* vi. 462.   [2] 4 *Am. Arch.* vi. 1524.

watched with extraordinary attention. John
Adams said, at the time, "We all look up to Virginia for examples." [1] Besides, in Virginia itself,
as well as in the other colonies, there was an un-
settled question as to the nature of the state governments which were then to be instituted. Should
they be strongly aristocratic and conservative, with
a possible place left for the monarchical feature;
or should the popular elements in each colony be
more largely recognized, and a decidedly democratic character given to these new constitutions?
On this question, two strong parties existed in
Virginia. In the first place, there were the old
aristocratic families, and those who sympathized
with them. These people, numerous, rich, culti-
vated, influential, in objecting to the unfair encroachments of British authority, had by no means
intended to object to the nature of the British
constitution, and would have been pleased to see
that constitution, in all its essential features, retained in Virginia. This party was led by such
men as Robert Carter Nicholas, Carter Braxton,
and Edmund Pendleton. In the second place,
there were the democrats, the reformers, the radicals, — who were inclined to take the opportunity
furnished by Virginia's rejection of British authority as the occasion for rejecting, within the new
State of Virginia, all the aristocratic and monarchical features of the British Constitution itself.
This party was led by such men as Patrick Henry,

[1] *Works of John Adams*, ix. 387.

Richard Henry Lee, Thomas Jefferson, and George Mason. Which party was to succeed in stamping its impress the more strongly on the new plan for government in Virginia?

Furthermore, it is important to observe that, on this very question then at issue in Virginia, two pamphlets, taking opposite sides, were, just at that moment, attracting the notice of Virginians, — both pamphlets being noble in tone, of considerable learning, very suggestive, and very well expressed. The first, entitled "Thoughts on Government," though issued anonymously, was soon known to be by John Adams. It advocated the formation of state constitutions on the democratic model; a lower house elected for a single year by the people; this house to elect an upper house of twenty or thirty members, who were to have a negative on the lower house, and to serve, likewise, for a single year; these two houses to elect a governor, who was to have a negative on them both, and whose term of office should also end with the year; while the judges, and all other officers, civil or military, were either to be appointed by the governor with the advice of the upper house, or to be chosen directly by the two houses themselves.[1] The second pamphlet, which was in part a reply to the first, was entitled "Address to the Convention of the Colony and Ancient Dominion of Virginia, on the subject of Government in general, and recommending a particular form to their con-

[1] John Adams's pamphlet is given in his *Works*, iv. 189-200.

sideration." It purported to be by "A native of the Colony." Although the pamphlet was sent into Virginia under strong recommendations from Carter Braxton, one of the Virginian delegates in Congress, the authorship was then unknown to the public. It advocated the formation of state constitutions on a model far less democratic: first, a lower house, the members of which were to be elected for three years by the people; secondly, an upper house of twenty-four members, to be elected for life by the lower house; thirdly, a governor, to be elected for life by the lower house; fourthly, all judges, all military officers, and all inferior civil ones, to be appointed by the governor.[1]

Such was the question over which the members of the committee, appointed on the 15th of May, must soon have come into sharp conflict. At its earliest meetings, apparently, Henry found the aristocratic tendencies of some of his associates so strong as to give him considerable uneasiness; and by his letter to John Adams, written on the 20th of the month, we may see that he was then complaining of the lack of any associate of adequate ability on his own side of the question. When we remember, however, that both James Madison and George Mason were members of that committee, we can but read Patrick Henry's words with some astonishment.[2] The explanation is probably

[1] The pamphlet is given in 4 *Am. Arch.* vi. 748–754.
[2] See the unfavorable comment of Rives, *Life and Times of Madison*, i. 147, 148.

to be found in the fact that Madison was not placed
on the committee until the 16th, and, being very
young and very unobtrusive, did not at first make
his true weight felt; while Mason was not placed
on the committee until the working day just before
Henry's letter was written, and very likely had
not then met with it, and may not, at the moment,
have been remembered by Henry as a member of
it. At any rate, this is the way in which our
eager Virginia democrat, in that moment of anxious conflict over the form of the future government of his State, poured out his anxieties to his
two most congenial political friends in Congress.
To Richard Henry Lee he wrote: —

" The grand work of forming a constitution for Virginia is now before the convention, where your love of
equal liberty and your skill in public counsels might so
eminently serve the cause of your country. Perhaps
I 'm mistaken, but I fear too great a bias to aristocracy
prevails among the opulent. I own myself a democratic
on the plan of our admired friend, J. Adams, whose
pamphlet I read with great pleasure. A performance
from Philadelphia is just come here, ushered in, I 'm
told, by a colleague of yours, B——, and greatly recommended by him. I don't like it. Is the author a
Whig? One or two expressions in the book make me
ask. I wish to divide you, and have you here to ani-
mate, by your manly eloquence, the sometimes drooping
spirits of our country, and in Congress to be the ornament of your native country, and the vigilant, determined foe of tyranny. To give you colleagues of kindred sentiments, is my wish. I doubt you have them

not at present. A confidential account of the matter to Colonel Tom,[1] desiring him to use it according to his discretion, might greatly serve the public and vindicate Virginia from suspicions. Vigor, animation, and all the powers of mind and body must now be summoned and collected together into one grand effort. Moderation, falsely so called, hath nearly brought on us final ruin. And to see those, who have so fatally advised us, still guiding, or at least sharing, our public counsels, alarms me."[2]

On the same day, he wrote as follows to John Adams: —

WILLIAMSBURG, May 20, 1776.

MY DEAR SIR, — Your favor, with the pamphlet, came safe to hand. I am exceedingly obliged to you for it; and I am not without hopes it may produce good here, where there is among most of our opulent families a strong bias to aristocracy. I tell my friends you are the author. Upon that supposition, I have two reasons for liking the book. The sentiments are precisely the same I have long since taken up, and they come recommended by you. Go on, my dear friend, to assail the strongholds of tyranny; and in whatever form oppression may be found, may those talents and that firmness, which have achieved so much for America, be pointed against it. . . .

Our convention is now employed in the great work of forming a constitution. My most esteemed republican form has many and powerful enemies. A silly thing, published in Philadelphia, by a native of Virginia, has

[1] Probably Thomas Ludwell Lee.

[2] S. Lit. Messenger for 1842. Reprinted in Campbell, Hist. Va. 647.

just made its appearance here, strongly recommended, 't is said, by one of our delegates now with you, — Braxton. His reasonings upon and distinction between private and public virtue, are weak, shallow, evasive, and the whole performance an affront and disgrace to this country; and, by one expression, I suspect his whiggism.

Our session will be very long, during which I cannot count upon one coadjutor of talents equal to the task. Would to God you and your Sam Adams were here! It shall be my incessant study so to form our portrait of government that a kindred with New England may be discerned in it; and if all your excellences cannot be preserved, yet I hope to retain so much of the likeness, that posterity shall pronounce us descended from the same stock. I shall think perfection is obtained, if we have your approbation.

I am forced to conclude; but first, let me beg to be presented to my ever-esteemed S. Adams. Adieu, my dear sir; may God preserve you, and give you every good thing.

P. HENRY, JR.

P. S. Will you and S. A. now and then write?[1]

To this hearty and even brotherly letter John Adams wrote from Philadelphia, on the 3d of June, a fitting reply, in the course of which he said, with respect to Henry's labors in making a constitution for Virginia: "The subject is of infinite moment, and perhaps more than adequate to the abilities of any man in America. I know of none so competent to the task as the author of the first Virginia resolutions against the Stamp Act,

[1] *Works of John Adams*, iv. 201, 202.

who will have the glory with posterity of beginning and concluding this great revolution. Happy
Virginia, whose constitution is to be framed by so
masterly a builder!" Then, with respect to the
aristocratic features in the Constitution, as proposed by "A Native of the Colony," John Adams
exclaims:—

"The dons, the bashaws, the grandees, the patricians,
the sachems, the nabobs, call them by what name you
please, sigh, and groan, and fret, and sometimes stamp,
and foam, and curse, but all in vain. The decree is
gone forth, and it cannot be recalled, that a more equal
liberty than has prevailed in other parts of the earth,
must be established in America. That exuberance of
pride which has produced an insolent domination in a
few, a very few, opulent, monopolizing families, will be
brought down nearer to the confines of reason and moderation than they have been used to. . . . I shall ever
be happy in receiving your advice by letter, until I can
be more completely so in seeing you here in person,
which I hope will be soon." [1]

On the 12th of June, the convention adopted
without a dissenting voice its celebrated "declaration of rights," a compact, luminous, and powerful statement, in sixteen articles, of those great
fundamental rights that were henceforth to be
"the basis and foundation of government" in
Virginia, and were to stamp their character upon
that constitution on which the committee were even
then engaged. Perhaps no political document of

[1] *Works of John Adams*, ix. 386-388.

that time is more worthy of study in connection with the genesis, not only of our state constitutions, but of that of the nation likewise. That the first fourteen articles of the declaration were written by George Mason has never been disputed: that he also wrote the fifteenth and the sixteenth articles is now claimed by his latest and ablest biographer,[1] but in opposition to the testimony of Edmund Randolph, who was a member both of the convention itself and of the particular committee in charge of the declaration, and who has left on record the statement that those articles were the work of Patrick Henry.[2] The fifteenth article was in these words: "That no free government, or the blessings of liberty, can be preserved to any people but by a firm adherence to justice, moderation, temperance, frugality, and virtue, and by frequent recurrence to fundamental principles." The sixteenth article is an assertion of the doctrine of religious liberty, — the first time that it was ever asserted by authority in Virginia. The original draft, in which the writer followed very closely the language used on that subject by the Independents in the Assembly of Westminster, stood as follows: —

"That religion, or the duty we owe our Creator, and the manner of discharging it, can be directed only by reason and conviction, and not by force or violence; and,

[1] Kate Mason Rowland, *Life of Mason*, i. 228–241.
[2] Edmund Randolph, MS. *Hist. Va.* See, also, W. W. Henry, *Life of P. Henry*, i. 422–436.

therefore, that all men should enjoy the fullest toleration in the exercise of religion, according to the dictates of conscience, unpunished and unrestrained by the magistrate, unless, under color of religion, any man disturb the peace, the happiness, or the safety of society; and that it is the mutual duty of all to practise Christian forbearance, love, and charity towards each other." [1]

The historic significance of this stately assertion of religious liberty in Virginia can be felt only by those who remember that, at that time, the Church of England was the established church of Virginia, and that the laws of Virginia then restrained the exercise there of every form of religious dissent, unless compliance had been made with the conditions of the toleration act of the first year of William and Mary. At the very moment, probably, when the committee were engaged in considering the tremendous innovation contained in this article, "sundry persons of the Baptist church in the county of Prince William" were putting their names to a petition earnestly imploring the convention, "That they be allowed to worship God in their own way, without interruption; that they be permitted to maintain their own ministers and none others; that they may be married, buried, and the like, without paying the clergy of other denominations;" and that, by the concession to them of such religious freedom, they be enabled to "unite with their brethren, and to the utmost

[1] Edmund Randolph, MS. *Hist. Va.* See, also, W. W. Henry, *Life of P. Henry*, i. 422–436.

of their ability promote the common cause" of
political freedom.[1]   Of course the adoption of the
sixteenth article virtually carried with it every
privilege which these people asked for.   The author of that article, whether it was George Mason
or Patrick Henry, was a devout communicant of
the established church of Virginia; and thus, the
first great legislative act for the reform of the
civil constitution of that church, and for its deliv-
erance from the traditional duty and curse of per-
secution, was an act which came from within the
church itself.

On Monday, the 24th of June, the committee,
through Archibald Cary, submitted to the convention their plan of a constitution for the new State
of Virginia; and on Saturday, the 29th of June,
this plan passed its third reading, and was unanimously adopted.   A glance at the document will
show that in the sharp struggle between the aristocratic and the democratic forces in the convention,
the latter had signally triumphed.   It provided
for a lower House of Assembly, whose members
were to be elected annually by the people, in the
proportion of two members from each county; for
an upper House of Assembly to consist of twenty-
four members, who were to be elected annually by
the people, in the proportion of one member from
each of the senatorial districts into which the several counties should be grouped; for a governor,
to be elected annually by joint ballot of both

[1] 4 *Am. Arch.* vi. 1582.

houses, and not to "continue in that office longer than three years successively," nor then to be eligible again for the office until after the lapse of four years from the close of his previous term; for a privy council of eight members, for delegates in Congress, and for judges in the several courts, all to be elected by joint ballot of the two Houses; for justices of the peace to be appointed by the governor and the privy council; and, finally, for an immediate election, by the convention itself, of a governor, and a privy council, and such other officers as might be necessary for the introduction of the new government. [1]

In accordance with the last provision of this Constitution, the convention at once proceeded to cast their ballots for governor, with the following result: —

For Patrick Henry	60
For Thomas Nelson	45
For John Page	1

By resolution, Patrick Henry was then formally declared to be the governor of the commonwealth of Virginia, to continue in office until the close of that session of the Assembly which should be held after the end of the following March.

On the same day on which this action was taken, he wrote, in reply to the official notice of his election, the following letter of acceptance, — a graceful, manly, and touching composition: —

[1] *Am. Arch.* vi. 1598–1601, note.

TO THE HONORABLE THE PRESIDENT AND HOUSE OF
CONVENTION.

GENTLEMEN, — The vote of this day, appointing me
governor of this commonwealth, has been notified to
me, in the most polite and obliging manner, by George
Mason, Henry Lee, Dudley Digges, John Blair, and
Bartholomew Dandridge, Esquires.

A sense of the high and unmerited honor conferred
upon me by the convention fills my heart with gratitude,
which I trust my whole life will manifest. I take this
earliest opportunity to express my thanks, which I wish
to convey to you, gentlemen, in the strongest terms of
acknowledgment.

When I reflect that the tyranny of the British king
and parliament hath kindled a formidable war, now ra-
ging throughout the wide-extended continent, and in the
operations of which this commonwealth must bear so
great a part, and that from the events of this war the
lasting happiness or misery of a great proportion of the
human species will finally result; that, in order to preserve this commonwealth from anarchy, and its attend-
ant ruin, and to give vigor to our councils and effect to
all our measures, government hath been necessarily assumed and new modelled; that it is exposed to numberless hazards and perils in its infantine state; that it can
never attain to maturity or ripen into firmness, unless
it is guarded by affectionate assiduity, and managed by
great abilities, — I lament my want of talents; I feel
my mind filled with anxiety and uneasiness to find myself so unequal to the duties of that important station to
which I am called by favor of my fellow citizens at this
truly critical conjuncture. The errors of my conduct

shall be atoned for, so far as I am able, by unwearied endeavors to secure the freedom and happiness of our common country.

I shall enter upon the duties of my office whenever you, gentlemen, shall be pleased to direct, relying upon the known wisdom and virtue of your honorable house to supply my defects, and to give permanency and success to that system of government which you have formed, and which is so wisely calculated to secure equal liberty, and advance human happiness.

I have the honor to be, gentlemen, your most obedient and very humble servant,

P. HENRY, JR.

WILLIAMSBURG, June 29, 1776.[1]

[1] 4 *Am. Arch.* vi. 1129, 1130.

CHAPTER XIII

FIRST GOVERNOR OF THE STATE OF VIRGINIA

ON Friday, the 5th of July, 1776, Patrick Henry took the oath of office,[1] and entered upon his duties as governor of the commonwealth of Virginia. The salary attached to the position was fixed at one thousand pounds sterling for the year; and the governor was invited to take up his residence in the palace at Williamsburg. No one had resided in the palace since Lord Dunmore had fled from it; and the people of Virginia could hardly fail to note the poetic retribution whereby the very man whom, fourteen months before, Lord Dunmore had contemptuously denounced as "a certain Patrick Henry of Hanover County," should now become Lord Dunmore's immediate successor in that mansion of state, and should be able, if he chose, to write proclamations against Lord Dunmore upon the same desk on which Lord Dunmore had so recently written the proclamation against himself.

Among the first to bring their congratulations to the new governor, were his devoted friends, the first and second regiments of Virginia, who told

[1] Burk, *Hist. Va.* iv. 154.

him that they viewed "with the sincerest sentiments of respect and joy" his accession to the
highest office in the State, and who gave to him
likewise this affectionate assurance: "our hearts
are willing, and arms ready, to maintain your
authority as chief magistrate."[1] On the 29th of
July, the erratic General Charles Lee, who was
then in Charleston, sent on his congratulations in
a letter amusing for its tart cordiality and its pep-
pery playfulness: —

"I most sincerely congratulate you on the noble conduct of your countrymen; and I congratulate your country on having citizens deserving of the high honor to
which you are exalted. For the being elected to the
first magistracy of a free people is certainly the pinnacle
of human glory; and I am persuaded that they could
not have made a happier choice. Will you excuse me,
— but I am myself so extremely democratical, that I think
it a fault in your constitution that the governor should be
eligible for three years successively. It appears to me
that a government of three years may furnish an opportunity of acquiring a very dangerous influence. But this
is not the worst. . . . A man who is fond of office, and
has his eye upon reëlection, will be courting favor and
popularity at the expense of his duty. . . . There is a
barbarism crept in among us that extremely shocks me:
I mean those tinsel epithets with which (I come in for
my share) we are so beplastered, — 'his excellency,'
and 'his honor,' 'the honorable president of the honorable congress,' or 'the honorable convention.' This ful-
some. nauseating cant may be well enough adapted to

[1] 4 *Am. Arch.* vi. 1602, 1603, note.

barbarous monarchies, or to gratify the adulterated pride
of the 'magnifici' in pompous aristocracies; but in a
great, free, manly, equal commonwealth, it is quite
abominable. For my own part, I would as lief they
would put ratsbane in my mouth as the 'excellency'
with which I am daily crammed. How much more true
dignity was there in the simplicity of address amongst
the Romans, — 'Marcus Tullius Cicero,' 'Decimo Bruto
Imperatori,' or 'Caio Marcello Consuli,' — than to 'his
excellency Major-General Noodle,' or to 'the honorable
John Doodle.' . . . If, therefore, I should sometimes
address a letter to you without the 'excellency' tacked,
you must not esteem it a mark of personal or official dis-
respect, but the reverse." [1]

Of all the words of congratulation which poured
in upon the new governor, probably none came so
straight from the heart, and none could have been
quite so sweet to him, as those which, on the 12th
of August, were uttered by some of the persecuted
dissenters in Virginia, who, in many an hour of
need, had learned to look up to Patrick Henry as
their strong and splendid champion, in the legislature and in the courts. On the date just mentioned, "the ministers and delegates of the Baptist
churches" of the State, being met in convention
at Louisa, sent to him this address: —

MAY IT PLEASE YOUR EXCELLENCY, — As your ad-
vancement to the honorable and important station as
governor of this commonwealth affords us unspeakable
pleasure, we beg leave to present your excellency with
our most cordial congratulations.

[1] 5 *Am. Arch.* i. 631.

Your public virtues are such that we are under no temptation to flatter you. Virginia has done honor to her judgment in appointing your excellency to hold the reins of government at this truly critical conjuncture, as you have always distinguished yourself by your zeal and activity for her welfare, in whatever department has been assigned you.

As a religious community, we have nothing to request of you. Your constant attachment to the glorious cause of liberty and the rights of conscience, leaves us no room to doubt of your excellency's favorable regards while we worthily demean ourselves.

May God Almighty continue you long, very long, a public blessing to this your native country, and, after a life of usefulness here, crown you with immortal felicity in the world to come.

Signed by order: JEREMIAH WALKER, *Moderator.*
JOHN WILLIAMS, *Clerk.*

To these loving and jubilant words, the governor replied in an off-hand letter, the deep feeling of which is not the less evident because it is restrained, — a letter which is as choice and noble in diction as it is in thought: —

TO THE MINISTERS AND DELEGATES OF THE BAPTIST CHURCHES, AND THE MEMBERS OF THAT COMMUNION.

GENTLEMEN, — I am exceedingly obliged to you for your very kind address, and the favorable sentiments you are pleased to entertain respecting my conduct and the principles which have directed it. My constant endeavor shall be to guard the rights of all my fellow-citizens from every encroachment.

I am happy to find a catholic spirit prevailing in our country, and that those religious distinctions, which formerly produced some heats, are now forgotten. Happy must every friend to virtue and America feel himself, to perceive that the only contest among us, at this most critical and important period, is, who shall be foremost to preserve our religious and civil liberties.

My most earnest wish is, that Christian charity, forbearance, and love, may unite all our different persuasions, as brethren who must perish or triumph together; and I trust that the time is not far distant when we shall greet each other as the peaceable possessors of that just and equal system of liberty adopted by the last convention, and in support of which may God crown our arms with success.

I am, gentlemen, your most obedient and very humble servant,   P. HENRY, JUN.[1]

August 13, 1776.

On the day on which Governor Henry was sworn into office, the convention finally adjourned, having made provision for the meeting of the General Assembly on the first Monday of the following October. In the mean time, therefore, all the interests of the State were to be in the immediate keeping of the governor and privy council; and, for a part of that time, as it turned out, the governor himself was disabled for service. For we now encounter in the history of Patrick Henry, the first mention of that infirm health from which he seems to have suffered, in some degree, during the remaining twenty-three years of his life. Before

[1] 5 *Am. Arch.* i. 905, 906.

taking full possession of the governor's palace, which had to be made ready for his use, he had likewise to prepare for this great change in his life by returning to his home in the county of Hanover. There he lay ill for some time; [1] and upon his recovery he removed with his family to Williamsburg, which continued to be their home for the next three years.

The people of Virginia had been accustomed, for more than a century, to look upon their governors as personages of very great dignity. Several of those governors had been connected with the English peerage; all had served in Virginia in a vice-regal capacity; many had lived there in a sort of vice-regal pomp and magnificence. It is not to be supposed that Governor Henry would be able or willing to assume so much state and grandeur as his predecessors had done; and yet he felt, and the people of Virginia felt, that in the transition from royal to republican forms the dignity of that office should not be allowed to decline in any important particular. Moreover, as a contemporary observer mentions, Patrick Henry had been "accused by the big-wigs of former times as being a coarse and common man, and utterly destitute of dignity; and perhaps he wished to show them that they were mistaken." [2] At any rate, by the testimony of all, he seems to have displayed his usual judgment and skill in adapting himself to the re-

[1] George Rogers Clark's *Campaign in the Illinois*, 11.
[2] Spencer Roane, MS.

quirements of his position; and, while never losing
his gentleness and his simplicity of manner, to
have borne himself as the impersonation, for the
time being, of the executive authority of a great and
proud commonwealth. He ceased to appear frequently upon the streets; and whenever he did
appear, he was carefully arrayed in a dressed wig,
in black small-clothes, and in a scarlet cloak; and
his presence and demeanor were such as to sustain,
in the popular mind, the traditional respect for
his high office.

He had so far recovered from the illness which
had prostrated him during the summer, as to be
at his post of duty when the General Assembly
of the State began its first session, on Monday,
the 7th of October, 1776. His health, however,
was still extremely frail; for on the 30th of that
month he was obliged to notify the House "that
the low state of his health rendered him unable to
attend to the duties of his office, and that his phy-
sicians had recommended to him to retire there-
from into the country, till he should recover his
strength." [1] His absence seems not to have been
very long. By the 16th of November, as one may
infer from entries in the journal of the House,[2] he
was able to resume his official duties.

The summer and autumn of that year proved to
be a dismal period for the American cause. Before our eyes, as we now look back over those
days, there marches this grim procession of dates:

[1] *Jour. Va. House Del.* 32.   [2] *Ibid.* 57–59.

August 27, the battle of Long Island; August 29, Washington's retreat across East River; September 15, the panic among the American troops at Kip's Bay, and the American retreat from New York; September 16, the battle of Harlem Plains; September 20, the burning of New York; October 28, the battle of White Plains; November 16, the surrender of Fort Washington; November 20, the abandonment of Fort Lee, followed by Washington's retreat across the Jerseys. In the midst of these disasters, Washington found time to write, from the Heights of Harlem, on the 5th of October, to his old friend, Patrick Henry, congratulating him on his election as governor of Virginia and on his recovery from sickness; explaining the military situation at headquarters; advising him about military appointments in Virginia; and especially giving to him important suggestions concerning the immediate military defence of Virginia "against the enemy's ships and tenders, which," as Washington says to the governor, "may go up your rivers in quest of provisions, or for the purpose of destroying your towns."[1] Indeed, Virginia was just then exposed to hostile attacks on all sides;[2] and it was so plain that any attack by water would have found an easy approach to Williamsburg, that, in the course of the next few months, the public records and the public stores

[1] *Writings of Washington*, iv. 138.

[2] See Letters from the president of Va. Privy Council and from General Lewis, in 5 *Am. Arch.* i. 736.

were removed to Richmond, as being, on every account, a "more secure site." [1] Apparently, however, the prompt recognition of this danger by Governor Henry, early in the autumn of 1776, and his vigorous military preparations against it, were interpreted by some of his political enemies as a sign both of personal cowardice and of official self-glorification, — as is indicated by a letter written by the aged Landon Carter to General Washington, on the 31st of October, and filled with all manner of caustic garrulity and insinuation, — a letter from which it may be profitable for us to quote a few sentences, as qualifying somewhat that stream of honeyed testimony respecting Patrick Henry which commonly flows down upon us so copiously from all that period.

"If I don't err in conjecture," says Carter, "I can't help thinking that the head of our Commonwealth has as great a palace of fear and apprehension as can possess the heart of any being ; and if we compare rumor with actual movements, I believe it will prove itself to every sensible man. As soon as the Congress sent for our first, third, fourth, fifth, and sixth regiments to assist you in contest against the enemy where they really were . . . there got a report among the soldiery that Dignity had declared it would not reside in Williamsburg without two thousand men under arms to guard him. This had like to have occasioned a mutiny. A desertion of many from the several companies did follow ; boisterous fellows resisting, and swearing they would not leave their

[1] Burk, *Hist. Va.* iv. 229.

county. . . . What a finesse of popularity was this?
. . . As soon as the regiments were gone, this great man
found an interest with the council of state, perhaps tim-
orous as himself, to issue orders for the militia of twenty-
six counties, and five companies of a minute battalion, to
march to Williamsburg, to protect him only against his
own fears; and to make this the more popular, it was
endeavored that the House of Delegates should give it a
countenance, but, as good luck would have it, it was
with difficulty refused.[1] . . . Immediately then, . . . a
bill is brought in to remove the seat of government, —
some say, up to Hanover, to be called Henry-Town." [2]

This gossip of a disappointed Virginian aristo-
crat, in vituperation of the public character of
Governor Henry, naturally leads us forward in
our story to that more stupendous eruption of gossip which relates, in the first instance, to the latter
part of December, 1776, and which alleges that a
conspiracy was then formed among certain members of the General Assembly to make Patrick
Henry the dictator of Virginia. The first intimation ever given to the public concerning it, was
given by Jefferson several years afterward, in his
"Notes on Virginia," a fascinating brochure which
was written by him in 1781 and 1782, was first
printed privately in Paris in 1784, and was first
published in England in 1787, in America in
1788.[3] The essential portions of his statement are
as follows: —

[1] Compare *Jour. Va. House Del.* 8.
[2] 5 *Am. Arch.* ii. 1305–1306.
[3] Randall, *Life of Jefferson,* i. 363, 413; and *Hist. Mag.* i. 52.

"In December, 1776, our circumstances being much distressed, it was proposed in the House of Delegates to create a dictator, invested with every power legislative, executive, and judiciary, civil and military, of life and death, over our persons and over our properties. . . . One who entered into this contest from a pure love of liberty, and a sense of injured rights, who determined to make every sacrifice and to meet every danger, for the reëstablishment of those rights on a firm basis, . . . must stand confounded and dismayed when he is told that a considerable portion of " the House " had meditated the surrender of them into a single hand, and in lieu of a limited monarchy, to deliver him over to a despotic one. . . . The very thought alone was treason against the people; was treason against man in general; as riveting forever the chains which bow down their necks, by giving to their oppressors a proof, which they would have trumpeted through the universe, of the imbecility of republican government, in times of pressing danger, to shield them from harm. . . . Those who meant well, of the advocates of this measure (and most of them meant well, for I know them personally, had been their fellow-laborer in the common cause, and had often proved the purity of their principles), had been seduced in their judgment by the example of an ancient republic, whose constitution and circumstances were fundamentally different." [1]

With that artistic tact and that excellent prudence which seem never to have failed Jefferson in any of his enterprises for the disparagement of his

[1] *Writings of Jefferson*, viii. 368–371; also Phila. ed. of *Notes*, 1825, 172–176.

associates, he here avoids, as will be observed, all mention of the name of the person for whose fatal promotion this classic conspiracy was formed, — leaving that interesting item to come out, as it did many years afterward, when the most of those who could have borne testimony upon the subject were in their graves, and when the damning stigma could be comfortably fastened to the name of Patrick Henry without the direct intervention of Jefferson's own hands. Accordingly, in 1816, a French gentleman, Girardin, a near neighbor of Jefferson's, who enjoyed "the incalculable benefit of a free access to Mr. Jefferson's library,"[1] and who wrote the continuation of Burk's "History of Virginia" under Jefferson's very eye,[2] gave in that work a highly wrought account of the alleged conspiracy of December, 1776, as involving "nothing less than the substitution of a despotic in lieu of a limited monarch;" and then proceeded to bring the accusation down from those lurid generalities of condemnation in which Jefferson himself had cautiously left it, by adding this sentence: "That Mr. Henry was the person in view for the dictatorship, is well ascertained."[3]

Finally, in 1817, William Wirt, whose "Life of Henry" was likewise composed under nearly the same inestimable advantages as regards in-

[1] Burk, *Hist. Va.* iv. Pref. Rem. vi.

[2] See Jefferson's explicit endorsement of Girardin's book in his own *Writings*, i. 50.

[3] Burk, *Hist. Va.* 189, 190.

struction and oversight furnished by Jefferson, repeated the fearful tale, and added some particulars; but, in doing so, Wirt could not fail — good lawyer and just man, as he was — to direct attention to the absence of all evidence of any collusion on the part of Patrick Henry with the projected folly and crime.

"Even the heroism of the Virginia legislature," says Wirt, "gave way; and, in a season of despair, the mad project of a dictator was seriously meditated. That Mr. Henry was thought of for this office, has been alleged, and is highly probable; but that the project was suggested by him, or even received his countenance, I have met with no one who will venture to affirm. There is a tradition that Colonel Archibald Cary, the speaker of the Senate, was principally instrumental in crushing this project; that meeting Colonel Syme, the step-brother of Colonel Henry, in the lobby of the House, he accosted him very fiercely in terms like these: 'I am told that your brother wishes to be dictator. Tell him from me, that the day of his appointment shall be the day of his death; — for he shall feel my dagger in his heart before the sunset of that day.' And the tradition adds that Colonel Syme, in great agitation, declared that 'if such a project existed, his brother had no hand in it; for that nothing could be more foreign to him, than to countenance any office which could endanger, in the most distant manner, the liberties of his country.' The intrepidity and violence of Colonel Cary's character renders the tradition probable; but it furnishes no proof of Mr. Henry's implication in the scheme."[1]

[1] Wirt, *Life of Henry*, 204–205.

A disinterested study of this subject, in the light of all the evidence now attainable, will be likely to convince any one that this enormous scandal must have been very largely a result of the extreme looseness at that time prevailing in the use of the word "dictator," and of its being employed, on the one side, in an innocent sense, and, on the other side, in a guilty one. In strict propriety, of course, the word designates a magistrate created in an emergency of public peril, and clothed for a time with unlimited power. It is an extreme remedy, and in itself a remedy extremely dangerous, and can never be innocently resorted to except when the necessity for it is indubitable; and it may well be questioned whether, among people and institutions like our own, a necessity can ever arise which would justify the temporary grant of unlimited power to any man. If this be true, it follows that no man among us can, without dire political guilt, ever consent to bestow such power; and that no man can, without the same guilt, ever consent to receive it.

Yet it is plain that even among us, between the years 1776 and 1783, emergencies of terrific public peril did arise, sufficient to justify, nay, even to compel, the bestowment either upon the governor of some State, or upon the general of the armies, not of unlimited power, certainly, but of extraordinary power, — such extraordinary power, for example, as was actually conferred by the Continental Congress, more than once, on Washington;

as was conferred by the legislature of South Carolina on Governor John Rutledge; as was repeatedly
conferred by the legislature of Virginia upon Governor Patrick Henry; and afterward, in still higher
degree, by the same legislature, on Governor
Thomas Jefferson himself.   Nevertheless, so loose
was the meaning then attached to the word "dictator," that it was not uncommon for men to speak
of these very cases as examples of the bestowment
of a dictatorship, and of the exercise of dictatorial
power; although, in every one of the cases mentioned, there was lacking the essential feature of
a true dictatorship, namely, the grant of unlimited
power to one man.   It is perfectly obvious, likewise, that when, in those days, men spoke thus of
a dictatorship, and of dictatorial power, they attached no suggestion of political guilt either to the
persons who bestowed such power, or to the persons who severally accepted it, — the tacit understanding being that, in every instance, the public
danger required and justified some grant of extraordinary power; that no more power was granted
than was necessary; and that the man to whom,
in any case, the grant was made, was a man to
whom, there was good reason to believe, the grant
could be made with safety.   Obviously, it was
upon this tacit understanding of its meaning that
the word was used, for instance, by Edmund Randolph, in 1788, in the Virginia Constitutional
Convention, when, alluding to the extraordinary
power bestowed by Congress on Washington, he

said: "We had an American dictator in 1781." Surely, Randolph did not mean to impute political crime, either to the Congress which made Washington a dictator, or to Washington himself who consented to be made one. It was upon the same tacit understanding, also, that Patrick Henry, in reply to Randolph, took up the word, and extolled the grant of dictatorial power to Washington on the occasion referred to: "In making a dictator," said Henry, "we followed the example of the most glorious, magnanimous, and skilful nations. In great dangers, this power has been given. Rome has furnished us with an illustrious example. America found a person for that trust: she looked to Virginia for him. We gave a dictatorial power to hands that used it gloriously, and which were rendered more glorious by surrendering it up."[1]

Thus it is apparent that the word "dictator" was frequently used in those times in a sense perfectly innocent. As all men know, however, the word is one capable of suggesting the possibilities of dreadful political crime; and it is not hard to see how, when employed by one person to describe the bestowment and acceptance of extraordinary power, — implying a perfectly innocent proposition, it could be easily taken by another person as describing the bestowment and acceptance of unlimited power, — implying a proposition which among us, probably, would always be a criminal one.

[1] Elliot's *Debates*, iii. 160.

With the help which this discussion may give us, let us now return to the General Assembly of Virginia, at Williamsburg, approaching the close of its first session, in the latter part of December, 1776. It was on the point of adjourning, not to meet again until the latter part of March, 1777. At that moment, by the arrival of most alarming news from the seat of war, it was forced to make special provision for the public safety during the interval which must elapse before its next session. Its journal indicates that, prior to the 20th of December, it had been proceeding with its business in a quiet way, under no apparent consciousness of imminent peril. On that day, however, there are traces of a panic; for, on that day, "The Virginia Gazette" announced to them the appalling news of "the crossing of the Delaware by the British forces, from twelve to fifteen thousand strong; the position of General Washington, at Bristol, on the south side of the river, with only six thousand men;" and the virtual flight of Congress from Philadelphia.[1] At this rate, how long would it be before the Continental army would be dispersed or captured, and the troops of the enemy sweeping in vengeance across the borders of Virginia? Accordingly, the House of Delegates immediately resolved itself into "a committee to take into their consideration the state of America;" but not being able to reach any decision that day, it voted to resume the subject on the day following, and for

[1] Cited by William Wirt Henry, *Hist. Mag.* for 1873, 349.

that purpose to meet an hour earlier than usual. So, on Saturday, the 21st of December, the House passed a series of resolutions intended to provide for the crisis into which the country was plunged, and, among the other resolutions, this: —

" And whereas the present imminent danger of America, and the ruin and misery which threatens the good people of this Commonwealth, and their posterity, calls for the utmost exertion of our strength, and it is become necessary for the preservation of the State that the usual forms of government be suspended during a limited time, for the more speedy execution of the most vigorous and effectual measures to repel the invasion of the enemy ;

" *Resolved, therefore,* That the governor be, and he is hereby fully authorized and empowered, by and with the advice and consent of the privy council, from henceforward, until ten days next after the first meeting of the General Assembly, to carry into execution such requisitions as may be made to this Commonwealth by the American Congress for the purpose of encountering or repelling the enemy; to order the three battalions on the pay of this Commonwealth to march, if necessary, to join the Continental army, or to the assistance of any of our sister States ; to call forth any and such greater military force as they shall judge requisite, either by embodying and arraying companies or regiments of volunteers, or by raising additional battalions, appointing and commissioning the proper officers, and to direct their operations within this Commonwealth, under the command of the Continental generals or other officers according to their respective ranks, or order them to march to join and act in concert with the Continental army, or the troops of any of the American States; and to provide for their pay, supply of provisions, arms, and other necessaries, at the charge of this Commonwealth, by drawing on the treasurer for the money which may be necessary from time to time; and the said treasurer is authorized to pay such warrants out of any public money which may be in his hands, and the General Assembly will, at their next session, make ample provision for any deficiency which may happen. But that this departure from the constitution of government, being in this instance founded only on the most evident and urgent necessity, ought not hereafter to be drawn into precedent."

These resolutions, having been pressed rapidly through the forms of the House, were at once carried up to the Senate for its concurrence. The answer of the Senate was promptly returned, agreeing to all the resolutions of the lower House, but proposing an important amendment in the phraseology of the particular resolution which we have just quoted. Instead of this clause — "the usual forms of government should be suspended," it suggested the far more accurate and far more prudent expression which here follows, — "additional powers be given to the governor and council." This amendment was assented to by the House; and almost immediately thereafter it adjourned until the last Thursday in March, 1777, "then to meet in the city of Williamsburg, or at such other place as the governor and council, for good reasons, may appoint."[1]

[1] *Jour. Va. House of Del.* 106–108.

Such, undoubtedly, was the occasion on which, if at any time during that session, the project for a dictatorship in Virginia was under consideration by the House of Delegates. The only evidence for the reality of such a project is derived from the testimony of Jefferson; and Jefferson, though a member of the House, was not then in attendance, having procured, on the 29th of the previous month, permission to be absent during the remainder of the session.[1] Is it not probable that the whole terrible plot, as it afterward lay in the mind of Jefferson, may have originated in reports which reached him elsewhere, to the effect that, in the excitement of the House over the public danger and over the need of energetic measures against that danger, some members had demanded that the governor should be invested with what they perhaps called dictatorial power, meaning thereby no more than extraordinary power; and that all the criminal accretions to that meaning, which Jefferson attributed to the project, were simply the work of his own imagination, always sensitive and quick to take alarm on behalf of human liberty, and, on such a subject as this, easily set on fire by examples of awful political crime which would occur to him from Roman history? This suggestion, moreover, is not out of harmony with one which has been made by a thorough and most candid student of the subject, who says: "I am very much inclined to think that some sneering

[1] *Jour. Va. H. Del.* 75; and Randall, *Life of Jefferson,* i. 205.

remark of Colonel Cary, on that occasion, has given rise to the whole story about a proposed dictator at that time." [1]

At any rate, this must not be forgotten: if the project of a dictatorship, in the execrable sense affirmed by Jefferson, was, during that session, advocated by any man or by any cabal in the Assembly, history must absolve Patrick Henry of all knowledge of it, and of all responsibility for it. Not only has no tittle of evidence been produced, involving his connivance at such a scheme, but the Assembly itself, a few months later, unwittingly furnished to posterity the most conclusive proof that no man in that body could have believed him to be smirched with even the suggestion of so horrid a crime. Had Patrick Henry been suspected, during the autumn and early winter of 1776, of any participation in the foul plot to create a despotism in Virginia, is it to be conceived that, at its very next session, in the spring of 1777, that Assembly, composed of nearly the same members as before, would have reëlected to the governorship so profligate and dangerous a man, and that too without any visible opposition in either House? Yet that is precisely what the Virginia Assembly did in May, 1777. Moreover, one year later, this same Assembly reëlected this same profligate and dangerous politician for his third and last permissible year in the governorship, and it did so with the same unbroken unanimity. Moreover, during

[1] William Wirt Henry, *Hist. Mag.* for 1873, 350.

all that time, Thomas Jefferson was a member, and a most conspicuous and influential member, of the Virginia Assembly. If, indeed, he then believed that his old friend, Patrick Henry, had stood ready in 1776, to commit "treason against the people" of America, and "treason against mankind in general," why did he permit the traitor to be twice reëlected to the chief magistracy, without the record of even one brave effort against him on either occasion?

On the 26th of December, 1776, in accordance with the special authority thus conferred upon him by the General Assembly, Governor Henry issued a vigorous proclamation, declaring that the "critical situation of American affairs" called for "the utmost exertion of every sister State to put a speedy end to the cruel ravages of a haughty and inveterate enemy, and secure our invaluable rights," and "earnestly exhorting and requiring" all the good people of Virginia to assist in the formation of volunteer companies for such service as might be required.[1] The date of that proclamation was also the date of Washington's famous matutinal surprise of the Hessians at Trenton, — a bit of much-needed good luck, which was followed by his fortunate engagement with the enemy near Princeton, on the 3d of January, 1777. On these and a very few other extremely small crumbs of comfort, the struggling revolutionists had to nourish their burdened hearts for many a month there-

[1] 5 *Am. Arch.* iii. 1425–1426.

after; Washington himself, during all that time, with his little army of tattered and barefoot warriors, majestically predominating over the scene from the heights of Morristown; while the good-humored British commander, Sir William Howe, considerately abstained from any serious military disturbance until the middle of the following summer. Thus the chief duty of the governor of Virginia, during the winter and spring of 1777, as it had been in the previous autumn, was that of trying to keep in the field Virginia's quota of troops, and of trying to furnish Virginia's share of military supplies, — no easy task, it should seem, in those times of poverty, confusion, and patriotic languor. The official correspondence of the governor indicates the unslumbering anxiety, the energy, the fertility of device with which, in spite of defective health, he devoted himself to these hard tasks.[1]

In his great desire for exact information as to the real situation at headquarters, Governor Henry had sent to Washington a secret messenger by the name of Walker, who was to make his observations at Morristown and to report the results to himself. Washington at once perceived the embarrassments to which such a plan might lead; and accordingly, on the 24th of February, 1777,

[1] I refer, for example, to his letters of Oct. 11, 1776; of Nov. 19, 1776; of Dec. 6, 1776; of Jan. 8, 1777; of March 20, 1777; of March 28, 1777; of June 20, 1777; besides the letters cited in the text.

he wrote to the governor, gently explaining why he could not receive Mr. Walker as a mere visiting observer: —

"To avoid the precedent, therefore, and from your character of Mr. Walker, and the high opinion I myself entertain of his abilities, honor, and prudence, I have taken him into my family as an extra aide-de-camp, and shall be happy if, in this character, he can answer your expectations. I sincerely thank you, sir, for your kind congratulations on the late success of the Continental arms (would to God it may continue), and for your polite mention of me. Let me earnestly entreat that the troops raised in Virginia for this army be forwarded on by companies, or otherwise, without delay, and as well equipped as possible for the field, or we shall be in no condition to open the campaign." [1]

On the 29th of the following month, the governor wrote to Washington of the overwhelming difficulty attending all his efforts to comply with the request mentioned in the letter just cited: —

"I am very sorry to inform you that the recruiting business of late goes on so badly, that there remains but little prospect of filling the six new battalions from this State, voted by the Assembly. The Board of Council see this with great concern, and, after much reflection on the subject, are of opinion that the deficiency in our regulars can no way be supplied so properly as by enlisting volunteers. There is reason to believe a considerable number of these may be got to serve six or eight months. . . . I believe you can receive no assistance by

[1] *Writings of Washington*, iv. 330.

drafts from the militia. From the battalions of the
Commonwealth none can be drawn as yet, because they
are not half full. . . . Virginia will find some apology
with you for this deficiency in her quota of regulars,
when the difficulties lately thrown in our way are considered. The Georgians and Carolinians have enlisted
[in Virginia] probably two battalions at least. A regiment of artillery is in great forwardness. Besides these,
Colonels Baylor and Grayson are collecting regiments;
and three others are forming for this State. Add to all
this our Indian wars and marine service, almost total
want of necessaries, the false accounts of deserters, —
many of whom lurk here, — the terrors of the small-
pox and the many deaths occasioned by it, and the deficient enlistments are accounted for in the best manner I
can. As no time can be spared, I wish to be honored
with your answer as soon as possible, in order to promote the volunteer scheme, if it meets your approbation.
I should be glad of any improvements on it that may
occur to you. I believe about four of the six battalions
may be enlisted, but have seen no regular [return] of
their state. Their scattered situation, and being many
of them in broken quotas, is a reason for their slow
movement. I have issued repeated orders for their
march long since." [1]

The General Assembly of Virginia, at its session
in the spring of 1777, was required to elect a governor, to serve for one year from the day on which
that session should end. As no candidate was
named in opposition to Patrick Henry, the Senate
proposed to the House of Delegates that he should

[1] Sparks, *Corr. Rev.* i. 361, 362.

be reappointed without ballot.   This, accordingly, was done, by resolution of the latter body on the 29th of May, and by that of the Senate on the 1st of June.   On the 5th of June, the committee appointed to inform the governor of this action laid before the House his answer: —

GENTLEMEN, — The signal honor conferred on me by the General Assembly, in their choice of me to be governor of this Commonwealth, demands my best acknowledgments, which I beg the favor of you to convey to them in the most acceptable manner.

I shall execute the duties of that high station to which I am again called by the favor of my fellow-citizens, according to the best of my abilities, and I shall rely upon the candor and wisdom of the Assembly to excuse and supply my defects.   The good of the Commonwealth shall be the only object of my pursuit, and I shall measure my happiness according to the success which shall attend my endeavors to establish the public liberty.   I beg to be presented to the Assembly, and that they and you will be assured that I am, with every sentiment of the highest regard, their and your most obedient and very humble servant,

P. HENRY.[1]

After a perusal of this nobly written letter, the gentle reader will have no difficulty in concluding that, if indeed the author of it was then lying in wait for an opportunity to set up a despotism in Virginia, he had already become an adept in the hypocrisy which enabled him, not only to conceal the fact, but to convey an impression quite the opposite.

[1] *Jour. Va. House Del.* 61.

CHAPTER XIV

GOVERNOR A SECOND TIME

PATRICK HENRY'S second term as governor extended from the 28th of June, 1777, to the 28th of June, 1778: a twelvemonth of vast and even decisive events in the struggle for national independence, — its awful disasters being more than relieved by the successes, both diplomatic and military, which were compressed within that narrow strip of time. Let us try, by a glance at the chief items in the record of that year, to bring before our eyes the historic environment amid which the governor of Virginia then wrought at his heavy tasks: July 6, 1777, American evacuation of Ticonderoga at the approach of Burgoyne; August 6, defeat of Herkimer by the British under St. Leger; August 16, Stark's victory over the British at Bennington; September 11, defeat of Washington at Brandywine; September 27, entrance of the British into Philadelphia; October 4, defeat of Washington at Germantown; October 16, surrender of Burgoyne and his entire army; December 11, Washington's retirement into winter quarters at Valley Forge; February 6, 1778, American treaty of alliance with France; May 11, death of Lord

Chatham; June 13, Lord North's peace commissioners propose to Congress a cessation of hostilities; June 18, the British evacuate Philadelphia;
June 28, the battle of Monmouth.

The story of the personal life of Patrick Henry
during those stern and agitating months is lighted
up by the mention of his marriage, on the 9th
of October, 1777, to Dorothea Dandridge, a grand-
daughter of the old royal governor, Alexander
Spotswood, — a lady who was much younger than
her husband, and whose companionship proved to
be the solace of all the years that remained to him
on earth.

The pressure of official business upon him can
hardly have been less than during the previous
year.   The General Assembly was in session from
the 20th of October, 1777, until the 24th of January, 1778, and from the 4th of May to the 1st of
June, 1778, — involving, of course, a long strain
of attention by the governor to the work of the two
houses.   Moreover, the prominence of Virginia
among the States, and, at the same time, her ex-
emption from the most formidable assaults of the
enemy, led to great demands being made upon her
both for men and for supplies.   To meet these
demands, either by satisfying them or by explaining his failure to do so, involved a copious and
laborious correspondence on the part of Governor
Henry, not only with his own official subordinates
in the State, but with the president of Congress,
with the board of war, and with the general of the

army. The official letters which he thus wrote are a monument of his ardor and energy as a war governor, his attention to details, his broad practical sense, his hopefulness and patience under galling disappointments and defeats.[1]

Perhaps nothing in the life of Governor Henry during his second term of office has so touching an interest for us now, as has the course which he took respecting the famous intrigue, which was developed into alarming proportions during the winter of 1777 and 1778, for the displacement of Washington, and for the elevation of the shallow and ill-balanced Gates to the supreme command of the armies. It is probable that several men of prominence in the army, in Congress, and in the several state governments, were drawn into this cabal, although most of them had too much caution to commit themselves to it by any documentary evidence which could rise up and destroy them in case of its failure. The leaders in the plot very naturally felt the great importance of securing the secret support of men of high influence in Washington's own State; and by many it was then be-

---

[1] Of the official letters of Governor Henry, doubtless many have perished; a few have been printed in Sparks, Force, Wirt, and elsewhere; a considerable number, also, are preserved in manuscript in the archives of the Department of State at Washington. Copies of the latter are before me as I write. As justifying the statement made in the text, I would refer to his letters of August 30, 1777; of October 29, 1777; of October 30, 1777; of December 6, 1777; of December 9, 1777; of January 20, 1778; of January 28, 1778; and of June 18, 1778.

lieved that they had actually won over no less a man than Richard Henry Lee. Of course, if also the sanction of Governor Patrick Henry could be secured, a prodigious advantage would be gained. Accordingly, from the town of York, in Pennsylvania, whither Congress had fled on the advance of the enemy towards Philadelphia, the following letter was sent to him, — a letter written in a disguised hand, without signature, but evidently by a personal friend, a man of position, and a master of the art of plausible statement: —

YORKTOWN, 12 January, 1778.

DEAR SIR, — The common danger of our country first brought you and me together. I recollect with pleasure the influence of your conversation and eloquence upon the opinions of this country in the beginning of the present controversy. You first taught us to shake off our idolatrous attachment to royalty, and to oppose its encroachments upon our liberties with our very lives. By these means you saved us from ruin. The independence of America is the offspring of that liberal spirit of thinking and acting, which followed the destruction of the sceptres of kings, and the mighty power of Great Britain.

But, Sir, we have only passed the Red Sea. A dreary wilderness is still before us; and unless a Moses or a Joshua are raised up in our behalf, we must perish before we reach the promised land. We have nothing to fear from our enemies on the way. General Howe, it is true, has taken Philadelphia, but he has only changed his prison. His dominions are bounded on all sides by his out-sentries. America can only be undone by herself. She looks up to her councils and arms for protection; but, alas! what are they? Her representation in Congress dwindled to only twenty-one members; her Adams, her Wilson, her Henry are no more among them. Her councils weak, and partial remedies applied constantly for universal diseases. Her army, what is it? A major-general belonging to it called it a few days ago, in my hearing, a mob. Discipline unknown or wholly neglected. The quartermaster's and commissary's departments filled with idleness, ignorance, and peculation; our hospitals crowded with six thousand sick, but half provided with necessaries or accommodations, and more dying in them in one month than perished in the field during the whole of the last campaign. The money depreciating, without any effectual measures being taken to raise it; the country distracted with the Don Quixote attempts to regulate the price of provisions; an artificial famine created by it, and a real one dreaded from it; the spirit of the people failing through a more intimate acquaintance with the causes of our misfortunes; many submitting daily to General Howe; and more wishing to do it, only to avoid the calamities which threaten our country. But is our case desperate? By no means. We have wisdom, virtue and strength enough to save us, if they could be called into action. The northern army has shown us what Americans are capable of doing with a General at their head. The spirit of the southern army is no way inferior to the spirit of the northern. A Gates, a Lee, or a Conway, would in a few weeks render them an irresistible body of men. The last of the above officers has accepted of the new office of inspector-general of our army, in order to reform abuses; but the remedy is only a palliative

one. In one of his letters to a friend he says, 'A great
and good God hath decreed America to be free, or the
[General] and weak counsellors would have ruined her
long ago.' You may rest assured of each of the facts
related in this letter. The author of it is one of your
Philadelphia friends. A hint of his name, if found out
by the handwriting, must not be mentioned to your most
intimate friend. Even the letter must be thrown into the
fire. But some of its contents ought to be made public,
in order to awaken, enlighten, and alarm our country.
I rely upon your prudence, and am, dear Sir, with my
usual attachment to you, and to our beloved independence,

Yours sincerely.

How was Patrick Henry to deal with such a letter as this? Even though he should reject its reasoning, and spurn the temptation with which it
assailed him, should he merely burn it, and be
silent? The incident furnished a fair test of his
loyalty in friendship, his faith in principle, his
soundness of judgment, his clear and cool grasp of
the public situation, — in a word, of his manliness
and his statesmanship. This is the way in which
he stood the test: —

PATRICK HENRY TO GEORGE WASHINGTON.

WILLIAMSBURG, 20 February, 1778.

DEAR SIR, — You will, no doubt, be surprised at
seeing the enclosed letter, in which the encomiums bestowed on me are as undeserved, as the censures aimed
at you are unjust. I am sorry there should be one man
who counts himself my friend, who is not yours.

Perhaps I give you needless trouble in handing you this paper. The writer of it may be too insignificant to deserve any notice. If I knew this to be the case, I should not have intruded on your time, which is so precious. But there may possibly be some scheme or party forming to your prejudice. The enclosed leads to such a suspicion. Believe, me, Sir, I have too high a sense of the obligations America has to you, to abet or countenance so unworthy a proceeding. The most exalted merit has ever been found to attract envy. But I please myself with the hope that the same fortitude and greatness of mind, which have hitherto braved all the difficulties and dangers inseparable from your station, will rise superior to every attempt of the envious partisan. I really cannot tell who is the writer of this letter, which not a little perplexes me. The handwriting is altogether strange to me.

To give you the trouble of this gives me pain. It would suit my inclination better to give you some assistance in the great business of the war. But I will not conceal anything from you, by which you may be affected; for I really think your personal welfare and the happiness of America are intimately connected. I beg you will be assured of that high regard and esteem with which I ever am, dear sir, your affectionate friend and very humble servant.

Fifteen days passed after the dispatch of that letter, when, having as yet no answer, but with a heart still full of anxiety respecting this mysterious and ill-boding cabal against his old friend, Governor Henry wrote again: —

PATRICK HENRY TO GEORGE WASHINGTON.

WILLIAMSBURG, 5 March, 1778.

DEAR SIR, — By an express, which Colonel Finnie sent to camp, I enclosed to you an anonymous letter which I hope got safe to hand. I am anxious to hear something that will serve to explain the strange affair, which I am now informed is taken up respecting you. Mr. Custis has just paid us a visit, and by him I learn sundry particulars concerning General Mifflin, that much surprised me. It is very hard to trace the schemes and windings of the enemies to America. I really thought that man its friend ; however, I am too far from him to judge of his present temper.

While you face the armed enemies of our liberty in the field, and by the favor of God have been kept unhurt, I trust your country will never harbor in her bosom the miscreant, who would ruin her best supporter. I wish not to flatter ; but when arts, unworthy honest men, are used to defame and traduce you, I think it not amiss, but a duty, to assure you of that estimation in which the public hold you. Not that I think any testimony I can bear is necessary for your support, or private satisfaction ; for a bare recollection of what is past must give you sufficient pleasure in every circumstance of life. But I cannot help assuring you, on this occasion, of the high sense of gratitude which all ranks of men in this our native country bear to you. It will give me sincere pleasure to manifest my regards, and render my best services to you or yours. I do not like to make a parade of these things, and I know you are not fond of it ; however, I hope the occasion will plead my excuse. Wishing you all possible felicity, I am, my dear

Sir, your ever affectionate friend and very humble servant.

Before Washington received this second letter, he had already begun to write the following reply to the first: —

GEORGE WASHINGTON TO PATRICK HENRY.

VALLEY FORGE, 27 March, 1778.

DEAR SIR, — About eight days ago I was honored with your favor of the 20th ultimo. Your friendship, sir, in transmitting to me the anonymous letter you had received, lays me under the most grateful obligations, and if my acknowledgments can be due for anything more, it is for the polite and delicate terms in which you have been pleased to communicate the matter.

I have ever been happy in supposing that I had a place in your esteem, and the proof you have afforded on this occasion makes me peculiarly so. The favorable light in which you hold me is truly flattering; but I should feel much regret, if I thought the happiness of America so intimately connected with my personal welfare, as you so obligingly seem to consider it. All I can say is, that she has ever had, and I trust she ever will have, my honest exertions to promote her interest. I cannot hope that my services have been the best; but my heart tells me they have been the best that I could render.

That I may have erred in using the means in my power for accomplishing the objects of the arduous, exalted station with which I am honored, I cannot doubt; nor do I wish my conduct to be exempted from reprehension farther than it may deserve. Error is the portion of humanity, and to censure it, whether committed by this or that public character, is the prerogative of freemen. However, being intimately acquainted with the man I conceive to be the author of the letter transmitted, and having always received from him the strongest professions of attachment and regard, I am constrained to consider him as not possessing, at least, a great degree of candor and sincerity, though his views in addressing you should have been the result of conviction, and founded in motives of public good. This is not the only secret, insidious attempt that has been made to wound my reputation. There have been others equally base, cruel, and ungenerous, because conducted with as little frankness, and proceeding from views, perhaps, as personally interested. I am, dear sir, with great esteem and regard, your much obliged friend, etc.

The writing of the foregoing letter was not finished, when Governor Henry's second letter reached him; and this additional proof of friendship so touched the heart of Washington that, on the next day, he wrote again, this time with far less self-restraint than before: —

GEORGE WASHINGTON TO PATRICK HENRY

CAMP, 28 March, 1778.

DEAR SIR, — Just as I was about to close my letter of yesterday, your favor of the 5th instant came to hand. I can only thank you again, in the language of the most undissembled gratitude, for your friendship; and assure you, that the indulgent disposition, which Virginia in particular, and the States in general, entertain towards me, gives me the most sensible pleasure. The approbation of my country is what I wish; and as

far as my abilities and opportunities will permit, I hope
I shall endeavor to deserve it. It is the highest reward
to a feeling mind; and happy are they, who so conduct
themselves as to merit it.

The anonymous letter with which you were pleased
to favor me, was written by Dr. Rush, so far as I can
judge from a similitude of hands. This man has been
elaborate and studied in his professions of regard for
me; and long since the letter to you. My caution to
avoid anything which could injure the service, prevented me from communicating, but to a very few of
my friends, the intrigues of a faction which I know was
formed against me, since it might serve to publish our
internal dissensions; but their own restless zeal to advance their views has too clearly betrayed them, and
made concealment on my part fruitless. I cannot precisely mark the extent of their views, but it appeared,
in general, that General Gates was to be exalted on the
ruin of my reputation and influence. This I am authorized to say, from undeniable facts in my own possession, from publications, the evident scope of which
could not be mistaken, and from private detractions industriously circulated. General Mifflin, it is commonly
supposed, bore the second part in the cabal; and General Conway, I know, was a very active and malignant
partisan; but I have good reason to believe that their
machinations have recoiled most sensibly upon themselves. With sentiments of great esteem and regard,
I am, dear sir, your affectionate humble servant.[1]

This incident in the lives of Washington and
Patrick Henry is to be noted by us, not only for

[1] *Writings of Washington*, v. 495–497; 512–515.

its own exquisite delicacy and nobility, but likewise as the culminating fact in the growth of a
very deep and true friendship between the two
men, — a friendship which seems to have begun
many years before, probably in the House of Burgesses, and which lasted with increasing strength
and tenderness, and with but a single episode of
estrangement, during the rest of their lives.
Moreover, he who tries to interpret the later career of Patrick Henry, especially after the establishment of the government under the Constitution,
and who leaves out of the account Henry's profound friendship for Washington, and the basis
of moral and intellectual congeniality on which
that friendship rested, will lose an important clew
to the perfect naturalness and consistency of
Henry's political course during his last years.   A
fierce partisan outcry was then raised against him
in Virginia, and he was bitterly denounced as a
political apostate, simply because, in the parting
of the ways of Washington and of Jefferson, Patrick Henry no longer walked with Jefferson.   In
truth, Patrick Henry was never Washington's follower nor Jefferson's : he was no man's follower.
From the beginning, he had always done for himself his own thinking, whether right or wrong.
At the same time, a careful student of the three
men may see that, in his thinking, Patrick Henry
had a closer and a truer moral kinship with Washington than with Jefferson.   At present, however,
we pause before the touching incident that has just

been narrated in the relations between Washington and Henry, in order to mark its bearing on their subsequent intercourse.   Washington, in whose nature confidence was a plant of slow growth, and who was quick neither to love nor to cease from loving, never forgot that proof of his friend's friendship.   Thenceforward, until that one year in which they both died, the letters which passed between them, while never effusive, were evidently the letters of two strong men who loved and trusted each other without reserve.

Not long before the close of the governor's second term in office, he had occasion to write to Richard Henry Lee two letters, which are of considerable interest, not only as indicating the cordial intimacy between these two great rivals in oratory, but also for the light they throw both on the under-currents of bitterness then ruffling the politics of Virginia, and on Patrick Henry's attitude towards the one great question at that time uppermost in the politics of the nation.   During the previous autumn, it seems, also, Lee had fallen into great disfavor in Virginia, from which he had so far emerged by the 23d of January, 1778, as to be then reëlected to Congress, to fill out an unexpired term.[1]   Shortly afterward, however, harsh speech against him was to be heard in Virginia once more, of which his friend, the governor, thus informed him, in a letter dated April 4, 1778 : —

[1] *Jour. Va. House Del.* 131.

"You are again traduced by a certain set who have drawn in others, who say that you are engaged in a scheme to discard General Washington. I know you too well to suppose that you would engage in anything not evidently calculated to serve the cause of whiggism. . . . But it is your fate to suffer the constant attacks of disguised Tories who take this measure to lessen you. Farewell, my dear friend. In praying for your welfare, I pray for that of my country, to which your life and service are of the last moment." [1]

Furthermore, on the 30th of May, the General Assembly made choice of their delegates in Congress for the following year. Lee was again elected, but by so small a vote that his name stood next to the lowest on the list.[2] Concerning this stinging slight, he appears to have spoken in his next letters to the governor; for, on the 18th of June, the latter addressed to him, from Williamsburg, this reply : —

MY DEAR SIR, — Both your last letters came to hand to-day. I felt for you, on seeing the order in which the balloting placed the delegates in Congress. It is an effect of that rancorous malice that has so long followed you, through that arduous path of duty which you have invariably travelled, since America resolved to resist her oppressors.

Is it any pleasure to you to remark, that at the same era in which these men figure against you, public spirit seems to have taken its flight from Virginia ? It is too

---

[1] Given in Grigsby, *Va. Conv. of* 1776, 142 note.
[2] *Jour. Va. House Del.* 27, 33.

much the case ; for the quota of our troops is not half made up, and no chance seems to remain for completing it. The Assembly voted three hundred and fifty horse, and two thousand men, to be forthwith raised, and to join the grand army. Great bounties are offered ; but, I fear, the only effect will be to expose our state to contempt, — for I believe no soldiers will enlist, especially in the infantry.

Can you credit it ? — no effort was made for supporting or restoring public credit. I pressed it warmly on some, but in vain. This is the reason we get no soldiers.

We shall issue fifty or sixty thousand dollars in cash to equip the cavalry, and their time is to expire at Christmas. I believe they will not be in the field before that time.

Let not Congress rely on Virginia for soldiers. I tell you my opinion : they will not be got here, until a different spirit prevails.

In the next paragraph of his letter, the governor passes from these local matters to what was then the one commanding topic in national affairs. Lord North's peace commissioners had already arrived, and were seeking to win back the Americans into free colonial relations with the mother country, and away from their new-formed friendship with perfidious France. With what energy Patrick Henry was prepared to reject all these British blandishments, may be read in the passionate sentences which conclude his letter : —

I look at the past condition of America, as at a dreadful precipice, from which we have escaped by

means of the generous French, to whom I will be ever-
lastingly bound by the most heartfelt gratitude.   But I
must mistake matters, if some of those men who traduce
you, do not prefer the offers of Britain.   You will have
a different game to play now with the commissioners.
How comes Governor Johnstone there ?   I do not see
how it comports with his past life.

Surely Congress will never recede from our French
friends.   Salvation to America depends upon our holding fast our attachment to them.   I shall date our ruin
from the moment that it is exchanged for anything
Great Britain can say, or do.   She can never be cordial
with us.   Baffled, defeated, disgraced by her colonies,
she will ever meditate revenge.   We can find no safety
but in her ruin, or, at least, in her extreme humiliation ;
which has not happened, and cannot happen, until she
is deluged with blood, or thoroughly purged by a revolution, which shall wipe from existence the present king
with his connections, and the present system with those
who aid and abet it.

For God's sake, my dear sir, quit not the councils of
your country, until you see us forever disjoined from
Great Britain.   The old leaven still works.   The flesh-
pots of Egypt are still savory to degenerate palates.
Again we are undone, if the French alliance is not religiously observed.   Excuse my freedom.   I know your
love to our country, — and this is my motive.   May
Heaven give you health and prosperity.

I am yours affectionately,

PATRICK HENRY. [1]

Before coming to the end of our story of Gov-

[1] Lee, *Life of Richard Henry Lee*, i. 195 196.

ernor Henry's second term, it should be mentioned
that twice during this period did the General Assembly confide to him those extraordinary powers
which by many were spoken of as dictatorial; first,
on the 22d of January, 1778,[1] and again, on the
28th of May, of the same year.[2] Finally, so safe
had been this great trust in his hands, and so effi-
ciently had he borne himself, in all the labors and
responsibilities of his high office, that, on the 29th
of May, the House of Delegates, by resolution,
unanimously elected him as governor for a third
term, — an act in which, on the same day, the
Senate voted its concurrence. On the 30th of
May, Thomas Jefferson, from the committee appointed to notify the governor of his reëlection, reported to the House the following answer : —

GENTLEMEN, — The General Assembly, in again elect-
ing me governor of this commonwealth, have done me
very signal honor. I trust that their confidence, thus
continued in me, will not be misplaced. I beg you
will be pleased, gentlemen, to present me to the General Assembly in terms of grateful acknowledgment for
this fresh instance of their favor towards me ; and to
assure them, that my best endeavors shall be used to
promote the public good, in that station to which they
have once more been pleased to call me.[3]

[1] *Jour. Va. House Del.* 72, 81, 85, 125, 126.
[2] *Ibid.* 15, 16, 17.
[3] *Ibid.* 26, 30.

CHAPTER XV

GOVERNOR HENRY'S third official year was marked, in the great struggle then in progress, by the arrival of the French fleet, and by its futile attempts to be of any use to those hard-pressed rebels whom the king of France had undertaken to encourage in their insubordination; by awful scenes of carnage and desolation in the outlying settlements at Wyoming, Cherry Valley, and Schoharie; by British predatory expeditions along the Connecticut coast; by the final failure and departure of Lord North's peace commissioners; and by the transfer of the chief seat of war to the South, beginning with the capture of Savannah by the British on the 29th of December, 1778, followed by their initial movement on Charleston, in May, 1779. In the month just mentioned, likewise, the enemy, under command of General Matthews and of Sir George Collier, suddenly swooped down on Virginia, first seizing Portsmouth and Norfolk, and then, after a glorious military debauch of robbery, ruin, rape, and murder, and after spreading terror and anguish among the undefended populations of Suffolk, Kemp's Landing, Tanner's Creek, and Gosport, as suddenly gathered up their booty, and went back in great glee to New York.

In the autumn of 1778, the governor had the happiness to hear of the really brilliant success of the expedition which, with statesmanlike sagacity, he had sent out under George Rogers Clark, into the Illinois country, in the early part of the year.[1] Some of the more important facts connected with this expedition, he thus announced to the Virginia delegates in Congress : —

WILLIAMSBURG, November 14, 1778.

GENTLEMEN, — The executive power of this State having been impressed with a strong apprehension of incursions on the frontier settlements from the savages situated about the Illinois, and supposing the danger would be greatly obviated by an enterprise against the English forts and possessions in that country, which were well known to inspire the savages with their bloody purposes against us, sent a detachment of militia, consisting of one hundred and seventy or eighty men commanded by Colonel George Rogers Clark, on that service some time last spring. By despatches which I have just received from Colonel Clark, it appears that his success has equalled the most sanguine expectations. He has not only reduced Fort Chartres and its dependencies, but has struck such a terror into the Indian tribes between that settlement and the lakes that no less than five of them, viz., the Puans, Sacks, Renards, Powtowantanies, and Miamis, who had received the hatchet from the English emissaries, have submitted to our arms

[1] Clark's *Campaign in the Illinois*, 95–97, where Governor Henry's public and private instructions are given in full.

all their English presents, and bound themselves by
treaties and promises to be peaceful in the future.

The great Blackbird, the Chappowow chief, has also
sent a belt of peace to Colonel Clark, influenced, he
supposes, by the dread of Detroit's being reduced by
American arms. This latter place, according to Colonel
Clark's representation, is at present defended by so inconsiderable a garrison and so scantily furnished with
provisions, for which they must be still more distressed
by the loss of supplies from the Illinois, that it might
be reduced by any number of men above five hundred.
The governor of that place, Mr. Hamilton, was exerting
himself to engage the savages to assist him in retaking
the places that had fallen into our hands; but the favorable impression made on the Indians in general in that
quarter, the influence of the French on them, and the
reënforcement of their militia Colonel Clark expected,
flattered him that there was little danger to be appre-
hended. . . . If the party under Colonel Clark can
coöperate in any respect with the measures Congress are
pursuing or have in view, I shall with pleasure give
him the necessary orders. In order to improve and
secure the advantages gained by Colonel Clark, I propose to support him with a reënforcement of militia.
But this will depend on the pleasure of the Assembly, to
whose consideration the measure is submitted.

The French inhabitants have manifested great zeal
and attachment to our cause, and insist on garrisons remaining with them under Colonel Clark. This I am
induced to agree to, because the safety of our own fron-
tiers as well as that of these people demands a compliance with this request. Were it possible to secure the
St. Lawrence and prevent the English attempts up that

river by seizing some post on it, peace with the Indians would seem to me to be secured.

With great regard I have the honor to be, Gentⁿ,

Your most obedient servant,

P. HENRY.[1]

During the autumn session of the General Assembly, that body showed its continued confidence in the governor by passing several acts conferring on him extraordinary powers, in addition to those already bestowed.[2]

A letter which the governor wrote at this period to the president of Congress, respecting military aid from Virginia to States further south, may give us some idea, not only of his own practical discernment in the matters involved, but of the confusion which, in those days, often attended military plans issuing from a many-headed executive : —

WILLIAMSBURG, November 28, 1778.

SIR, — Your favor of the 16th instant is come to hand, together with the acts of Congress of the 26th of August for establishing provision for soldiers and sailors maimed or disabled in the public service, — of the 26th of September for organizing the treasury, a proclamation for a general thanksgiving, and three copies of the alliance between his most Christian Majesty and these United States.

I lost no time in laying your letter before the privy council, and in deliberating with them on the subject of

[1] MS.

[2] *Jour. Va. House Del.* 30, 36, 66 ; also Hening, ix. 474-476; 477-478; 530-532; 584-585.

sending 1000 militia to Charlestown, South Carolina. I beg to assure Congress of the great zeal of every member of the executive here to give full efficacy to their designs on every occasion. But on the present, I am very sorry to observe, that obstacles great and I fear unsurmountable are opposed to the immediate march of the men. Upon requisition to the deputy quartermaster-general in this department for tents, kettles, blankets, and wagons, he informs they cannot be had. The season when the march must begin will be severe and inclement, and, without the forementioned necessaries, impracticable to men indifferently clad and equipped as they are in the present general scarcity of clothes.

The council, as well as myself, are not a little perplexed on comparing this requisition to defend South Carolina and Georgia from the assaults of the enemy, with that made a few days past for galleys to conquer East Florida. The galleys have orders to rendezvous at Charlestown, which I was taught to consider as a place of acknowledged safety; and I beg leave to observe, that there seems some degree of inconsistency in marching militia such a distance in the depth of winter, under the want of necessaries, to defend a place which the former measures seemed to declare safe.

The act of Assembly whereby it is made lawful to order their march, confines the operations to measures merely defensive to a sister State, and of whose danger there is certain information received.

However, as Congress have not been pleased to explain the matters herein alluded to, and altho' a good deal of perplexity remains with me on the subject, I have by advice of the privy council given orders for 1000 men to be instantly got into readiness to march to

Charlestown, and they will march as soon as they are
furnished with tents, kettles, and wagons. In the mean
time, if intelligence is received that their march is essential to the preservation of either of the States of
South Carolina or Georgia the men will encounter every
difficulty, and have orders to proceed in the best way
they can without waiting to be supplied with those
necessaries commonly afforded to troops even on a summer's march.

I have to beg that Congress will please to remember
the state of embarrassment in which I must necessarily
remain with respect to the ordering galleys to Charlestown, in their way to invade Florida, while the militia
are getting ready to defend the States bordering on it,
and that they will please to favor me with the earliest
intelligence of every circumstance that is to influence the
measures either offensive or defensive.

I have the honor to be, Sir, your most obedient and
very humble servant,

P. HENRY.[1]

By the early spring of 1779, it became still more
apparent that the purpose of the enemy was to
shift the scene of their activity from the middle
States to the South, and that Virginia, whose soil
had never thus far been bruised by the tread of
a hostile army, must soon experience that dire
calamity. Perhaps no one saw this more clearly
than did Governor Henry. At the same time, he
also saw that Virginia must in part defend herself
by helping to defend her sister States at the South,
across whose territories the advance of the enemy

[1] MS.

into Virginia was likely to be attempted. His clear grasp of the military situation, in all the broad relations of his own State to it, is thus revealed in a letter to Washington, dated at Williamsburg, 13th of March, 1779: —

"My last accounts from the South are unfavorable. Georgia is said to be in full possession of the enemy, and South Carolina in great danger. The number of disaffected there is said to be formidable, and the Creek Indians inclining against us. One thousand militia are ordered thither from our southern counties; but a doubt is started whether they are by law obliged to march. I have also proposed a scheme to embody volunteers for this service; but I fear the length of the march, and a general scarcity of bread, which prevails in some parts of North Carolina and this State, may impede this service. About five hundred militia are ordered down the Tennessee River, to chastise some new settlements of renegade Cherokees that infest our southwestern frontier, and prevent our navigation on that river, from which we began to hope for great advantages. Our militia have full possession of the Illinois and the posts on the Wabash; and I am not without hopes that the same party may overawe the Indians as far as Detroit. They are independent of General McIntosh, whose numbers, although upwards of two thousand, I think could not make any great progress, on account, it is said, of the route they took, and the lateness of the season.

"The conquest of Illinois and Wabash was effected with less than two hundred men, who will soon be reenforced; and, by holding posts on the back of the Indians, it is hoped may intimidate them. Forts Natchez

and Morishac are again in the enemy's hands; and
from thence they infest and ruin our trade on the Mississippi, on which river the Spaniards wish to open a
very interesting commerce with us. I have requested
Congress to authorize the conquest of those two posts,
as the possession of them will give a colorable pretence
to retain all West Florida, when a treaty may be
opened." [1]

Within two months after that letter was written,
the dreaded warships of the enemy were ploughing
the waters of Virginia : it was the sorrow-bringing
expedition of Matthews and Sir George Collier.
The news of their arrival was thus conveyed by
Governor Henry to the president of Congress : —

WILLIAMSBURG, 11 May, 1779.

SIR, — On Saturday last, in the evening, a British
fleet amounting to about thirty sail . . . came into the
Bay of Chesapeake, and the next day proceeded to
Hampton Road, where they anchored and remained
quiet until yesterday about noon, when several of the
ships got under way, and proceeded towards Portsmouth, which place I have no doubt they intend to attack by water or by land or by both, as they have many
flat-bottomed boats with them for the purpose of landing
their troops. As I too well know the weakness of that
garrison, I am in great pain for the consequences, there
being great quantities of merchandise, the property of
French merchants and others in this State, at that place,
as well as considerable quantities of military stores,
which, tho' measures some time since were taken to

[1] Sparks, *Corr. Rev.* ii. 261–262.

remove, may nevertheless fall into the enemy's hands. Whether they may hereafter intend to fortify and maintain this post is at present unknown to me, but the consequences which will result to this State and to the United States finally if such a measure should be adopted must be obvious. Whether it may be in the power of Congress to adopt any measures which can in any manner counteract the design of the enemy is submitted to their wisdom. At present, I cannot avoid intimating that I have the greatest reason to think that many vessels from France with public and private merchandise may unfortunately arrive while the enemy remain in perfect possession of the Bay of Chesapeake, and fall victims unexpectedly.

Every precaution will be taken to order lookout boats on the seacoasts to furnish proper intelligence; but the success attending this necessary measure will be precarious in the present situation of things.[1]

On the next day the governor had still heavier tidings for the same correspondent: —

WILLIAMSBURG, May 12, 1779.

SIR, — I addressed you yesterday upon a subject of the greatest consequence. The last night brought me the fatal account of Portsmouth being in possession of the enemy. Their force was too great to be resisted, and therefore the fort was evacuated after destroying one capital ship belonging to the State and one or two private ones loaded with tobacco. Goods and merchandise, however, of very great value fall into the enemy's hands. If Congress could by solicitations procure a

[1] MS.

fleet superior to the enemy's force to enter Chesapeake at this critical period, the prospect of gain and advantage would be great indeed. I have the honor to be, with the greatest regard, Sir,

> Your most humble and obedient servant,
>
> P. HENRY.[1]

To meet this dreadful invasion, the governor attempted to arouse and direct vigorous measures, in part by a proclamation, on the 14th of May, announcing to the people of Virginia the facts of the case, "and requiring the county lieutenants and other military officers in the Commonwealth, and especially those on the navigable waters, to hold their respective militias in readiness to oppose the attempts of the enemy wherever they might be made." [2]

On the 21st of the month, in a letter to the president of Congress, he reported the havoc then wrought by the enemy : —

> WILLIAMSBURG, May 21, 1779.

SIR, — Being in the greatest haste to dispatch your express, I have not time to give you any very particular information concerning the present invasion. Let it suffice therefore to inform Congress that the number of the enemy's ships are nearly the same as was mentioned in my former letter; with regard to the number of the troops which landed and took Portsmouth, and afterwards proceeded and burnt, plundered, and destroyed Suffolk, committing various barbarities, etc., we are still ignorant, as the accounts from the deserters differ

[1] MS.   [2] Burk, *Hist. Va.* iv. 338.

widely; perhaps, however, it may not exceed 2000 or 2500 men.

I trust that a sufficient number of troops are embodied and stationed in certain proportions at this place, York, Hampton, and on the south side of James River. . . . When any further particulars come to my knowledge they shall be communicated to Congress without delay.

I have the honor to be, Sir, your humble servant,

P. HENRY.

P. S. I am pretty certain that the land forces are commanded by Gen'l Matthews and the fleet by Sir George Collier.[1]

In the very midst of this ugly storm, it was required that the ship of state should undergo a change of commanders. The third year for which Governor Henry had been elected was nearly at an end. There were some members of the Assembly who thought him eligible as governor for still another year, on the ground that his first election was by the convention, and that the year of office which that body gave to him " was merely provisory," and formed no proper part of his constitutional term.[2] Governor Henry himself, however, could not fail to perceive the unfitness of any struggle upon such a question at such a time, as well as the futility which would attach to that high office, if held, amid such perils, under a clouded title. Accordingly, on the 28th of May, he cut short all discussion by sending to the speaker of the House of Delegates the following letter: —

[1] MS.   [2] Burk, *Hist. Va.* iv. 350.

May 28, 1779.

Sir, — The term for which I had the honor to be elected governor by the late Assembly being just about to expire, and the Constitution, as I think, making me ineligible to that office, I take the liberty to communicate to the Assembly through you, Sir, my intention to retire in four or five days.

I have thought it necessary to give this notification of my design, in order that the Assembly may have the earliest opportunity of deliberating upon the choice of a successor to me in office.

With great regard, I have the honor to be, Sir, your most obedient servant, P. HENRY.[1]

On the first of June, Thomas Jefferson was elected to succeed him in office, but by a majority of only six votes out of one hundred and twenty-eight.[2] On the following day Patrick Henry, having received certain resolutions from the General Assembly[3] commending him for his conduct while governor, graciously closed this chapter of his official life by the following letter : —

GENTLEMEN, — The House of Delegates have done me very great honor in the vote expressive of their approbation of my public conduct. I beg the favor of you, gentlemen, to convey to that honorable house my most cordial acknowledgments, and to assure them that I shall ever retain a grateful remembrance of the high honor they have now conferred on me.[4]

[1] Wirt, 225.
[2] *Jour. Va. House Del.* 29.
[3] Burk, *Hist. Va.* 350.
[4] *Jour. Va. House Del.* 32.

In the midst of these frank voices of public appreciation over the fidelity and efficiency of his service as governor, there were doubtless the usual murmurs of partisan criticism or of personal ill-will. For example, a few days after Jefferson had taken his seat in the stately chair which Patrick Henry had just vacated, St. George Tucker, in a letter to Theophilus Bland, gave expression to this sneer: " *Sub rosa*, I wish his excellency's activity may be equal to the abilities he possesses in so eminent a degree. . . . But if he should tread in the steps of his predecessor, there is not much to be expected from the brightest talents." [1] Over against a taunt like this, one can scarcely help placing the fact that the general of the armies who, for three stern years, had been accustomed to lean heavily for help on this governor of Virginia, and who never paid idle compliments, nevertheless paid many a tribute to the intelligence, zeal, and vigorous activity of Governor Henry's administration. Thus, on the 27th of December, 1777, Washington writes to him: " In several of my late letters I addressed you on the distress of the troops for want of clothing. Your ready exertions to relieve them have given me the highest satisfaction." [2] On the 19th of February, 1778, Washington again writes to him: " I address myself to you, convinced that our alarming distresses will engage your most serious consideration, and that the full force of that zeal and vigor you have man-

[1] *Bland Papers*, ii. 11.　　　　　　[2] MS.

ifested upon every other occasion, will now operate for our relief, in a matter that so nearly affects the very existence of our contest." [1] On the 19th of April, 1778, Washington once more writes to him: " I hold myself infinitely obliged to the legislature for the ready attention which they have paid to my representation of the wants of the army, and to you for the strenuous manner in which you have recommended to the people an observance of my request." [2] Finally, if any men had even better opportunities than Washington for estimating correctly Governor Henry's efficiency in his great office, surely those men were his intimate associates, the members of the Virginia legislature. It is quite possible that their first election of him as governor may have been in ignorance of his real qualities as an executive officer; but this cannot be said of their second and of their third elections of him, each one of which was made, as we have seen, without one audible lisp of opposition. Is it to be believed that, if he had really shown that lack of executive efficiency which St. George Tucker's sneer implies, such a body of men, in such a crisis of public danger, would have twice and thrice elected him to the highest executive office in the State, and that, too, without one dissenting vote? To say so, indeed, is to fix a far more damning censure upon them than upon him.

[1] MS.   [2] MS.

CHAPTER XVI

AT HOME AND IN THE HOUSE OF DELEGATES

THE high official rank which Governor Henry had borne during the first three years of American independence was so impressive to the imaginations of the French allies who were then in the country, that some of them addressed their letters to him as "Son Altesse Royale, Monsieur Patrick Henri, Gouverneur de l'Etat de Virginie." [1] From this titular royalty he descended, as we have seen, about the 1st of June, 1779; and for the subsequent five and a half years, until his recall to the governorship, he is to be viewed by us as a very retired country gentleman in delicate health, with episodes of labor and of leadership in the Virginia House of Delegates.

A little more than a fortnight after his descent from the governor's chair, he was elected by the General Assembly as a delegate in Congress.[2] It is not known whether he at any time thought it possible for him to accept this appointment; but, on the 28th of the following October, the body that had elected him received from him a letter

[1] Rives, *Life of Madison*, i. 189, note.
[2] *Jour. Va. House Del.* 54.

declining the service.[1] Moreover, in spite of all
invitations and entreaties, Patrick Henry never
afterwards served in any public capacity outside
the State of Virginia.

During his three years in the governorship, he
had lived in the palace at Williamsburg. In the
course of that time, also, he had sold his estate of
Scotchtown, in Hanover County, and had purchased a large tract of land in the new county
of Henry, — a county situated about two hundred
miles southwest from Richmond, along the North
Carolina boundary, and named, of course, in honor
of himself. To his new estate there, called Leatherwood, consisting of about ten thousand acres,
he removed early in the summer of 1779. This
continued to be his home until he resumed the
office of governor in November, 1784.[2]

After the storm and stress of so many years of
public life, and of public life in an epoch of revolution, the invalid body, the care-burdened spirit,
of Patrick Henry must have found great refresh-
ment in this removal to a distant, wild, and moun-
tainous solitude. In undisturbed seclusion, he
there remained during the summer and autumn
of 1779, and even the succeeding winter and
spring, — scarcely able to hear the far-off noises of
the great struggle in which he had hitherto borne
so rugged a part, and of which the victorious issue
was then to be seen by him, though dimly, through
many a murky rack of selfishness, cowardice, and
crime.

[1] *Jour. Va. House Del.* 27.   [2] MS.

His successor in the office of governor was Thomas Jefferson, the jovial friend of his own jovial youth, bound to him still by that hearty friendship which was founded on congeniality of political sentiment, but was afterward to die away, at least on Jefferson's side, into alienation and hate. To this dear friend Patrick Henry wrote late in that winter, from his hermitage among the eastward fastnesses of the Blue Ridge, a remarkable letter, which has never before been in print, and which is full of interest for us on account of its impulsive and self-revealing words. Its tone of despondency, almost of misanthropy, — so unnatural to Patrick Henry, — is perhaps a token of that sickness of body which had made the soul sick too, and had then driven the writer into the wilderness, and still kept him there: —

TO THOMAS JEFFERSON.

LEATHERWOOD, 15th Feby., 1780.

DEAR SIR, — I return you many thanks for your favor by Mr. Sanders. The kind notice you were pleased to take of me was particularly obliging, as I have scarcely heard a word of public matters since I moved up in the retirement where I live.

I have had many anxieties for our commonwealth, principally occasioned by the depreciation of our money. To judge by this, which somebody has called the pulse of the state, I have feared that our body politic was dangerously sick. God grant it may not be unto death. But I cannot forbear thinking, the present increase of prices is in great part owing to a kind of habit, which

is now of four or five years' growth, which is fostered
by a mistaken avarice, and like other habits hard to
part with. For there is really very little money here-
abouts.

What you say of the practice of our distinguished
Tories perfectly agrees with my own observation, and
the attempts to raise prejudices against the French, I
know, were begun when I lived below. What gave me
the utmost pain was to see some men, indeed very many,
who were thought good Whigs, keep company with the
miscreants, — wretches who, I am satisfied, were laboring our destruction. This countenance shown them is
of fatal tendency. They should be shunned and ex-
ecrated, and this is the only way to supply the place of
legal conviction and punishment. But this is an effort
of virtue, small as it seems, of which our countrymen
are not capable.

Indeed, I will own to you, my dear Sir, that observing this impunity and even respect, which some wicked
individuals have met with while their guilt was clear
as the sun, has sickened me, and made me sometimes
wish to be in retirement for the rest of my life. I will,
however, be down, on the next Assembly, if I am
chosen. My health, I am satisfied, will never again
permit a close application to sedentary business, and
I even doubt whether I can remain below long enough
to serve in the Assembly. I will, however, make the
trial.

But tell me, do you remember any instance where
tyranny was destroyed and freedom established on its
ruins, among a people possessing so small a share of
virtue and public spirit? I recollect none, and this,
more than the British arms, makes me fearful of final

success without a reform. But when or how this is to be effected, I have not the means of judging. I most sincerely wish you health and prosperity. If you can spare time to drop me a line now and then, it will be highly obliging to, dear Sir, your affectionate friend and obedient servant, P. HENRY.[1]

The next General Assembly, which he thus promised to attend in case he should be chosen, met at Richmond on the 1st of May, 1780. It hardly needs to be mentioned that the people of Henry County were proud to choose him as one of their members in that body; but he seems not to have taken his seat there until about the 19th of May.[2] From the moment of his arrival in the House of Delegates, every kind of responsibility and honor was laid upon him. This was his first appearance in such an assembly since the proclamation of independence; and the prestige attaching to his name, as well as his own undimmed genius for leadership, made him not only the most conspicuous person in the house, but the nearly absolute director of its business in every detail of opinion and of procedure on which he should choose to express himself, — his only rival, in any particular, being Richard Henry Lee. It helps one now to understand the real reputation he had among his contemporaries for practical ability, and for a habit of shrinking from none of the commonplace drudgeries of legislative work, that during the first few days after his accession to the House

[1] MS.   [2] *Jour. Va. House Del.* 14.

he was placed on the committee of ways and means; on a committee " to inquire into the present state of the account of the commonwealth against the United States, and the most speedy and effectual method of finally settling the same;" on a committee to prepare a bill for the repeal of a part of the act " for sequestering British property, enabling those indebted to British subjects to pay off such debts, and directing the proceedings in suits where such subjects are parties;" on three several committees respecting the powers and duties of high sheriffs and of grand juries; and, finally, on a committee to notify Jefferson of his rcëlection as governor, and to report his answer to the House. On the 7th of June, however, after a service of little more than two weeks, his own sad apprehensions respecting his health seem to have been realized, and he was obliged to ask leave to withdraw from the House for the remainder of the session.[1]

At the autumn session of the legislature he was once more in his place. On the 6th of November, the day on which the House was organized, he was made chairman of the committee on privileges and elections, and also of a committee " for the better defence of the southern frontier," and was likewise placed on the committee on propositions and grievances, as well as on the committee on courts of justice. On the following day he was made a member of a committee for the defence of the east-

[1] *Jour. Va. House Del.* 14, 15, 18, 25, 28, 31, 39.

ern frontier.   On the 10th of November he was
placed on a committee to bring in a bill relating
to the enlistment of Virginia troops, and to the re-
demption of the state bills of credit then in circu-
lation, and the emission of new bills.   On the 22d
of November he was made a member of a committee to which was again referred the account between the State and the United States.   On the
9th of December he was made a member of a committee to draw up bills for the organization and
maintenance of a navy for the State, and the protection of navigation and commerce upon its waters.   On the 14th of December he was made
chairman of a committee to draw up a bill for the
better regulation and discipline of the militia, and
of still another committee to prepare a bill "for
supplying the army with clothes and provisions." [1]
On the 28th of December, the House having knowledge of the arrival in town of poor General Gates,
then drooping under the burden of those Southern
willows which he had so plentifully gathered at
Camden, Patrick Henry introduced the following
magnanimous resolution : —

"That a committee of four be appointed to wait on
Major General Gates, and to assure him of the high regard and esteem of this House; that the remembrance
of his former glorious services cannot be obliterated by
any reverse of fortune ; but that this House, ever mind-
ful of his great merit, will omit no opportunity of testi-
fying to the world the gratitude which, as a member of

[1] *Jour. Va. House Del.* 7, 8, 10, 14, 24, 45, 50, 51.

the American Union, this country owes to him in his
military character." [1]

On the 2d of January, 1781, the last day of the
session, the House adopted, on Patrick Henry's
motion, a resolution authorizing the governor to
convene the next meeting of the legislature at
some other place than Richmond, in case its assembling in that city should " be rendered incon-
venient by the operations of an invading enemy," [2]
a resolution reflecting their sense of the peril then
hanging over the State.

Before the legislature could again meet, events
proved that it was no imaginary danger against
which Patrick Henry's resolution had been intended to provide.   On the 2d of January, 1781,
the very day on which the legislature had adjourned, a hostile fleet conveyed into the James
River a force of about eight hundred men under
command of Benedict Arnold, whose eagerness to
ravage Virginia was still further facilitated by the
arrival, on the 26th of March, of two thousand
men under General Phillips.   Moreover, Lord
Cornwallis, having beaten General Greene at
Guildford, in North Carolina, on the 15th of
March, seemed to be gathering force for a speedy
advance into Virginia.   That the roar of his guns
would soon be heard in the outskirts of their capital, was what all Virginians then felt to be inevitable.

---

[1] *Jour. Va. House Del.* 71.   [2] *Ibid.* 79.

Under such circumstances, it is not strange that a session of the legislature, which is said to have been held on the 1st of March,[1] should have been a very brief one, or that when the 7th of May arrived — the day for its reassembling at Richmond — no quorum should have been present; or that, on the 10th of May, the few members who had arrived in Richmond should have voted, in deference to " the approach of an hostile army,"[2] to adjourn to Charlottesville, — a place of far greater security, ninety-seven miles to the northwest, among the mountains of Albemarle. By the 20th of May, Cornwallis reached Petersburg, twenty-three miles south of Richmond; and shortly afterward, pushing across the James and the Chickahominy, he encamped on the North Anna, in the county of Hanover. Thus, at last, the single county of Louisa then separated him from that county in which was the home of the governor of the State, and where was then convened its legislature, — Patrick Henry himself being present and in obvious direction of all its business. The opportunity to bag such game, Lord Cornwallis was not the man to let slip. Accordingly, on Sunday, the 3d of June, he dispatched a swift expedition under Tarleton, to surprise and capture the members of the legislature, " to seize on the person of the governor," and " to spread on his route devastation and terror."[3] In this entire scheme, doubt-

[1] Burk, *Hist. Va.* iv. 491.　　[2] *Jour. Va. House Del.* 1.
[3] Burk, *Hist. Va.* iv. 496–497.

less, Tarleton would have succeeded, had it not
been that as he and his troopers, on that fair Sab-
bath day, were hurrying past the Cuckoo tavern in
Louisa, one Captain John Jouette, watching from
behind the windows, espied them, divined their
object, and mounting a fleet horse, and taking a
shorter route, got into Charlottesville a few hours
in advance of them, just in time to give the alarm,
and to set the imperiled legislators a-flying to the
mountains for safety.

Then, by all accounts, was witnessed a display
of the locomotive energies of grave and potent
senators, such as this world has not often exhibited. Of this tragically comical incident, of course,
the journal of the House of Delegates makes only
the most placid and forbearing mention. For
Monday, June 4, its chief entry is as follows :
" There being reason to apprehend an immediate
incursion of the enemy's cavalry to this place,
which renders it indispensable that the General
Assembly should forthwith adjourn to a place of
greater security ; resolved, that this House be adjourned until Thursday next, then to meet at the
town of Staunton, in the county of Augusta," —
a town thirty-nine miles farther west, beyond a
chain of mountains, and only to be reached by
them or their pursuers through difficult passes in
the Blue Ridge. The next entry in the journal is
dated at Staunton, on the 7th of June, and, very
properly, is merely a prosaic and business-like

record of the reassembling of the House according to the adjournment aforesaid.[1]

But as to some of the things that happened in that interval of panic and of scrambling flight, popular tradition has not been equally forbearing; and while the anecdotes upon that subject, which have descended to our time, are very likely decorated by many tassels of exaggeration and of myth, they yet have, doubtless, some slight framework of truth, and do really portray for us the actual beliefs of many people in Virginia respecting a number of their celebrated men, and especially respecting some of the less celebrated traits of those men. For example, it is related that on the sudden adjournment of the House, caused by this dusty and breathless apparition of the speedful Jouette, and his laconic intimation that Tarleton was coming, the members, though somewhat accustomed to ceremony, stood not upon the order of their going, but went at once, — taking first to their horses, and then to the woods; and that, breaking up into small parties of fugitives, they thus made their several ways, as best they could, through the passes of the mountains leading to the much-desired seclusion of Staunton. One of these parties consisted of Benjamin Harrison, Colonel William Christian, John Tyler, and Patrick Henry. Late in the day, tired and hungry, they stopped their horses at the door of a small hut, in a gorge of the hills, and asked for food. An old woman,

[1] *Jour. Va. House Del.* 10.

who came to the door, and who was alone in the house, demanded of them who they were, and where they were from. Patrick Henry, who acted as spokesman of the party, answered: "We are members of the legislature, and have just been compelled to leave Charlottesville on account of the approach of the enemy." "Ride on, then, ye cowardly knaves," replied she, in great wrath; "here have my husband and sons just gone to Charlottesville to fight for ye, and you running away with all your might. Clear out — ye shall have nothing here." "But," rejoined Mr. Henry, in an expostulating tone, "we were obliged to fly. It would not do for the legislature to be broken up by the enemy. Here is Mr. Speaker Harrison; you don't think he would have fled had it not been necessary?" "I always thought a great deal of Mr. Harrison till now," answered the old woman; "but he'd no business to run from the enemy," and she was about to shut the door in their faces. "Wait a moment, my good woman," urged Mr. Henry; "you would hardly believe that Mr. Tyler or Colonel Christian would take to flight if there were not good cause for so doing?" "No, indeed, that I would n't," she replied. "But," exclaimed he, "Mr. Tyler and Colonel Christian are here." "They here? Well, I never would have thought it;" and she stood for a moment in doubt, but at once added, "No matter. We love these gentlemen, and I did n't suppose they would ever run away from the British; but since they have, they shall have nothing to eat in my house. You may ride along." In this desperate situation Mr. Tyler then stepped forward and said, " What would you say, my good woman, if I were to tell you that Patrick Henry fled with the rest of us ? " " Patrick Henry ! I should tell you there was n't a word of truth in it," she answered angrily ; " Patrick Henry would never do such a cowardly thing." " But this is Patrick Henry," said Mr. Tyler, pointing to him. The old woman was amazed ; but after some reflection, and with a convulsive twitch or two at her apron string, she said, " Well, then, if that's Patrick Henry, it must be all right. Come in, and ye shall have the best I have in the house." [1]

The pitiless tongue of tradition does not stop here, but proceeds to narrate other alleged experiences of this our noble, though somewhat disconcerted, Patrick. Arrived at last in Staunton, and walking through its reassuring streets, he is said to have met one Colonel William Lewis, to whom the face of the orator was then unknown ; and to have told to this stranger the story of the flight of the legislature from Albemarle. " If Patrick Henry had been in Albemarle," was the stranger's comment, " the British dragoons never would have passed over the Rivanna River." [2]

The tongue of tradition, at last grown quite reckless, perhaps, of its own credit, still further relates

---

[1] L. G. Tyler, *Letters and Times of the Tylers*, i. 81–83, where it is said to be taken from Abel's *Life of John Tyler*.

[2] Peyton, *Hist. Augusta Co.* 211.

that even at Staunton these illustrious fugitives
did not feel entirely sure that they were beyond
the reach of Tarleton's men. A few nights after
their arrival there, as the story runs, upon some
sudden alarm, several of them sprang from their
beds, and, imperfectly clapping on their clothes,
fled out of the town, and took refuge at the plantation of one Colonel George Moffett, near which,
they had been told, was a cave in which they might
the more effectually conceal themselves. Mrs.
Moffett, though not knowing the names of these
flitting Solons, yet received them with true Virginian hospitality; but the next morning, at breakfast, she made the unlucky remark that there was
one member of the legislature who certainly would
not have run from the enemy. "Who is he?"
was then asked. Her reply was, "Patrick Henry."
At that moment a gentleman of the party, himself
possessed of but one boot, was observed to blush
considerably. Futhermore, as soon as possible
after breakfast, these imperiled legislators departed
in search of the cave; shortly after which a negro
from Staunton rode up, carrying in his hand a
solitary boot, and inquiring earnestly for Patrick
Henry. In that way, as the modern reporter of
this very debatable tradition unkindly adds, the
admiring Mrs. Moffett ascertained who it was that
the boot fitted; and he further suggests that, whatever Mrs. Moffett's emotions were at that time,
those of Patrick must have been, "Give me liberty,
but not death." [1]

---

[1] Peyton, *Hist. Augusta Co.* 211.

Passing by these whimsical tales, we have now to add that the legislature, having on the 7th of June entered upon its work at Staunton, steadily continued it there until the 23d of the month, when it adjourned in orderly fashion, to meet again in the following October. Governor Jefferson, whose second year of office had expired two days before the flight of himself and the legislature from Charlottesville, did not accompany that body to Staunton, but pursued his own way to Poplar Forest and to Bedford, where, "remote from the legislature,"[1] he remained during the remainder of its session. On the 12th of June, Thomas Nelson was elected as his successor in office.[2]

It was during this period of confusion and terror that, as Jefferson alleges, the legislature once more had before it the project of a dictator, in the criminal sense of that word; and, upon Jefferson's private authority, both Wirt and Girardin long afterward named Patrick Henry as the man who was intended for this profligate honor.[3] We need not here repeat what was said, in our narrative of the closing weeks of 1776, concerning this terrible posthumous imputation upon the public and private character of Patrick Henry. Nearly everything which then appeared to the discredit of this charge in connection with the earlier date, is equally appli-

---

[1] Randall, *Life of Jefferson*, i. 352.

[2] *Jour. Va. House Del.* 15.

[3] *Jefferson's Writings*, viii. 368; Wirt, 231; Girardin, in Burk, *Hist. Va.* iv. App. pp. xi.-xii.; Randall, *Life of Jefferson*, i. 348-352.

cable to it in connection with the later date also.
Moreover, as regards this later date, there has recently been discovered a piece of contemporaneous
testimony which shows that, whatever may have
been the scheme for a dictatorship in Virginia in
1781, it was a great military chieftain who was
wanted for the position; and, apparently, that Patrick Henry was not then even mentioned in the
affair. On the 9th of June, 1781, Captain H.
Young, though not a member of the House of
Delegates, writes from Staunton to Colonel William Davies as follows: "Two days ago, Mr. Nicholas gave notice that he should this day move to
have a dictator appointed. General Washington
and General Greene are talked of. I dare say
your knowledge of these worthy gentlemen will be
sufficient to convince you that neither of them will,
or ought to, accept of such an appointment. . . .
We have but a thin House of Delegates; but they
are zealous, I think, in the cause of virtue." [1] Furthermore, the journal of that House contains no
record of any such motion having been made; and
it is probable that it never was made, and that the
subject never came before the legislature in any
such form as to call for its notice.

Finally, with respect to both the dates mentioned
by Jefferson for the appearance of the scheme,
Edmund Randolph has left explicit testimony to
the effect that such a scheme never had any substantial existence at all: "Mr. Jefferson, in his

[1] *Calendar Va. State Papers*, ii. 152.

Notes on Virginia, speaks with great bitterness against those members of the Assembly in the years 1776 and 1781, who espoused the erection of a dictator. Coming from such authority, the invective infects the character of the legislature, notwithstanding he has restricted the charge to less than a majority, and acknowledged the spotlessness of most of them. . . . The subject was never before them, except as an article of newspaper intelligence, and even then not in a form which called for their attention. Against this unfettered monster, which deserved all the impassioned reprobation of Mr. Jefferson, their tones, it may be affirmed, would have been loud and tremendous." [1]

For its autumn session, in 1781, the legislature did not reach an organization until the 19th of November, — just one month after the surrender of Cornwallis. Eight days after the organization of the House, Patrick Henry took his seat; [2] and after a service of less than four weeks, he obtained leave of absence for the remainder of the session. [3] During 1782 his attendance upon the House seems to have been limited to the spring session. At the organization of the House, on the 12th of May, 1783, he was in his place again, and during that session, as well as the autumnal one, his attendance was close and laborious. At both sessions of the House in 1784 he was present and in full force;

---

[1] MS. *Hist. Va.*
[2] *Jour. Va. House Del.* for Nov. 27.
[3] *Jour. Va. House Del.* for Dec. 21.

but in the very midst of these employments he was interrupted by his election as governor, on the 17th of November, — shortly after which, he withdrew to his country-seat in order to remove his family thence to the capital.

In the course of all these labors in the legislature, and amid a multitude of topics merely local and temporary, Patrick Henry had occasion to deal publicly, and under the peculiar responsibilities of leadership, with nearly all the most important and difficult questions that came before the American people during the later years of the war and the earlier years of the peace. The journal of the House for that period omits all mention of words spoken in debate; and although it does occasionally enable us to ascertain on which side of certain questions Patrick Henry stood, it leaves us in total ignorance of his reasons for any position which he chose to take. In trying, therefore, to estimate the quality of his statesmanship when dealing with these questions, we lack a part of the evidence which is essential to any just conclusion; and we are left peculiarly at the mercy of those sweeping censures which have been occasionally applied to his political conduct during that period.[1]

On the assurance of peace, in the spring of 1783, perhaps the earliest and the knottiest problem which had to be taken up was the one relating to that vast body of Americans who then bore the

[1] For example, *Bland Papers*, ii. 51; Rives, *Life of Madison,* i. 536; ii. 240, note.

contumelious name of Tories, — those Americans who, against all loss and ignominy, had steadily remained loyal to the unity of the British empire, unflinching in their rejection of the constitutional heresy of American secession. How should these execrable beings — the defeated party in a long and most rancorous civil war — be treated by the party which was at last victorious? Many of them were already in exile: should they be kept there? Many were still in this country: should they be banished from it? As a matter of fact, the exasperation of public feeling against the Tories was, at that time, so universal and so fierce that no statesman could then lift up his voice in their favor without dashing himself against the angriest currents of popular opinion and passion, and risking the loss of the public favor toward himself. Nevertheless, precisely this is what Patrick Henry had the courage to do. While the war lasted, no man spoke against the Tories more sternly than did he. The war being ended, and its great purpose secured, no man, excepting perhaps Alexander Hamilton, was so prompt and so energetic in urging that all animosities of the war should be laid aside, and that a policy of magnanimous forbearance should be pursued respecting these baffled opponents of American independence. It was in this spirit that, as soon as possible after the cessation of hostilities, he introduced a bill for the repeal of an act " to prohibit intercourse with, and the admission of British subjects into " Virginia,[1]

[1] *Jour. Va. House Del. 42.*

— language well understood to refer to the Tories.
This measure, we are told, not only excited surprise, but "was, at first, received with a repugnance apparently insuperable." Even his intimate
friend John Tyler, the speaker of the House,
hotly resisted it in the committee of the whole,
and in the course of his argument, turning to Patrick Henry, asked "how he, above all other men,
could think of inviting into his family an enemy
from whose insults and injuries he had suffered so
severely?"

In reply to this appeal, Patrick Henry declared
that the question before them was not one of personal feeling; that it was a national question; and
that in discussing it they should be willing to sacrifice all personal resentments, all private wrongs.
He then proceeded to unfold the proposition that
America had everything out of which to make a
great nation — except people.

"Your great want, sir, is the want of men; and these
you must have, and will have speedily, if you are wise.
Do you ask how you are to get them? Open your
doors, sir, and they will come in. The population of
the Old World is full to overflowing; that population
is ground, too, by the oppressions of the governments
under which they live. Sir, they are already standing
on tiptoe upon their native shores, and looking to your
coasts with a wishful and longing eye. . . . But gentlemen object to any accession from Great Britain, and
particularly to the return of the British refugees. Sir,
I feel no objection to the return of those deluded

people. They have, to be sure, mistaken their own interests most wofully, and most wofully have they suffered the punishment due to their offences. But the relations which we bear to them and to their native country are now changed. Their king hath acknowledged our independence. The quarrel is over. Peace hath returned, and found us a free people. Let us have the magnanimity, sir, to lay aside our antipathies and prejudices, and consider the subject in a political light. Those are an enterprising, moneyed people. They will be serviceable in taking off the surplus produce of our lands, and supplying us with necessaries during the infant state of our manufactures. Even if they be inimical to us in point of feeling and principle, I can see no objection, in a political view, in making them tributary to our advantage. And, as I have no prejudices to prevent my making this use of them, so, sir, I have no fear of any mischief that they can do us. Afraid of them? What, sir [said he, rising to one of his loftiest attitudes, and assuming a look of the most indignant and sovereign contempt], shall we, who have laid the proud British lion at our feet, now be afraid of his whelps?" [1]

In the same spirit he dealt with the restraints on British commerce imposed during the war, — a question similar to the one just mentioned, at least in this particular, that it was enveloped in the angry prejudices born of the conflict just ended. The journal for the 13th of May, 1783, has this entry: " Mr. Henry presented, according to order, a bill 'to repeal the several Acts of Assembly for

[1] John Tyler, in Wirt, 233, 236.

seizure and condemnation of British goods found on land ;' and the same was received and read the first time, and ordered to be read a second time." In advocating this measure, he seems to have lifted the discussion clear above all petty considerations to the plane of high and permanent principle, and, according to one of his chief antagonists in that debate, to have met all objections by arguments that were "beyond all expression eloquent and sublime." After describing the embarrassments and distresses of the situation and their causes, he took the ground that perfect freedom was as necessary to the health and vigor of commerce as it was to the health and vigor of citizenship. "Why should we fetter commerce? If a man is in chains, he droops and bows to the earth, for his spirits are broken; but let him twist the fetters from his legs, and he will stand erect. Fetter not commerce, sir. Let her be as free as air; she will range the whole creation, and return on the wings of the four winds of heaven, to bless the land with plenty." [1]

Besides these and other problems in the foreign relations of the country, there remained, of course, at the end of the war, several vast domestic problems for American statesmanship to grapple with, — one of these being the relations of the white race to their perpetual neighbors, the Indians. In the autumn session of 1784, in a series of efforts said to have been marked by "irresistible earnestness and eloquence," he secured the

[1] John Tyler, in Wirt, 237-238.

favorable attention of the House to this ancient problem, and even to his own daring and statesmanlike solution of it. The whole subject, as he thought, had been commonly treated by the superior race in a spirit not only mean and hard, but superficial also; the result being nearly two centuries of mutual suspicion, hatred, and slaughter. At last the time had come for the superior race to put an end to this traditional disaster and disgrace. Instead of tampering with the difficulty by remedies applied merely to the surface, he was for striking at the root of it, namely, at the deep divergence in sympathy and in interest between the two races. There was but one way in which to do this: it was for the white race to treat the Indians, consistently, as human beings, and as fast as possible to identify their interests with our own along the entire range of personal concerns, — in property, government, society, and, especially, in domestic life. In short, he proposed to encourage, by a system of pecuniary bounties, the practice of marriage between members of the two races, believing that such ties, once formed, would be an inviolable pledge of mutual friendship, fidelity, and forbearance, and would gradually lead to the transformation of the Indians into a civilized and Christian people. His bill for this purpose, elaborately drawn up, was carried through its second reading and " engrossed for its final passage," when, by his sudden removal from the floor of the House to the governor's chair, the measure was deprived of its all-conquering champion, and, on the third reading, it fell a sacrifice to the Caucasian rage and scorn of the members.

It is proper to note, also, that during this period of service in the legislature Patrick Henry marched straight against public opinion, and jeoparded his popularity, on two or three other subjects. For example, the mass of the people of Virginia were then so angrily opposed to the old connection between church and state that they occasionally saw danger even in projects which in no way involved such a connection. This was the case with Patrick Henry's necessary and most innocent measure " for the incorporation of all societies of the Christian religion which may apply for the same ; " likewise, his bill for the incorporation of the clergy of the Episcopal Church ; and, finally, his more questionable and more offensive resolution for requiring all citizens of the State to contribute to the expense of supporting some form of religious worship according to their own preference.

Whether, in these several measures, Patrick Henry was right or wrong, one thing, at least, is obvious : no politician who could thus beard in his very den the lion of public opinion can be accurately described as a demagogue.

With respect to those amazing gifts of speech by which, in the House of Delegates, he thus repeatedly swept all opposition out of his way, and made people think as he wished them to do, often in the very teeth of their own immediate interests or prepossessions, an amusing instance was mentioned, many years afterward, by President James Madison. During the war Virginia had paid her soldiers in certificates for the amounts due them, to be redeemed in cash at some future time. In many cases, the poverty of the soldiers had induced them to sell these certificates, for trifling sums in ready money, to certain speculators, who were thus making a traffic out of the public distress. For the purpose of checking this cruel and harmful business, Madison brought forward a suitable bill, which, as he told the story, Patrick Henry supported with an eloquence so irresistible that it was carried through the House without an opposing vote; while a notorious speculator in these very certificates, having listened from the gallery to Patrick Henry's speech, at its conclusion so far forgot his own interest in the question as to exclaim, "That bill ought to pass." [1]

Concerning his appearance and his manner of speech in those days, a bit of testimony comes down to us from Spencer Roane, who, as he tells us, first "met with Patrick Henry in the Assembly of 1783." He adds: —

"I also then met with R. H. Lee. . . . I lodged with Lee one or two sessions, and was perfectly acquainted with him, while I was yet a stranger to Mr. H. These two gentlemen were the great leaders in the House of Delegates, and were almost constantly opposed. Notwithstanding my habits of intimacy with Mr. Lee, I

[1] Howe, *Hist. Coll. Va.* 222.

found myself obliged to vote with P. H. against him in
'83, and against Madison in '84, . . . but with several
important exceptions. I voted against him (P. H.), I
recollect, on the subject of the refugees, — he was for
permitting their return; on the subject of a general
assessment; and the act incorporating the Episcopal
Church. I voted with him, in general, because he was,
I thought, a more practical statesman than Madison
(time has made Madison more practical), and a less
selfish one than Lee. As an orator, Mr. Henry demolished Madison with as much ease as Samson did the
cords that bound him before he was shorn. Mr. Lee
held a greater competition. . . . Mr. Lee was a polished
gentleman. His person was not very good; and he had
lost the use of one of his hands; but his manner was
perfectly graceful. His language was always chaste,
and, although somewhat too monotonous, his speeches
were always pleasing; yet he did not ravish your senses,
nor carry away your judgment by storm. . . . Henry
was almost always victorious. He was as much superior
to Lee in temper as in eloquence. . . . Mr. Henry was
inferior to Lee in the gracefulness of his action, and
perhaps also in the chasteness of his language; yet his
language was seldom incorrect, and his address always
striking. He had a fine blue eye; and an earnest manner which made it impossible not to attend to him. His
speaking was unequal, and always rose with the subject
and the exigency. In this respect, he entirely differed
from Mr. Lee, who always was equal. At some times,
Mr. Henry would seem to hobble, especially in the beginning of his speeches; and, at others, his tones would
be almost disagreeable; yet it was by means of his
tones, and the happy modulation of his voice, that his

speaking perhaps had its greatest effect. He had a
happy articulation, and a clear, distinct, strong voice;
and every syllable was distinctly uttered. He was very
unassuming as to himself, amounting almost to humility,
and very respectful towards his competitor; the consequence was that no feeling of disgust or animosity was
arrayed against him. His exordiums in particular were
often hobbling and always unassuming. He knew mankind too well to promise much. . . . He was great at a
reply, and greater in proportion to the pressure which
was bearing upon him. The resources of his mind and
of his eloquence were equal to any drafts which could
be made upon them. He took but short notes of what
fell from his adversaries, and disliked the drudgery of
composition; yet it is a mistake to say that he could
not write well." [1]

[1] MS.

CHAPTER XVII

SHALL THE CONFEDERATION BE MADE STRONGER?

We have now arrived at the second period of Patrick Henry's service as governor of Virginia, beginning with the 30th of November, 1784. For the four or five years immediately following that date, the salient facts in his career seem to group themselves around the story of his relation to that vast national movement which ended in an entire reorganization of the American Republic under a new Constitution. Whoever will take the trouble to examine the evidence now at hand bearing upon the case, can hardly fail to convince himself that the true story of Patrick Henry's opposition to that great movement has never yet been told. Men have usually misconceived, when they have not altogether overlooked, the motives for his opposition, the spirit in which he conducted it, and the beneficent effects which were accomplished by it; while his ultimate and firm approval of the new Constitution, after it had received the chief amendments called for by his criticisms, has been passionately described as an example of gross political fickleness and inconsistency, instead of being, as it really was, a most logical proceeding on his part, and in perfect harmony with the principles underlying his whole public career.

Before entering on a story so fascinating for the light it throws on the man and on the epoch, it is well that we should stay long enough to glance at what we may call the incidental facts in his life, for these four or five years now to be looked into.

Not far from the time of his thus entering once more upon the office of governor, occurred the death of his aged mother, at the home of his brother-in-law, Colonel Samuel Meredith of Winton, who, in a letter to the governor, dated November 22, 1784, speaks tenderly of the long illness which had preceded the death of the venerable lady, and especially of the strength and beauty of her character : —

" She has been in my family upwards of eleven years ; and from the beginning of that time to the end, her life appeared to me most evidently to be a continued manifestation of piety and devotion, guided by such a great share of good sense as rendered her amiable and agreeable to all who were so happy as to be acquainted with her. Never have I known a Christian character equal to hers." [1]

On bringing his family to the capital, in November, 1784, from the far-away solitude of Leatherwood, the governor established them, not within the city itself, but across the James River, at a place called Salisbury. What with children and with grandchildren, his family had now become

[1] MS.

a patriarchal one; and some slight glimpse of
himself and of his manner of life at that time is
given us in the memorandum of Spencer Roane.
In deference to "the ideas attached to the office of
governor, as handed down from the royal government," he is said to have paid careful attention to
his costume and personal bearing before the public,
never going abroad except in black coat, waistcoat,
and knee-breeches, in scarlet cloak, and in dressed
wig. Moreover, his family "were furnished with
an excellent coach, at a time when these vehicles
were not so common as at present. They lived as
genteelly, and associated with as polished society,
as that of any governor before or since has ever
done. He entertained as much company as others,
and in as genteel a style; and when, at the end of
two years, he resigned the office, he had greatly
exceeded the salary, and [was] in debt, which was
one cause that induced him to resume the practice
of the law." [1]

During his two years in the governorship, his
duties concerned matters of much local importance,
indeed, but of no particular interest at present. To
this remark one exception may be found in some
passages of friendly correspondence between the
governor and Washington, — the latter then enjoying the long-coveted repose of Mt. Vernon. In
January, 1785, the Assembly of Virginia vested in
Washington certain shares in two companies, just
then formed, for opening and extending the navi-

[1] MS.

gation of the James and Potomac rivers.[1] In response to Governor Henry's letter communicating this act, Washington wrote on the 27th of February, stating his doubts about accepting such a gratuity, but at the same time asking the governor as a friend to assist him in the matter by his advice. Governor Henry's reply is of interest to us, not only for its allusion to his own domestic anxieties at the time, but for its revelation of the frank and cordial relations between the two men : —

RICHMOND, March 12th, 1785.

DEAR SIR, — The honor you are pleased to do me, in your favor of the 27th ultimo, in which you desire my opinion in a friendly way concerning the act enclosed you lately, is very flattering to me. I did not receive the letter till Thursday, and since that my family has been very sickly. My oldest grandson, a fine boy indeed, about nine years old, lays at the point of death. Under this state of uneasiness and perturbation, I feel some unfitness to consider a subject of so delicate a nature as that you have desired my thoughts on. Besides, I have some expectation of a conveyance more proper, it may be, than the present, when I would wish to send you some packets received from Ireland, which I fear the post cannot carry at once. If he does not take them free, I shan't send them, for they are heavy. Captain Boyle, who had them from Sir Edward Newenham, wishes for the honor of a line from you, which I have promised to forward to him.

I will give you the trouble of hearing from me next

[1] Hening, xi. 525–526.

post, if no opportunity presents sooner, and, in the mean
time, I beg you to be persuaded that, with the most
sincere attachment, I am, dear sir, your most obedient
servant,

                                                    P. HENRY.[1]

GENERAL WASHINGTON.

The promise contained in this letter was fulfilled
on the 19th of the same month, when the governor
wrote to Washington a long and careful statement
of the whole case, urging him to accept the shares,
and closing his letter with an assurance of his
" unalterable affection" and "most sincere attachment,"[2] — a subscription not common among public men at that time.

On the 30th of November, 1786, having declined
to be put in nomination for a third year, as permitted by the Constitution, he finally retired from
the office of governor. The House of Delegates,
about the same time, by unanimous vote, crowned
him with the public thanks, "for his wise, prudent, and upright administration, during his last
appointment of chief magistrate of this Commonwealth; assuring him that they retain a perfect
sense of his abilities in the discharge of the duties
of that high and important office, and wish him all
domestic happiness on his return to private life."[3]

This return to private life meant, among other

[1] MS.
[2] Sparks, *Corr. Rev.* iv. 93–96. See, also, Washington's letter
to Henry, for Nov. 30, 1785, in *Writings of W.* xii. 277–278.
[3] *Jour. Va. House Del.* for Nov. 25, 1786.

things, his return, after an interruption of more than twelve years, to the practice of the law. For this purpose he deemed it best to give up his remote home at Leatherwood, and to establish himself in Prince Edward County, — a place about midway between his former residence and the capital, and much better suited to his convenience, as an active practitioner in the courts. Accordingly, in Prince Edward County he continued to reside from the latter part of 1786 until 1795. Furthermore, by that county he was soon elected as one of its delegates in the Assembly; and, resuming there his old position as leader, he continued to serve in every session until the end of 1790, at which time he finally withdrew from all official connection with public life. Thus it happened that, by his retirement from the governorship in 1786, and by his almost immediate restoration to the House of Delegates, he was put into a situation to act most aggressively and most powerfully on public opinion in Virginia during the whole period of the struggle over the new Constitution.

As regards his attitude toward that great business, we need, first of all, to clear away some obscurity which has gathered about the question of his habitual views respecting the relations of the several States to the general government. It has been common to suppose that, even prior to the movement for the new Constitution, Patrick Henry had always been an extreme advocate of the rights of the States as opposed to the central authority of the Union; and that the tremendous resistance which he made to the new Constitution in all stages of the affair prior to the adoption of the first group of amendments is to be accounted for as the effect of an original and habitual tendency of his mind.[1] Such, however, seems not to have been the case.

In general it may be said that, at the very outset of the Revolution, Patrick Henry was one of the first of our statesmen to recognize the existence and the imperial character of a certain cohesive central authority, arising from the very nature of the revolutionary act which the several colonies were then taking. As early as 1774, in the first Continental Congress, it was he who exclaimed: "All distinctions are thrown down. All America is thrown into one mass." "The distinctions between Virginians, Pennsylvanians, New Yorkers, and New Englanders are no more. I am not a Virginian, but an American." In the spring of 1776, at the approach of the question of independence, it was he who even incurred reproach by his anxiety to defer independence until after the basis for a general government should have been established, lest the several States, in separating from England, should lapse into a separation from one another also. As governor of Virginia from 1776 to 1779, his official correspondence with the president of Congress, with the board of war, and with the general of the army is pervaded by proofs of

[1] For example, Curtis, *Hist. Const.* ii. 553–554.

his respect for the supreme authority of the general government within its proper sphere. Finally, as a leader in the Virginia House of Delegates from 1780 to 1784, he was in the main a supporter of the policy of giving more strength and dignity to the general government. During all that period, according to the admission of his most unfriendly modern critic, Patrick Henry showed himself "much more disposed to sustain and strengthen the federal authority" than did, for example, his great rival in the House, Richard Henry Lee; and for the time those two great men became "the living and active exponents of two adverse political systems in both state and national questions."[1] In 1784, by which time the weakness of the general government had become alarming, Patrick Henry was among the foremost in Virginia to express alarm, and to propose the only appropriate remedy. For example, on the assembling of the legislature, in May of that year, he took pains to seek an early interview with two of his prominent associates in the House of Delegates, Madison and Jones, for the express purpose of devising with them some method of giving greater strength to the Confederation. "I find him," wrote Madison to Jefferson immediately after the interview, "strenuous for invigorating the federal government, though without any precise plan."[2] A more detailed account of the same interview was sent to Jefferson by another corre-

---

[1] Rives, *Life of Madison*, i. 536–537.
[2] Madison, *Letters*, etc. i. 80.

spondent. According to the latter, Patrick Henry then declared that " he saw ruin inevitable, unless something was done to give Congress a compulsory process on delinquent States;" that "a bold example set by Virginia" in that direction "would have influence on the other States;" and that " this conviction was his only inducement for coming into the present Assembly." Whereupon, it was then agreed between them that "Jones and Madison should sketch some plan for giving greater power to the federal government; and Henry promised to sustain it on the floor."[1] Finally, such was the impression produced by Patrick Henry's political conduct during all those years that, as late as in December, 1786, Madison could speak of him as having "been hitherto the champion of the federal cause."[2]

Not far, however, from the date last mentioned Patrick Henry ceased to be "the champion of the federal cause," and became its chief antagonist, and so remained until some time during Washington's first term in the presidency. What brought about this sudden and total revolution? It can be explained only by the discovery of some new influence which came into his life between 1784 and 1786, and which was powerful enough to reverse entirely the habitual direction of his political thought and conduct. Just what that influence was can now be easily shown.

[1] Bancroft, *Hist. Const.* i. 162.
[2] Madison, *Letters*, etc. i. 264.

On the 3d of August, 1786, John Jay, as secretary for foreign affairs, presented to Congress some results of his negotiations with the Spanish envoy, Gardoqui, respecting a treaty with Spain; and he then urged that Congress, in view of certain vast advantages to our foreign commerce, should consent to surrender the navigation of the Mississippi for twenty-five or thirty years,[1] — a proposal which, very naturally, seemed to the six Southern States as nothing less than a cool invitation to them to sacrifice their own most important interests for the next quarter of a century, in order to build up during that period the interests of the seven States of the North. The revelation of this project, and of the ability of the Northern States to force it through, sent a shock of alarm and of distrust into every Southern community. Moreover, full details of these transactions in Congress were promptly conveyed to Governor Henry by James Monroe, who added this pungent item, — that a secret project was then under the serious consideration of "committees" of Northern men, for a dismemberment of the Union, and for setting the Southern States adrift, after having thus bartered away from them the use of the Mississippi.[2]

On the same day that Monroe was writing from New York that letter to Governor Henry, Madison was writing from Philadelphia a letter to Jefferson. Having mentioned a plan for strengthening the Confederation, Madison says: —

[1] *Secret Jour. Cong.* iv. 44–63.
[2] Rives, *Life of Madison*, ii. 122.

"Though my wishes are in favor of such an event, yet I despair so much of its accomplishment at the present crisis, that I do not extend my views beyond a commercial reform. To speak the truth, I almost despair even of this. You will find the cause in a measure now before Congress, . . . a proposed treaty with Spain, one article of which shuts the Mississippi for twenty or thirty years. Passing by the other Southern States, figure to yourself the effect of such a stipulation on the Assembly of Virginia, already jealous of Northern politics, and which will be composed of thirty members from the Western waters, — of a majority of others attached to the Western country from interests of their own, of their friends, or their constituents. . . . Figure to yourself its effect on the people at large on the Western waters, who are impatiently waiting for a favorable result to the negotiation with Gardoqui, and who will consider themselves sold by their Atlantic brethren. Will it be an unnatural consequence if they consider themselves absolved from every federal tie, and court some protection for their betrayed rights ? " [1]

How truly Madison predicted the fatal construction which in the South, and particularly in Virginia, would be put upon the proposed surrender of the Mississippi, may be seen by a glance at some of the resolutions which passed the Virginia House of Delegates on the 29th of the following November : —

"That the common right of navigating the river Mississippi, and of communicating with other nations through that channel, ought to be considered as the

[1] Rives, *Life of Madison*, ii. 119–120.

bountiful gift of nature to the United States, as proprie-
tors of the territories watered by the said river and its
eastern branches, and as moreover secured to them by
the late revolution.

" That the Confederacy, having been formed on the
broad basis of equal rights, in every part thereof, to the
protection and guardianship of the whole, a sacrifice of
the rights of any one part, to the supposed or real interest of another part, would be a flagrant violation of justice, a direct contravention of the end for which the
federal government was instituted, and an alarming innovation in the system of the Union." [1]

One day after the passage of those resolutions,
Patrick Henry ceased to be the governor of Virginia ; and five days afterward he was chosen by
Virginia as one of its seven delegates to a convention to be held at Philadelphia in the following
May for the purpose of revising the federal Constitution. But amid the widespread excitement,
amid the anger and the suspicion then prevailing
as to the liability of the Southern States, even
under a weak confederation, to be slaughtered, in
all their most important concerns, by the superior
weight and number of the Northern States, it is
easy to see how little inclined many Southern
statesmen would be to increase that liability by
making this weak confederation a strong one. In
the list of such Southern statesmen Patrick Henry
must henceforth be reckoned ; and, as it was never
his nature to do anything tepidly or by halves, his

[1] *Jour. Va. House Del.* 66-67.

hostility to the project for strengthening the Confederation soon became as hot as it was comprehensive. On the 7th of December, only three days after he was chosen as a delegate to the Philadelphia convention, Madison, then at Richmond, wrote concerning him thus anxiously to Washington: —

"I am entirely convinced from what I observe here, that unless the project of Congress can be reversed, the hopes of carrying this State into a proper federal system will be demolished. Many of our most federal leading men are extremely soured with what has already passed. Mr. Henry, who has been hitherto the champion of the federal cause, has become a cold advocate, and, in the event of an actual sacrifice of the Mississippi by Congress, will unquestionably go over to the opposite side." [1]

But in spite of this change in his attitude toward the federal cause, perhaps he would still go to the great convention. On that subject he appears to have kept his own counsel for several weeks; but by the 1st of March, 1787, Edmund Randolph, at Richmond, was able to send this word to Madison, who was back in his place in Congress: "Mr. Henry peremptorily refuses to go;" and Randolph mentions as Henry's reasons for this refusal, not only his urgent professional duties, but his repugnance to the proceedings of Congress in the matter of the Mississippi.[2] Five days later, from the same city, John Marshall

---

[1] Madison, *Letters*, etc. i. 264.
[2] Rives, *Life of Madison*, ii. 238–239.

wrote to Arthur Lee : " Mr. Henry, whose opinions have their usual influence, has been heard to say that he would rather part with the Confederation than relinquish the navigation of the Mississippi." [1] On the 18th of the same month, in a letter to Washington, Madison poured out his solicitude respecting the course which Henry was going to take: "I hear from Richmond, with much concern, that Mr. Henry has positively declined his mission to Philadelphia. Besides the loss of his services on that theatre, there is danger, I fear, that this step has proceeded from a wish to leave his conduct unfettered on another theatre, where the result of the convention will receive its destiny from his omnipotence." [2] On the next day, Madison sent off to Jefferson, who was then in Paris, an account of the situation : " But although it appears that the intended sacrifice of the Mississippi will not be made, the consequences of the intention and the attempt are likely to be very serious. I have already made known to you the light in which the subject was taken up by Virginia. Mr. Henry's disgust exceeds all measure, and I am not singular in ascribing his refusal to attend the convention, to the policy of keeping himself free to combat or espouse the result of it according to the result of the Mississippi business, among other circumstances." [3]

[1] R. H. Lee, *Life of A. Lee*, ii. 321.
[2] Sparks, *Corr. Rev.* iv. 168.
[3] *Madison Papers*, ii. 623.

Finally, on the 25th of March Madison wrote to Randolph, evidently in reply to the information given by the latter on the 1st of the month: "The refusal of Mr. Henry to join in the task of revising the Confederation is ominous; and the more so, I fear, if he means to be governed by the event which you conjecture." [1]

That Patrick Henry did not attend the great convention, everybody knows; but the whole meaning of his refusal to do so, everybody may now understand somewhat more clearly, perhaps, than before.

[1] *Madison Papers*, 627.

CHAPTER XVIII

THE BATTLE IN VIRGINIA OVER THE NEW CONSTI-
TUTION

THE great convention at Philadelphia, after a session of four months, came to the end of its noble labors on the 17th of September, 1787. Washington, who had been not merely its presiding officer but its presiding genius, then hastened back to Mt. Vernon, and, in his great anxiety to win over to the new Constitution the support of his old friend Patrick Henry, he immediately dispatched to him a copy of that instrument, accompanied by a very impressive and conciliatory letter,[1] to which, about three weeks afterwards, was returned the following reply: —

RICHMOND, October 19, 1787.

DEAR SIR, — I was honored by the receipt of your favor, together with a copy of the proposed federal Constitution, a few days ago, for which I beg you to accept my thanks. They are also due to you from me as a citizen, on account of the great fatigue necessarily attending the arduous business of the late convention.

I have to lament that I cannot bring my mind to accord with the proposed Constitution. The concern I

[1] *Writings of Washington*, ix. 265–266.

feel on this account is really greater than I am able to express. Perhaps mature reflections may furnish me with reasons to change my present sentiments into a conformity with the opinions of those personages for whom I have the highest reverence. Be that as it may, I beg you will be persuaded of the unalterable regard and attachment with which I shall be,

Dear Sir, your obliged and very humble servant,

P. HENRY.[1]

Four days before the date of this letter the legislature of Virginia had convened at Richmond for its autumn session, and Patrick Henry had there taken his usual place on the most important committees, and as the virtual director of the thought and work of the House. Much solicitude was felt concerning the course which he might advise the legislature to adopt on the supreme question then before the country, — some persons even fearing that he might try to defeat the new Constitution in Virginia by simply preventing the call of a state convention. Great was Washington's satisfaction on receiving from one of his correspondents in the Assembly, shortly after the session began, this cheerful report : —

" I have not met with one in all my inquiries (and I have made them with great diligence) opposed to it, except Mr. Henry, who I have heard is so, but could only conjecture it from a conversation with him on the subject. . . . The transmissory note of Congress was before us to-day, when Mr. Henry declared that it

[1] MS.

transcended our powers to decide on the Constitution, and that it must go before a convention. As it was insinuated he would aim at preventing this, much pleasure was discovered at the declaration." [1]

On the 24th of October, from his place in Congress, Madison sent over to Jefferson, in Paris, a full account of the results of the Philadelphia convention, and of the public feeling with reference to its work: "My information from Virginia is as yet extremely imperfect. . . . The part which Mr. Henry will take is unknown here. Much will depend on it. I had taken it for granted, from a variety of circumstances, that he would be in the opposition, and still think that will be the case. There are reports, however, which favor a contrary supposition." [2] But, by the 9th of December, Madison was able to send to Jefferson a further report, which indicated that all doubt respecting the hostile attitude of Patrick Henry was then removed. After mentioning that a majority of the people of Virginia seemed to be in favor of the Constitution, he added: "What change may be produced by the united influence and exertions of Mr. Henry, Mr. Mason, and the governor, with some pretty able auxiliaries, is uncertain. . . . Mr. Henry is the great adversary who will render the event precarious. He is, I find, with his usual address, working up every possible interest into a spirit of opposition." [3]

---

[1] *Writings of Washington*, ix. 273.
[2] Madison, *Letters*, etc. i. 356.
[3] *Ibid.* i. 364–365.

Long before the date last mentioned, the legislature had regularly declared for a state convention, to be held at Richmond on the first Monday in June, 1788, then and there to determine whether or not Virginia would accept the new Constitution. In view of that event, delegates were in the mean time to be chosen by the people; and thus, for the intervening months, the fight was to be transferred to the arena of popular debate. In such a contest Patrick Henry, being once aroused, was not likely to take a languid or a hesitating part; and of the importance then attached to the part which he did take, we catch frequent glimpses in the correspondence of the period. Thus, on the 19th of February, 1788, Madison, still at New York, sent this word to Jefferson: "The temper of Virginia, as far as I can learn, has undergone but little change of late. At first, there was an enthusiasm for the Constitution. The tide next took a sudden and strong turn in the opposite direction. The influence and exertions of Mr. Henry, Colonel Mason, and some others, will account for this. . . . I am told that a very bold language is held by Mr. Henry and some of his partisans." [1] On the 10th of April, Madison, then returned to his home in Virginia, wrote to Edmund Randolph: "The declaration of Henry, mentioned in your letter, is a proof to me that desperate measures will be his game." [2] On the 22d of the same month Madison wrote to Jefferson: "The adversaries take very

[1] Madison, *Letters*, etc. i. 378.   [2] *Ibid.* i. 387.

different grounds of opposition. Some are opposed to the substance of the plan; others, to particular modifications only. Mr. Henry is supposed to aim at disunion." [1] On the 24th of April, Edward Carrington, writing from New York, told Jefferson: "Mr. H. does not openly declare for a dismemberment of the Union, but his arguments in support of his opposition to the Constitution go directly to that issue. He says that three confederacies would be practicable, and better suited to the good of commerce than one." [2] On the 28th of April, Washington wrote to Lafayette on account of the struggle then going forward; and after naming some of the leading champions of the Constitution, he adds sorrowfully: "Henry and Mason are its great adversaries." [3] Finally, as late as on the 12th of June, the Rev. John Blair Smith, at that time president of Hampden-Sidney College, conveyed to Madison, an old college friend, his own deep disapproval of the course which had been pursued by Patrick Henry in the management of the canvass against the Constitution: —

"Before the Constitution appeared, the minds of the people were artfully prepared against it; so that all opposition [to Mr. Henry] at the election of delegates to consider it, was in vain. That gentleman has descended to lower artifices and management on the occasion than I thought him capable of. . . . If Mr. Innes has shown

[1] Madison, *Letters*, i. 388.
[2] Bancroft, *Hist. Const.* ii. 465.
[3] *Writings of Washington*, ix. 356.

you a speech of Mr. Henry to his constituents, which I
sent him, you will see something of the method he has
taken to diffuse his poison. . . . It grieves me to see
such great natural talents abused to such purposes." [1]

On Monday, the 2d of June, 1788, the long-
expected convention assembled at Richmond. So
great was the public interest in the event that a
full delegation was present, even on the first day;
and in order to make room for the throngs of citizens from all parts of Virginia and from other
States, who had flocked thither to witness the impending battle, it was decided that the convention
should hold its meetings in the New Academy, on
Shockoe Hill, the largest assembly-room in the
city.

Eight States had already adopted the Constitution. The five States which had yet to act upon
the question were New Hampshire, Rhode Island,
New York, North Carolina, and Virginia. For
every reason, the course then to be taken by Virginia would have great consequences. Moreover,
since the days of the struggle over independence,
no question had so profoundly moved the people of
Virginia; none had aroused such hopes and such
fears; none had so absorbed the thoughts, or so
embittered the relations of men. It is not strange,
therefore, that this convention, consisting of one
hundred and seventy members, should have been
thought to represent, to an unusual degree, the intelligence, the character, the experience, the repu-

[1] Rives, *Life of Madison*, ii. 544, note.

tation of the State. Perhaps it would be true to say that, excepting Washington, Jefferson, and Richard Henry Lee, no Virginian of eminence was absent from it.

Furthermore, the line of division, which from the outset parted into two hostile sections these one hundred and seventy Virginians, was something quite unparalleled. In other States it had been noted that the conservative classes, the men of education and of property, of high office, of high social and professional standing, were nearly all on the side of the new Constitution. Such was not the case in Virginia. Of the conservative classes throughout that State, quite as many were against the new Constitution as were in favor of it. Of the four distinguished citizens who had been its governors, since Virginia had assumed the right to elect governors, — Patrick Henry, Jefferson, Nelson, and Harrison, — each in turn had denounced the measure as unsatisfactory and dangerous; while Edmund Randolph, the governor then in office, having attended the great convention at Philadelphia, and having there refused to sign the Constitution, had published an impressive statement of his objections to it, and, for several months thereafter, had been counted among its most formidable opponents. Concerning the attitude of the legal profession, — a profession always inclined to conservatism, — Madison had written to Jefferson: "The general and admiralty courts, with most of the bar, oppose the Constitution."[1] Finally, among

[1] Rives, *Life of Madison*, ii. 541.

Virginians who were at that time particularly hon-
ored and trusted for patriotic services during the
Revolution, such men as these, Theodoric Bland,
William Grayson, John Tyler, Meriwether Smith,
James Monroe, George Mason, and Richard Henry
Lee, had declared their disapproval of the docu-
ment.

Nevertheless, within the convention itself, at the
opening of the session, it was claimed by the friends
of the new government that they then outnumbered their opponents by at least fifty votes.[1] Their
great champion in debate was James Madison, who
was powerfully assisted, first or last, by Edmund
Pendleton, John Marshall, George Nicholas, Francis Corbin, George Wythe, James Innes, General
Henry Lee, and especially by that same Governor
Randolph who, after denouncing the Constitution
for "features so odious" that he could not "agree
to it,"[2] had finally swung completely around to its
support.

Against all this array of genius, learning, character, logical acumen, and eloquence, Patrick Henry
held the field as protagonist for twenty-three days,
— his chief lieutenants in the fight being Mason,
Grayson, and John Dawson, with occasional help
from Harrison, Monroe, and Tyler. Upon him
alone fell the brunt of the battle. Out of the
twenty-three days of that splendid tourney, there
were but five days in which he did not take the

[1] *Hist. Mag.* for 1873, 274.
[2] Elliot, *Debates*, i. 491 ; v. 502, 534-535.

floor. On each of several days he made three speeches; on one day he made five speeches; on another day eight. In one speech alone, he was on his legs for seven hours. The words of all who had any share in that debate were taken down, according to the imperfect art of the time, by the stenographer, David Robertson, whose reports, however, are said to be little more than a pretty full outline of the speeches actually made: but in the volume which contains these abstracts, one of Patrick Henry's speeches fills eight pages, another ten pages, another sixteen, another twenty-one, another forty; while, in the aggregate, his speeches constitute nearly one quarter of the entire book, — a book of six hundred and sixty-three pages.[1]

Any one who has fallen under the impression, so industriously propagated by the ingenious enmity of Jefferson's old age, that Patrick Henry was a man of but meagre information and of extremely slender intellectual resources, ignorant especially of law, of political science, and of history, totally lacking in logical power and in precision of statement, with nothing to offset these deficiencies excepting a strange gift of overpowering, dithyrambic eloquence, will find it hard, as he turns over the leaves on which are recorded the debates of the Virginia convention, to understand just how such a person could have made the speeches which are there attributed to Patrick Henry, or how a mere rhapsodist could have thus held his ground, in close

[1] Elliot, *Debates*, iii.

hand-to-hand combat, for twenty-three days, against such antagonists, on all the difficult subjects of law, political science, and history involved in the Constitution of the United States, — while showing at the same time every quality of good generalship as a tactician and as a party leader. "There has been, I am aware," says an eminent historian of the Constitution, "a modern scepticism concerning Patrick Henry's abilities; but I cannot share it. . . . The manner in which he carried on the opposition to the Constitution in the convention of Virginia, for nearly a whole month, shows that he possessed other powers besides those of great natural eloquence." [1]

But, now, what were Patrick Henry's objections to the new Constitution?

First of all, let it be noted that his objections did not spring from any hostility to the union of the thirteen States, or from any preference for a separate union of the Southern States. Undoubtedly there had been a time, especially under the provocations connected with the Mississippi business, when he and many other Southern statesmen sincerely thought that there might be no security for their interests even under the Confederation, and that this lack of security would be even more glaring and disastrous under the new Constitution. Such, for example, seems to have been the opinion of Governor Benjamin Harrison, as late as October the 4th, 1787, on which date he thus wrote to

---

[1] Curtis, *Hist. Const.* ii. 561, note.

Washington: "I cannot divest myself of an opinion that . . . if the Constitution is carried into effect, the States south of the Potomac will be little more than appendages to those to the northward of it."[1] It is very probable that this sentence accurately reflects, likewise, Patrick Henry's mood of thought at that time. Nevertheless, whatever may have been his thought under the sectional suspicions and alarms of the preceding months, it is certain that, at the date of the Virginia convention, he had come to see that the thirteen States must, by all means, try to keep together. "I am persuaded," said he, in reply to Randolph, "of what the honorable gentleman says, ' that separate confederacies will ruin us.' " " Sir," he exclaimed on another occasion, "the dissolution of the Union is most abhorrent to my mind. The first thing I have at heart is American liberty; the second thing is American union." Again he protested: " I mean not to breathe the spirit, nor utter the language, of secession."[2]

In the second place, he admitted that there were great defects in the old Confederation, and that those defects ought to be cured by proper amendments, particularly in the direction of greater strength to the federal government. But did the proposed Constitution embody such amendments? On the contrary, that Constitution, instead of properly amending the old Confederation, simply anni-

[1] *Writings of Washington*, ix. 266, note.
[2] Elliot, *Debates*, iii. 161, 57, 63.

hilated it, and replaced it by something radically different and radically dangerous.

" The federal convention ought to have amended the old system; for this purpose they were solely delegated; the object of their mission extended to no other consideration." " The distinction between a national government and a confederacy is not sufficiently discerned. Had the delegates who were sent to Philadelphia a power to propose a consolidated government, instead of a confederacy ? " " Here is a resolution as radical as that which separated us from Great Britain. It is radical in this transition ; our rights and privileges are endangered, and the sovereignty of the States will be relinquished : and cannot we plainly see that this is actually the case ? The rights of conscience, trial by jury, liberty of the press, all your immunities and franchises, all pretensions to human rights and privileges, are rendered insecure, if not lost, by this change, so loudly talked of by some, so inconsiderately by others." " A number of characters, of the greatest eminence in this country, object to this government for its consolidating tendency. This is not imaginary. It is a formidable reality. If consolidation proves to be as mischievous to this country as it has been to other countries, what will the poor inhabitants of this country do ? This government will operate like an ambuscade. It will destroy the state governments, and swallow the liberties of the people, without giving previous notice. If gentlemen are willing to run the hazard, let them run it ; but I shall exculpate myself by my opposition and monitory warnings within these walls." [1]

[1] Elliot, *Debates*, iii. 23, 52, 44, 156.

But, in the third place, besides transforming the old confederacy into a centralized and densely consolidated government, and clothing that government with enormous powers over States and over individuals, what had this new Constitution provided for the protection of States and of individuals? Almost nothing. It had created a new and a tremendous power over us; it had failed to cover us with any shield, or to interpose any barrier, by which, in case of need, we might save ourselves from the wanton and fatal exercise of that power. In short, the new Constitution had no bill of rights. But "a bill of rights," he declared, is " indispensably necessary."

"A general positive provision should be inserted in the new system, securing to the States and the people every right which was not conceded to the general government." "I trust that gentlemen, on this occasion, will see the great objects of religion, liberty of the press, trial by jury, interdiction of cruel punishments, and every other sacred right, secured, before they agree to that paper." " Mr. Chairman, the necessity of a bill of rights appears to me to be greater in this government than ever it was in any government before. I have observed already that the sense of European nations, and particularly Great Britain, is against the construction of rights being retained which are not expressly relinquished. I repeat, that all nations have adopted the construction, that all rights not expressly and unequivocally reserved to the people are impliedly and incidentally relinquished to rulers, as necessarily inseparable from delegated powers. . . . Let us consider the sentiments which have been entertained by the people of America on this subject. At the Revolution, it must be admitted that it was their sense to set down those great rights which ought, in all countries, to be held inviolable and sacred. Virginia did so, we all remember. She made a compact to reserve, expressly, certain rights. . . . She most cautiously and guardedly reserved and secured those invaluable, inestimable rights and privileges which no people, inspired with the least glow of patriotic liberty, ever did, or ever can, abandon. She is called upon now to abandon them, and dissolve that compact which secured them to her. . . . Will she do it? This is the question. If you intend to reserve your unalienable rights, you must have the most express stipulation; for, if implication be allowed, you are ousted of those rights. If the people do not think it necessary to reserve them, they will be supposed to be given up. . . . If you give up these powers, without a bill of rights, you will exhibit the most absurd thing to mankind that ever the world saw, — a government that has abandoned all its powers, — the powers of direct taxation, the sword, and the purse. You have disposed of them to Congress, without a bill of rights, without check, limitation, or control. And still you have checks and guards; still you keep barriers — pointed where? Pointed against your weakened, prostrated, enervated, state government! You have a bill of rights to defend you against the state government — which is bereaved of all power, and yet you have none against Congress — though in full and exclusive possession of all power. You arm yourselves against the weak and defenceless, and expose yourselves naked to the armed and powerful. Is not this a conduct of unexampled absurdity?" [1]

[1] Elliot, *Debates*, iii. 150, 462, 445–446.

Again and again, in response to his demand for an express assertion, in the instrument itself, of the rights of individuals and of States, he was told that every one of those rights was secured, since it was naturally and fairly implied. "Even say," he rejoined, "it is a natural implication, — why not give us a right . . . in express terms, in language that could not admit of evasions or subterfuges? If they can use implication for us, they can also use implication against us. We are giving power; they are getting power; judge, then, on which side the implication will be used." "Implication is dangerous, because it is unbounded; if it be admitted at all, and no limits prescribed, it admits of the utmost extension." "The existence of powers is sufficiently established. If we trust our dearest rights to implication, we shall be in a very unhappy situation." [1]

Then, in addition to his objections to the general character of the Constitution, namely, as a consolidated government, unrestrained by an express guarantee of rights, he applied his criticisms in great detail, and with merciless rigor, to each department of the proposed government, — the legislative, the executive, and the judicial; and with respect to each one of these he insisted that its intended functions were such as to inspire distrust and alarm. Of course, we cannot here follow this fierce critic of the Constitution into all the detail of his criticisms; but, as a single example, we may cite a

[1] Elliot, *Debates*, iii. 149–150.

portion of his assault upon the executive department, — an assault, as will be seen, far better suited
to the political apprehensions of his own time than
of ours : —

"The Constitution is said to have beautiful features;
but when I come to examine these features, sir, they
appear to me horribly frightful. Among other deformi-
ties, it has an awful squinting; it squints towards monarchy. And does not this raise indignation in the breast
of every true American? Your president may easily
become king. . . . Where are your checks in this government? Your strongholds will be in the hands of
your enemies. It is on a supposition that your American
governors shall be honest, that all the good qualities of
this government are founded; but its defective and imperfect construction puts it in their power to perpetrate
the worst of mischiefs, should they be bad men. And,
sir, would not all the world, from the eastern to the
western hemispheres, blame our distracted folly in resting
our rights upon the contingency of our rulers being good
or bad? Show me that age and country where the
rights and liberties of the people were placed on the sole
chance of their rulers being good men, without a consequent loss of liberty. . . . If your American chief be
a man of ambition and abilities, how easy is it for him
to render himself absolute! The army is in his hands;
and if he be a man of address, it will be attached to
him, and it will be the subject of long meditation with
him to seize the first auspicious moment to accomplish
his design. And, sir, will the American spirit solely
relieve you when this happens ? I would rather infinitely
— and I am sure most of this convention are of the

same opinion — have a king, lords, and commons, than a government so replete with such insupportable evils. If we make a king, we may prescribe the rules by which he shall rule his people, and interpose such checks as shall prevent him from infringing them; but the president, in the field, at the head of his army, can prescribe the terms on which he shall reign master, so far that it will puzzle any American ever to get his neck from under the galling yoke. . . . Will not the recollection of his crimes teach him to make one bold push for the American throne? Will not the immense difference between being master of everything, and being ignominiously tried and punished, powerfully excite him to make this bold push? But, sir, where is the existing force to punish him? Can he not, at the head of his army, beat down every opposition? Away with your president! we shall have a king. The army will salute him monarch. Your militia will leave you, and assist in making him king, and fight against you. And what have you to oppose this force? What will then become of you and your rights? Will not absolute despotism ensue?" [1]

Without reproducing here, in further detail, Patrick Henry's objections to the new Constitution, it may now be stated that they all sprang from a single idea, and all revolved about that idea, namely, that the new plan of government, as it then stood, seriously endangered the rights and liberties of the people of the several States. And in holding this opinion he was not at all peculiar. Very many of the ablest and noblest statesmen of

[1] Elliot, *Debates*, iii. 58–60.

the time shared it with him. Not to name again his chief associates in Virginia, nor to cite the language of such men as Burke and Rawlins Lowndes, of South Carolina; as Timothy Bloodworth, of North Carolina; as Samuel Chase and Luther Martin, of Maryland; as George Clinton, of New York; as Samuel Adams, John Hancock, and Elbridge Gerry, of Massachusetts; as Joshua Atherton, of New Hampshire, it may sufficiently put us into the tone of contemporary opinion upon the subject, to recall certain grave words of Jefferson, who, watching the whole scene from the calm distance of Paris, thus wrote on the 2d of February, 1788, to an American friend: —

" I own it astonishes me to find such a change wrought in the opinions of our countrymen since I left them, as that three fourths of them should be contented to live under a system which leaves to their governors the power of taking from them the trial by jury in civil cases, freedom of religion, freedom of the press, freedom of commerce, the habeas corpus laws, and of yoking them with a standing army. That is a degeneracy in the principles of liberty, to which I had given four centuries, instead of four years." [1]

Holding such objections to the proposed Constitution, what were Patrick Henry and his associates in the Virginia convention to do? Were they to reject the measure outright? Admitting that it had some good features, they yet thought that the best course to be taken by Virginia would be to

[1] Bancroft, *Hist. Const.* ii. 459–460.

remit the whole subject to a new convention of the States, — a convention which, being summoned after a year or more of intense and universal discussion, would thus represent the later, the more definite, and the more enlightened desires of the American people. But despairing of this, Patrick Henry and his friends concentrated all their forces upon this single and clear line of policy: so to press their objections to the Constitution as to induce the convention, not to reject it, but to postpone its adoption until they could refer to the other States in the American confederacy the following momentous proposition, namely, " a declaration of rights, asserting, and securing from encroachment, the great principles of civil and religious liberty, and the undeniable rights of the people, together with amendments to the most exceptionable parts of the said constitution of government." [1]

Such, then, was the real question over which in that assemblage, from the first day to the last, the battle raged. The result of the battle was reached on Wednesday, the 25th of June; and that result was a victory for immediate adoption, but by a majority of only ten votes, instead of the fifty votes that were claimed for it at the beginning of the session. Moreover, even that small majority for immediate adoption was obtained only by the help, first, of a preamble solemnly affirming it to be the understanding of Virginia in this act that it retained every power not expressly granted to the

[1] Elliot, *Debates*, iii. 653.

general government; and, secondly, of a subsidiary resolution promising to recommend to Congress "whatsoever amendments may be deemed necessary."

Just before the decisive question was put, Patrick Henry, knowing that the result would be against him, and knowing, also, from the angry things uttered within that House and outside of it, that much solicitude was abroad respecting the course likely to be taken by the defeated party, then and there spoke these noble words: —

"I beg pardon of this House for having taken up more time than came to my share, and I thank them for the patience and polite attention with which I have been heard. If I shall be in the minority, I shall have those painful sensations which arise from a conviction of being overpowered in a good cause. Yet I will be a peaceable citizen. My head, my hand, and my heart shall be at liberty to retrieve the loss of liberty, and remove the defects of that system in a constitutional way. I wish not to go to violence, but will wait, with hopes that the spirit which predominated in the Revolution is not yet gone, nor the cause of those who are attached to the Revolution yet lost. I shall therefore patiently wait in expectation of seeing that government changed, so as to be compatible with the safety, liberty, and happiness of the people." [1]

Those words of the great Virginian leader proved to be a message of reassurance to many an anxious citizen, in many a State, — not least so to that

[1] Elliot, *Debates*, iii. 652.

great citizen who, from the slopes of Mount Vernon, was then watching, night and day, for signs of some abatement in the storm of civil discord. Those words, too, have, in our time, won for the orator who spoke them the deliberate, and the almost lyrical, applause of the greatest historian who has yet laid hand on the story of the Constitution : " Henry showed his genial nature, free from all malignity. He was like a billow of the ocean on the first bright day after the storm, dashing itself against the rocky cliff, and then, sparkling with light, retreating to its home." [1]

Long after the practical effects of the Virginia convention of 1788 had been merged in the general political life of the country, that convention was still proudly remembered for the magnificent exertions of intellectual power, and particularly of eloquence, which it had called forth. So lately as the year 1857, there was still living a man who, in his youth, had often looked in upon that famous convention, and whose enthusiasm, in recalling its great scenes, was not to be chilled even by the frosts of his ninety winters : —

"The impressions made by the powerful arguments of Madison and the overwhelming eloquence of Henry can never fade from my mind. I thought them almost supernatural. They seemed raised up by Providence, each in his way, to produce great results: the one by his grave, dignified, and irresistible arguments to convince and enlighten mankind; the other, by his brilliant

[1] Bancroft, *Hist. Const.* ii. 316–317.

and enrapturing eloquence to lead whithersoever he would." [1]

Those who had heard Patrick Henry on the other great occasions of his career were ready to say that his eloquence in the convention of 1788 was, upon the whole, fully equal to anything ever exhibited by him in any other place. The official reports of his speeches in that assemblage were always declared to be inferior in " strength and beauty " to those actually made by him there. [2] " In forming an estimate of his eloquence," says one gentleman who there heard him, " no reliance can be placed on the printed speeches. No reporter whatever could take down what he actually said ; and if he could, it would fall far short of the original." [3]

In his arguments against the Constitution Patrick Henry confined himself to no systematic order. The convention had indeed resolved that the document should be discussed, clause by clause, in a regular manner ; but in spite of the complaints and reproaches of his antagonists, he continually broke over all barriers, and delivered his " multiform and protean attacks " in such order as suited the workings of his own mind.

In the course of that long and eager controversy, he had several passages of sharp personal collision with his opponents, particularly with Governor Randolph, whose vacillating course respecting the

[1] Rives, *Life of Madison*, ii. 610.
[2] Kennedy, *Life of Wirt*, i. 345.
[3] Spencer Roane, MS.

Constitution had left him exposed to the most galling comments, and who on one occasion, in his anguish, turned upon Patrick Henry with the exclamation: " I find myself attacked in the most illiberal manner by the honorable gentleman. I disdain his aspersions and his insinuations. His asperity is warranted by no principle of parliamentary decency, nor compatible with the least shadow of friendship; and if our friendship must fall, let it fall, like Lucifer, never to rise again." [1] Like all very eloquent men, he was taunted, of course, for having more eloquence than logic; for " his declamatory talents; " for his " vague discourses and mere sports of fancy; " for discarding " solid argument; " and for " throwing those bolts" which he had " so peculiar a dexterity at discharging." [2] On one occasion, old General Adam Stephen tried to burlesque the orator's manner of speech; [3] on another occasion, that same petulant warrior bluntly told Patrick that if he did " not like this government," he might " go and live among the Indians," and even offered to facilitate the orator's self-expatriation among the savages: " I know of several nations that live very happily; and I can furnish him with a vocabulary of their language." [4]

Knowing, as he did, every passion and prejudice of his audience, he adopted, it appears, almost every conceivable method of appeal. " The va-

---

[1] Elliot, *Debates*, iii. 187.   [2] *Ibid.* iii. 406, 104, 248, 177.
[3] St. George Tucker, MS.   [4] Elliot, *Debates*, iii. 580.

riety of arguments," writes one witness, "which Mr. Henry generally presented in his speeches, addressed to the capacities, prejudices, and individual interests of his hearers, made his speeches very unequal. He rarely made in that convention a speech which Quintilian would have approved. If he soared at times, like the eagle, and seemed like the bird of Jove to be armed with thunder, he did not disdain to stoop like the hawk to seize his prey, — but the instant that he had done it, rose in pursuit of another quarry." [1]

Perhaps the most wonderful example of his eloquence, if we may judge by contemporary descriptions, was that connected with the famous scene of the thunder-storm, on Tuesday, the 24th of June, only one day before the decisive vote was taken. The orator, it seems, had gathered up all his forces for what might prove to be his last appeal against immediate adoption, and was portraying the disasters which the new system of government, unless amended, was to bring upon his countrymen, and upon all mankind : " I see the awful immensity of the dangers with which it is pregnant. I see it. I feel it. I see beings of a higher order anxious concerning our decision. When I see beyond the horizon that bounds human eyes, and look at the final consummation of all human things, and see those intelligent beings which inhabit the ethereal mansions reviewing the political decisions and revolutions which, in the progress of time, will

[1] St. George Tucker, MS.

happen in America, and the consequent happiness
or misery of mankind, I am led to believe that
much of the account, on one side or the other, will
depend on what we now decide. Our own happiness alone is not affected by the event. All
nations are interested in the determination. We
have it in our power to secure the happiness of one
half of the human race. Its adoption may involve
the misery of the other hemisphere." Thus far
the stenographer had proceeded, when he suddenly
stopped, and placed within brackets the following
note: "[Here a violent storm arose, which put
the House in such disorder, that Mr. Henry was
obliged to conclude.]"[1] But the scene which is
thus quietly despatched by the official reporter of
the convention was again and again described, by
many who were witnesses of it, as something most
sublime and even appalling. After having deline-
ated with overpowering vividness the calamities
which were likely to befall mankind from their
adoption of the proposed frame of government,
the orator, it is said, as if wielding an enchanter's
wand, suddenly enlarged the arena of the debate
and the number of his auditors; for, peering
beyond the veil which shuts in mortal sight, and
pointing "to those celestial beings who were hov-
ering over the scene," he addressed to them "an
invocation that made every nerve shudder with
supernatural horror, when, lo! a storm at that
instant rose, which shook the whole building, and

[1] Elliot, *Debates*, iii. 625.

the spirits whom he had called seemed to have come at his bidding. Nor did his eloquence, or the storm, immediately cease; but availing himself of the incident, with a master's art, he seemed to mix in the fight of his ethereal auxiliaries, and, 'rising on the wings of the tempest, to seize upon the artillery of heaven, and direct its fiercest thunders against the heads of his adversaries.' The scene became insupportable; and the House rose without the formality of adjournment, the members rushing from their seats with precipitation and confusion." [1]

[1] Wirt, 296–297.   Also Spencer Roane, MS.

CHAPTER XIX

THE AFTER-FIGHT FOR AMENDMENTS

THUS, on the question of adopting the new Constitution, the fight was over; but on the question of amending that Constitution, now that it had been adopted, the fight, of course, was only just begun.

For how could this new Constitution be amended? A way was provided, — but an extremely strait and narrow way. No amendment whatsoever could become valid until it had been accepted by three fourths of the States; and no amendment could be submitted to the States for their consideration until it had first been approved, either by two thirds of both houses of Congress, or else by a majority of a convention specially called by Congress at the request of two thirds of the States.

Clearly, the framers of the Constitution intended that the supreme law of the land, when once agreed to, should have within it a principle of fixedness almost invincible. At any rate, the process by which alone alterations can be made, involves so wide an area of territory, so many distinct groups of population, and is withal, in itself, so manifold and complex, so slow, and so liable to entire stoppage, that any proposition looking toward change must inevitably perish long before reaching the far-away goal of final endorsement, unless that proposition be really impelled by a public demand not only very energetic and persistent, but well-nigh universal. Indeed, the constitutional provision for amendments seemed, at that time, to many, to be almost a constitutional prohibition of amendments.

It was, in part, for this very reason that Patrick Henry had urged that those amendments of the Constitution which, in his opinion, were absolutely necessary, should be secured before its adoption, and not be left to the doubtful chance of their being obtained afterward, as the result of a process ingeniously contrived, as it were, to prevent their being obtained at all. But at the close of that June day on which he and his seventy-eight associates walked away from the convention wherein, on this very proposition, they had just been voted down, how did the case stand? The Constitution, now become the supreme law of the land, was a Constitution which, unless amended, would, as they sincerely believed, effect the political ruin of the American people. As good citizens, as good men, what was left for them to do? They had fought hard to get the Constitution amended before adoption. They had failed. They must now fight hard to get it amended after adoption. Disastrous would it be, to assume that the needed amendments would now be carried at any rate. True, the Virginia convention, like the conventions of several other States, had voted to recommend amendments. But the hostility to amendments, as Patrick Henry believed, was too deeply rooted to yield to mere recommendations. The necessary amendments would not find their way through all the hoppers and tubes and valves of the enormous mill erected within the Constitution, unless forced onward by popular agitation, — and by popular agitation widespread, determined, vehement, even alarming. The powerful enemies of amendments must be convinced that, until amendments were carried through that mill, there would be no true peace or content among the surrounding inhabitants.

This gives us the clew to the policy steadily and firmly pursued by Patrick Henry as a party leader, from June, 1788, until after the ratification of the first ten amendments, on the 15th of December, 1791. It was simply a strategic policy dictated by his honest view of the situation; a bold, manly, patriotic policy; a policy, however, which was greatly misunderstood, and grossly misrepresented, at the time; a policy, too, which grieved the heart of Washington, and for several years raised between him and his ancient friend the one cloud of distrust that ever cast a shadow upon their intercourse.

In fact, at the very opening of the Virginia convention, and in view of the possible defeat of his demand for amendments, Patrick Henry had formed a clear outline of this policy, even to the

extent of organizing throughout the State local
societies for stirring up, and for keeping up, the
needed agitation.   All this is made evident by an
important letter written by him to General John
Lamb of New York, and dated at Richmond,
June 9, 1788, — when the convention had been in
session just one week.   In this letter, after some
preliminary words, he says : —

It is matter of great consolation to find that the sentiments of a vast majority of Virginians are in unison
with those of our Northern friends.   I am satisfied four
fifths of our inhabitants are opposed to the new scheme
of government.   Indeed, in the part of this country
lying south of James River, I am confident, nine tenths
are opposed to it.   And yet, strange as it may seem, the
numbers in convention appear equal on both sides: so
that the majority, which way soever it goes, will be small.
The friends and seekers of power have, with their usual
subtilty, wriggled themselves into the choice of the
people, by assuming shapes as various as the faces of
the men they address on such occasions.

If they shall carry their point, and preclude previous
amendments, which we have ready to offer, it will become highly necessary to form the society you mention.
Indeed, it appears the only chance for securing a rem-
nant of those invaluable rights which are yielded by the
new plan.   Colonel George Mason has agreed to act
as chairman of our republican society.   His character I
need not describe.   He is every way fit; and we have
concluded to send you by Colonel Oswald a copy of the
Bill of Rights, and of the particular amendments we
intend to propose in our convention.   The fate of them

is altogether uncertain; but of that you will be informed. To assimilate our views on this great subject is of the last moment; and our opponents expect much from our dissension. As we see the danger, I think it is easily avoided.

I can assure you that North Carolina is more decidedly opposed to the new government than Virginia. The people there seem rife for hazarding all, before they submit. Perhaps the organization of our system may be so contrived as to include lesser associations dispersed throughout the State. This will remedy in some degree the inconvenience arising from our dispersed situation. Colonel Oswald's short stay here prevents my saying as much on the subject as I could otherwise have done. And after assuring you of my ardent wishes for the happiness of our common country, and the best interests of humanity, I beg leave to subscribe myself, with great respect and regard,

Sir, your obedient, humble servant,

P. HENRY.[1]

On the 27th of June, within a few hours, very likely, after the final adjournment of the convention, Madison hastened to report to Washington the great and exhilarating result, but with this anxious and really unjust surmise respecting the course then to be pursued by Patrick Henry: —

"Mr. H——y declared, previous to the final question, that although he should submit as a quiet citizen, he should seize the first moment that offered for shaking off the yoke in a constitutional way. I suspect the plan will be to encourage two thirds of the legislatures

[1] Leake, *Life of Gen. John Lamb*, 307–308.

in the task of undoing the work ; or to get a Congress appointed in the first instance that will commit suicide on their own authority." [1]

At the same sitting, probably, Madison sent off to Hamilton, at New York, another report, in which his conjecture as to Patrick Henry's intended policy is thus stated : —

"I am so uncharitable as to suspect that the ill-will to the Constitution will produce every peaceable effort to disgrace and destroy it. Mr. Henry declared . . . that he should wait with impatience for the favorable moment of regaining, in a constitutional way, the lost liberties of his country." [2]

Two days afterward, by which time, doubtless, Madison's letter had reached Mount Vernon, Washington wrote to Benjamin Lincoln of Massachusetts, respecting the result of the convention : —

"Our accounts from Richmond are that . . . the final decision exhibited a solemn scene, and that there is every reason to expect a perfect acquiescence therein by the minority. Mr. Henry, the great leader of it, has signified that, though he can never be reconciled to the Constitution in its present form, and shall give it every constitutional opposition in his power, yet he will submit to it peaceably." [3]

Thus, about the end of June, 1788, there came down upon the fierce political strife in Virginia a

[1] Madison, *Letters*, etc. i. 402.
[2] *Works of Hamilton*, i. 463.
[3] *Writings of Washington*, ix. 392.

lull, which lasted until the 20th of October, at which time the legislature assembled for its autumnal session. Meantime, however, the convention of New York had adopted the Constitution, but after a most bitter fight, and by a majority of only three votes, and only in consequence of the pledge that every possible effort should be made to obtain speedily those great amendments that were at last called for by a determined public demand. One of the efforts contemplated by the New York convention took the form of a circular letter to the governors of the several States, urging almost pathetically that "effectual measures be immediately taken for calling a convention" to propose those amendments which are necessary for allaying "the apprehensions and discontents" then so prevalent.[1]

This circular letter "rekindled," as Madison then wrote to Jefferson, "an ardor among the opponents of the federal Constitution for an immediate revision of it by another general convention. . . . Mr. Henry and his friends in Virginia enter with great zeal into the scheme."[2] In a letter written by Washington, nearly a month before the meeting of the legislature, it is plainly indicated that his mind was then grievously burdened by the anxieties of the situation, and that he was disposed to put the very worst construction upon the expected conduct of Patrick Henry and his party in the approaching session : —

[1] Elliot, *Debates*, ii. 414.
[2] Madison, *Letters*, etc. i. 418.

"Their expedient will now probably be an attempt to procure the election of so many of their own junto under the new government, as, by the introduction of local and embarrassing disputes, to impede or frustrate its operation. . . . I assure you I am under painful apprehensions from the single circumstance of Mr. H. having the whole game to play in the Assembly of this State; and the effect it may have in others should be counteracted if possible."[1]

No sooner had the Assembly met, than Patrick Henry's ascendency became apparent. His sway over that body was such that it was described as "omnipotent." And by the time the session had been in progress not quite a month, Washington informed Madison that "the accounts from Richmond" were "very unpropitious to federal measures." "In one word," he added, "it is said that the edicts of Mr. H. are enregistered with less opposition in the Virginia Assembly than those of the grand monarch by his parliaments. He has only to say, Let this be law, and it is law."[2] Within ten days from the opening of the session, the House showed its sensitive response to Patrick Henry's leadership by adopting a series of resolutions, the chief purpose of which was to ask Congress to call immediately a national convention for proposing to the States the required amendments. In the debate on the subject, he is said to have declared "that he should oppose every measure tending to

[1] *Writings of Washington*, ix. 433.
[2] Bancroft, *Hist. Const.* ii. 483.

the organization of the government, unless accompanied with measures for the amendment of the Constitution." [1]

Some phrases in one of his resolutions were most offensive to those members of the House who had "befriended the new Constitution," and who, by implication at least, were held forth as "betrayers of the dearest rights of the people." "If Mr. Henry pleases," so wrote a correspondent of Washington, "he will carry the resolution in its present terms, than which none, in my opinion, can be more exceptionable or inflammatory; though, as he is sometimes kind and condescending, he may perhaps be induced to alter it." [2]

In accordance with these resolutions, a formal application to Congress for a national convention was prepared by Patrick Henry, and adopted by the House on the 14th of November. Every word of that document deserves now to be read, as his own account of the spirit and purpose of a measure then and since then so profoundly and so cruelly misinterpreted : —

"The good people of this commonwealth, in convention assembled, having ratified the Constitution submitted to their consideration, this legislature has, in conformity to that act, and the resolutions of the United States in Congress assembled to them transmitted, thought proper to make the arrangements that were necessary for carrying it into effect. Having thus shown themselves obedient to the voice of their constituents, all

[1] *Corr. Rev.* iv. 240-241.   [2] *Ibid.* iv. 241.

America will find that, so far as it depends on them, that plan of government will be carried into immediate operation.

"But the sense of the people of Virginia would be but in part complied with, and but little regarded, if we went no further. In the very moment of adoption, and coeval with the ratification of the new plan of government, the general voice of the convention of this State pointed to objects no less interesting to the people we represent, and equally entitled to your attention. At the same time that, from motives of affection for our sister States, the convention yielded their assent to the ratification, they gave the most unequivocal proofs that they dreaded its operation under the present form.

"In acceding to a government under this impression, painful must have been the prospect, had they not derived consolation from a full expectation of its imperfections being speedily amended. In this resource, therefore, they placed their confidence, — a confidence that will continue to support them whilst they have reason to believe they have not calculated upon it in vain.

"In making known to you the objections of the people of this Commonwealth to the new plan of government, we deem it unnecessary to enter into a particular detail of its defects, which they consider as involving all the great and unalienable rights of freemen: for their sense on this subject, we refer you to the proceedings of their late convention, and the sense of this General Assembly, as expressed in their resolutions of the   day of

"We think proper, however, to declare that in our opinion, as those objections were not founded in speculative theory, but deduced from principles which have been established by the melancholy example of other nations, in different ages, so they will never be removed until the cause itself shall cease to exist. The sooner, therefore, the public apprehensions are quieted, and the government is possessed of the confidence of the people, the more salutary will be its operations, and the longer its duration.

"The cause of amendments we consider as a common cause; and since concessions have been made from political motives, which we conceive may endanger the republic, we trust that a commendable zeal will be shown for obtaining those provisions which, experience has taught us, are necessary to secure from danger the unalienable rights of human nature.

"The anxiety with which our countrymen press for the accomplishment of this important end, will ill admit of delay. The slow forms of congressional discussion and recommendation, if indeed they should ever agree to any change, would, we fear, be less certain of success. Happily for their wishes, the Constitution hath presented an alternative, by admitting the submission to a convention of the States. To this, therefore, we resort, as the source from whence they are to derive relief from their present apprehensions. We do, therefore, in behalf of our constituents, in the most earnest and solemn manner, make this application to Congress, that a convention be immediately called, of deputies from the several States, with full power to take into their consideration the defects of this Constitution, that have been suggested by the state conventions, and report such amendments thereto, as they shall find best suited to promote our common interests, and secure to ourselves and our latest posterity the great and unalienable rights of mankind."[1]

Such was the purpose, such was the temper, of Virginia's appeal, addressed to Congress, and written by Patrick Henry, on behalf of immediate measures for curing the supposed defects of the Constitution. Was it not likely that this appeal would be granted? One grave doubt haunted the mind of Patrick Henry. If, in the elections for senators and representatives then about to occur in the several States, very great care was not taken, it might easily happen that a majority of the members of Congress would be composed of men who would obstruct, and perhaps entirely defeat, the desired amendments. With the view of doing his part towards the prevention of such a result, he determined that both the senators from Virginia, and as many as possible of its representatives, should be persons who could be trusted to help, and not to hinder, the great project.

Accordingly, when the day came for the election of senators by the Assembly of Virginia, he just stood up in his place and named " Richard Henry Lee and William Grayson, Esquires," as the two men who ought to be elected as senators; and, furthermore, he named James Madison as the one man who ought not to be elected as senator. Whereupon the vote was taken; "and after some time," as the journal expresses it, the committee to examine the ballot-boxes "returned into the

[1] *Jour. Va. House Del.* 42–43.

House, and reported that they had . . . found a majority of votes in favor of Richard Henry Lee and William Grayson, Esquires." [1] On the 8th of December, 1788, just one month afterward, Madison himself, in a letter to Jefferson, thus alluded to the incident: "They made me a candidate for the Senate, for which I had not allotted my pretensions. The attempt was defeated by Mr. Henry, who is omnipotent in the present legislature, and who added to the expedients common on such occassions a public philippic against my federal principles." [2]

Virginia's delegation in the Senate was thus made secure. How about her delegation in the lower house? That, also, was an affair to be sharply looked to. Above all things, James Madison, as the supposed foe of amendments, was to be prevented, if possible, from winning an election. Therefore the committee of the House of Delegates, which was appointed for the very purpose, among other things, of dividing the State into its ten congressional districts, so carved out those districts as to promote the election of the friends of the good cause, and especially to secure, as was hoped, the defeat of its great enemy. Of this committee Patrick Henry was not a member; but as a majority of its members were known to be his devoted followers, very naturally upon him, at the time, was laid the burden of the blame for practising this

[1] *Jour. Va. House Del.* 32.
[2] Madison, *Letters*, etc., i. 443–444.

ignoble device in politics, — a device which, when
introduced into Massachusetts several years afterward, also by a Revolutionary father, came to be
christened with the satiric name of "gerrymander-
ing." Surely it was a rare bit of luck, in the case
of Patrick Henry, that the wits of Virginia did not
anticipate the wits of Massachusetts by describing
this trick as "henrymandering;" and that he thus
narrowly escaped the ugly immortality of having
his name handed down from age to age in the
coinage of a base word which should designate a
base thing, — one of the favorite, shabby manœuvres of less scrupulous American politicians.[1]

Thus, however, within four weeks from the opening of the session, he had succeeded in pressing
through the legislature, in the exact form he
wished, all these measures for giving effect to
Virginia's demand upon Congress for amendments.
This being accomplished, he withdrew from the
service of the House for the remainder of the session, probably on account of the great urgency of
his professional engagements at that time. The
journal of the House affords us no trace of his
presence there after the 18th of November; and
although the legislature continued in session until
the 13th of December, its business did not digress
beyond local topics. To all these facts, rather

[1] For contemporary allusions to this first example of gerry-
mandering, see *Writings of Washington*, ix. 446–447; *Writings of
Jefferson*, ii. 574; Rives, *Life of Madison*, ii. 653–655; Bancroft,
Hist. Const. ii. 485.

bitter allusion is made in a letter to the governor of New Hampshire, written from Mount Vernon, on the 31st of January, 1789, by the private secretary of Washington, Tobias Lear, who thus reflected, no doubt, the mood of his chief : —

"Mr. Henry, the leader of the opposition in this State, finding himself beaten off the ground by fair argument in the state convention, and outnumbered upon the important question, collected his whole strength, and pointed his whole force against the government, in the Assembly. He here met with but a feeble opposition. . . . He led on his almost unresisted phalanx, and planted the standard of hostility upon the very battlements of federalism. In plain English, he ruled a majority of the Assembly; and his edicts were registered by that body with less opposition than those of the Grand Monarque have met with from his parliaments. He chose the two senators. . . . He divided the State into districts, . . . taking care to arrange matters so as to have the county, of which Mr. Madison is an inhabitant, thrown into a district of which a majority were supposed to be unfriendly to the government, and by that means exclude him from the representative body in Congress. He wrote the answer to Governor Clinton's letter, and likewise the circular letter to the executives of the several States. . . . And after he had settled everything relative to the government wholly, I suppose, to his satisfaction, he mounted his horse and rode home, leaving the little business of the State to be done by anybody who chose to give themselves the trouble of attending to it." [1]

[1] Bancroft, *Hist. Const.* ii. 488–489.

How great was the effect of these strategic measures, forced by Patrick Henry through the legislature of Virginia in the autumn of 1788, was not
apparent, of course, until after the organization of
the first Congress of the United States, in the
spring of 1789.   Not until the 5th of May could
time be found by that body for paying the least
attention to the subject of amendments.   On that
day Theodoric Bland, from Virginia, presented to
the House of Representatives the solemn application of his State for a new convention; and, after
some discussion, this document was entered on the
journals of the House.[1]   The subject was then
dropped until the 8th of June, when Madison, who
had been elected to Congress in spite of Patrick
Henry, and who had good reason to know how
dangerous it would be for Congress to trifle with
the popular demand for amendments, succeeded,
against much opposition, in getting the House to
devote that day to a preliminary discussion of the
business.   It was again laid aside for nearly six
weeks, and again got a slight hearing on the 21st
of July.   On the 13th of August it was once more
brought to the reluctant attention of the House,
and then proved the occasion of a debate which
lasted until the 24th of that month, when the
House finished its work on the subject, and sent
up to the Senate seventeen articles of amendment.
Only twelve of these articles succeeded in passing
the Senate; and of these twelve, only ten received

[1] Gales, *Debates*, i. 258–261.

from the States that approval which was necessary to their ratification. This was obtained on the 15th of December, 1791.

The course thus taken by Congress, in itself proposing amendments, was not at the time pleasing to the chiefs of that party which, in the several States, had been clamorous for amendments.[1] These men, desiring more radical changes in the Constitution than could be expected from Congress, had set their hearts on a new convention, — which, undoubtedly, had it been called, would have reconstructed, from top to bottom, the work done by the convention of 1787. Yet it should be noticed that the ten amendments, thus obtained under the initiative of Congress, embodied "nearly every material change suggested by Virginia;"[2] and that it was distinctly due, in no small degree, to the bitter and implacable urgency of the popular feeling in Virginia, under the stimulus of Patrick Henry's leadership, that Congress was induced by Madison to pay any attention to the subject. In the matter of amendments, therefore, Patrick Henry and his party did not get all that they demanded, nor in the way that they demanded; but even so much as they did get, they would not then have got at all, had they not demanded more, and demanded more, also, through the channel of a new convention, the dread of which, it is evident, drove Madison and

[1] Marshall, *Life of Washington*, v. 209–210; Story, *Const.* i. 211.

[2] Howison, *Hist. Va.* ii. 333.

his brethren in Congress into the prompt concession of amendments which they themselves did not care for. Those amendments were really a tub to the whale; but then that tub would not have been thrown overboard at all, had not the whale been there, and very angry, and altogether too troublesome with his foam-compelling tail, and with that huge head of his which could batter as well as spout.

CHAPTER XX

LAST LABORS AT THE BAR

THE incidents embraced within the last three chapters cover the period from 1786 to 1791, and have been thus narrated by themselves for the purpose of exhibiting as distinctly as possible, and in unbroken sequence, Patrick Henry's relations to each succeeding phase of that immense national movement which produced the American Constitution, with its first ten amendments.

During those same fervid years, however, in which he was devoting, as it might seem, every power of body and mind to his great labors as a party leader, and as a critic and moulder of the new Constitution, he had resumed, and he was sturdily carrying forward, most exacting labors in the practice of the law.

Late in the year 1786, as will be remembered, being then poor and in debt, he declined another election to the governorship, and set himself to the task of repairing his private fortunes, so sadly fallen to decay under the noble neglect imposed by his long service of the public. One of his kinsmen has left on record a pleasant anecdote to the effect that the orator happened to mention at that

time to a friend how anxious he was under the
great burden of his debts. "Go back to the bar,"
said his friend; "your tongue will soon pay your
debts. If you will promise to go, I will give you a
retaining fee on the spot."[1] This course, in fact,
he had already determined to take; and thus at the
age of fifty, at no time robust in health, and at that
time grown prematurely old under the storm and
stress of all those unquiet years, he again buckled
on his professional armor, rusty from long disuse,
and pluckily began his life over again, in the hope
of making some provision for his own declining
days, as well as for the honor and welfare of his
great brood of children and grandchildren. To
this task, accordingly, he then bent himself, with
a grim wilfulness that would not yield either to
bodily weakness, or to the attractions or the dis-
tractions of politics. It is delightful to be permitted to add, that his energy was abundantly
rewarded; and that in exactly eight years thereafter, namely in 1794, he was able to retire, in comfort and wealth, from all public and professional
employments of every sort.

Of course the mere announcement, in 1786, that
Patrick Henry was then ready once more to receive clients, was enough to excite the attention of
all persons in Virginia who might have important
interests in litigation. His great renown throughout the country, his high personal character, his
overwhelming gifts in argument, his incompara-

[1] Winston, in Wirt, 260.

ble gifts in persuasion, were such as to ensure an almost dominant advantage to any cause which he should espouse before any tribunal. Confining himself, therefore, to his function as an advocate, and taking only such cases as were worth his attention, he was immediately called to appear in the courts in all parts of the State.

It is not necessary for us to try to follow this veteran and brilliant advocate in his triumphal progress from one court-house to another, or to give the detail of the innumerable causes in which he was engaged during these last eight years of his practice at the bar. Of all the causes, however, in which he ever took part as a lawyer, in any period of his career, probably the most difficult and important, in a legal aspect, was the one commonly referred to as that of the British debts, argued by him in the Circuit Court of the United States at Richmond, first in 1791, and again, in the same place, in 1793.[1]

A glance at the origin of this famous cause will help us the better to understand the significance of his relation to it. By the treaty with Great Britain in 1783, British subjects were empowered "to recover debts previously contracted to them by our citizens, notwithstanding a payment of the debt into a state treasury had been made during the war, under the authority of a state law of sequestration." According to this provision a

[1] Ware, Administrator of Jones, Plaintiff in Error, *v.* Hylton *et al.*, Curtis, *Decisions*, i. 164-229.

British subject, one William Jones, brought an
action of debt in the federal court at Richmond,
against a citizen of Virginia, Thomas Walker, on
a bond dated May, 1772. The real question was
" whether payment of a debt due before the war
of the Revolution, from a citizen of Virginia to
British subjects, into the loan office of Virginia,
pursuant to a law of that State, discharged the
debtor."

The case, as will readily be seen, involved many
subtle and difficult points of law, municipal, national, and international; and the defence was
contained in the following five pleas: (1.) That
of payment, generally; (2.) That of the Virginia
act of sequestration, October 20, 1777; (3.) That
of the Virginia act of forfeiture, May 3, 1779;
(4.) That of British violations of the treaty of
1783; (5.) That of the necessary annulment of
the debt, in consequence of the dissolution of the
co-allegiance of the two parties, on the declaration
of independence.[1]

Some idea of the importance attached to the
case may be inferred from the assertion of Wirt,
that " the whole power of the bar of Virginia was
embarked " in it; and that the " learning, argument, and eloquence " exhibited in the discussion
were such " as to have placed that bar, in the estimation of the federal judges, . . . above all others
in the United States." [2]   Associated with Patrick
Henry, for the defendant, were John Marshall,
Alexander Campbell, and James Innes.

[1] Wirt, 316–318.   [2] Ibid. 312.

For several weeks before the trial of this cause in 1791, Patrick Henry secluded himself from all other engagements, and settled down to intense study in the retirement of his home in the country. A grandson of the orator, Patrick Henry Fontaine, who was there as a student of the law, relates that he himself was sent off on a journey of sixty miles to procure a copy of Vattel's Law of Nations. From this and other works of international law, the old lawyer " made many quotations; and with the whole syllabus of notes and heads of arguments, he filled a manuscript volume more than an inch thick, and closely written; a book . . . bound with leather, and convenient for carrying in his pocket. He had in his yard . . . an office, built at some distance from his dwelling, and an avenue of fine black locusts shaded a walk in front of it. . . He usually walked and meditated, when the weather permitted, in this shaded avenue. . . . For several days in succession, before his departure to Richmond to attend the court," the orator was seen " walking frequently in this avenue, with his note-book in his hand, which he often opened and read; and from his gestures, while promenading alone in the shade of the locusts," it was supposed that he was committing his speech to memory.[1] According to another account, so eager was his application to this labor that, in one stage of it, " he shut himself up in his office for three days, during which he did not

[1] Edward Fontaine, MS.

see his family; his food was handed by a servant through the office door." [1]   Of all this preparation, not unworthy to be called Demosthenic, the result was, if we may accept the opinion of one eminent lawyer, that Patrick Henry " came forth, on this occasion, a perfect master of every law, national and municipal, which touched the subject of investigation in the most distant point." [2]

It was on the 14th of November, 1791, that the cause came on to be argued in the court-house at Richmond, before Judges Johnson and Blair of the Supreme Court, and Judge Griffin of that district.   The case of the plaintiff was opened by Mr. Counsellor Baker, whose argument lasted till the evening of that day.   Patrick Henry was to begin his argument in reply the next morning.

" The legislature was then in session; but when eleven o'clock, the hour for the meeting of the court, arrived, the speaker found himself without a house to do business.   All his authority and that of his sergeant at arms were unavailing to keep the members in their seats : every consideration of public duty yielded to the anxiety which they felt, in common with the rest of their fellow citizens, to hear this great man on this truly great and extensively interesting question.   Accordingly, when the court was ready to proceed to business, the court-room of the capitol, large as it is, was insufficient to contain the vast concourse that was pressing to enter it.   The portico, and the area in which the statue of Washington stands, were filled with a disappointed

[1] Howe, *Hist. Coll. Va.* 221.   [2] Wirt, 312.

crowd, who nevertheless maintained their stand without. In the court-room itself, the judges, through condescension to the public anxiety, relaxed the rigor of respect which they were in the habit of exacting, and permitted the vacant seats of the bench, and even the windows behind it, to be occupied by the impatient multitude. The noise and tumult occasioned by seeking a more favorable station was at length hushed, and the profound silence which reigned within the room gave notice to those without that the orator had risen, or was on the point of rising. Every eye in front of the bar was riveted upon him with the most eager attention; and so still and deep was the silence that every one might hear the throbbing of his own heart. Mr. Henry, however, appeared wholly unconscious that all this preparation was on his account, and rose with as much simplicity and composure as if the occasion had been one of ordinary occurrence. . . . It may give the reader some idea of the amplitude of the argument, when he is told that Mr. Henry was engaged three days successively in its delivery; and some faint conception of the enchantment which he threw over it, when he learns that although it turned entirely on questions of law, yet the audience, mixed as it was, seemed so far from being wearied, that they followed him throughout with increased enjoyment. The room continued full to the last; and such was 'the listening silence' with which he was heard, that not a syllable that he uttered is believed to have been lost. When he finally sat down, the concourse rose, with a general murmur of admiration; the scene resembled the breaking up and dispersion of a great theatrical assembly, which had been enjoying, for the first time, the exhibition of some new and splendid drama; the speaker of the House of Delegates was at length able to command a quorum for business; and every quarter of the city, and at length every part of the State, was filled with the echoes of Mr. Henry's eloquent speech." [1]

In the spring of 1793 this cause was argued a second time, before the same district judge, and, in addition, before Mr. Chief Justice Jay, and Mr. Justice Iredell of the Supreme Court.   On this occasion, apparently, there was the same eagerness to hear Patrick Henry as before, — an eagerness which was shared in by the two visiting judges, as is indicated in part by a letter from Judge Iredell, who, on the 27th of May, thus wrote to his wife: " We began on the great British causes the second day of the court, and are now in the midst of them. The great Patrick Henry is to speak to-day." [2] Among the throng of people who then poured into the court-room was John Randolph of Roanoke, then a stripling of twenty years, who, having got a position very close to the judges, was made aware of their conversation with one another as the case proceeded.   He describes the orator as not expecting to speak at that time; " as old, very much wrapped up, and resting his head on the bar." Meanwhile the chief justice, who, in earlier days, had often heard Henry in the Continental Congress, told Iredell that that feeble old gentleman in mufflers, with his head bowed wearily down

---

[1] Wirt, 320–321 ; 368–369.
[2] McRee, *Life of Iredell*, ii. 394.

upon the bar, was "the greatest of orators." "Iredell doubted it; and, becoming impatient to hear him, they requested him to proceed with his argument, before he had intended to speak. . . . As he arose, he began to complain that it was a hardship, too great, to put the laboring oar into the hands of a decrepit old man, trembling, with one foot in the grave, weak in his best days, and far inferior to the able associate by him." Randolph then gives an outline of his progress through the earlier and somewhat tentative stages of his speech, comparing his movement to the exercise "of a first-rate, four-mile race-horse, sometimes displaying his whole power and speed for a few leaps, and then taking up again." "At last," according to Randolph, the orator "got up to full speed; and took a rapid view of what England had done, when she had been successful in arms; and what would have been our fate, had we been unsuccessful. The color began to come and go in the face of the chief justice; while Iredell sat with his mouth and eyes stretched open, in perfect wonder. Finally, Henry arrived at his utmost height and grandeur. He raised his hands in one of his grand and solemn pauses. . . . There was a tumultuous burst of applause; and Judge Iredell exclaimed, 'Gracious God! he is an orator indeed!'"[1] It is said, also, by another witness, that Henry happened that day to wear on his finger a diamond ring; and that

[1] Memorandum of J. W. Bouldin, in *Hist. Mag.* for 1873, 274–275.

in the midst of the supreme splendor of his eloquence, a distinguished English visitor who had
been given a seat on the bench, said with significant emphasis to one of the judges, " The diamond
is blazing ! " [1]

As examples of forensic eloquence, on a great
subject, before a great and a fit assemblage, his
several speeches in the case of the British debts
were, according to all the testimony, of the highest
order of merit. What they were as examples of
legal learning and of legal argumentation, may be
left for every lawyer to judge for himself, by reading, if he so pleases, the copious extracts which
have been preserved from the stenographic reports
of these speeches, as taken by Robertson. Even
from that point of view, they appear not to have
suffered by comparison with the efforts made, in
that cause, on the same side, by John Marshall
himself. No inconsiderable portion of his auditors
were members of the bar ; and those keen and
competent critics are said to have acknowledged
themselves as impressed " not less by the matter
than the manner " of his speeches.[2] Moreover,
though not expressly mentioned, Patrick Henry's
argument is pointedly referred to in the high compliment pronounced by Judge Iredell, when giving
his opinion in this case : —

"The cause has been spoken to, at the bar, with a
degree of ability equal to any occasion. . . . I shall, as

1 Howe, *Hist. Coll. Va.* 222.
2 Judge Spencer Roane, MS.

long as I live, remember with pleasure and respect the arguments which I have heard in this case. They have discovered an ingenuity, a depth of investigation, and a power of reasoning fully equal to anything I have ever witnessed; and some of them have been adorned with a splendor of eloquence surpassing what I have ever felt before. Fatigue has given way under its influence, and the heart has been warmed, while the understanding has been instructed." [1]

It will be readily understood, however, that while Patrick Henry's practice included important causes turning, like the one just described, on propositions of law, and argued by him before the highest tribunals, the larger part of the practice to be had in Virginia at that time must have been in actions tried before juries, in which his success was chiefly due to his amazing endowments of sympathy, imagination, tact, and eloquence. The testimony of contemporary witnesses respecting his power in this direction is most abundant, and also most interesting; and, for obvious reasons, such portions of it as are now to be reproduced should be given in the very language of the persons who thus heard him, criticised him, and made deliberate report concerning him.

First of all, in the way of preliminary analysis of Henry's genius and methods as an advocate before juries, may be cited a few sentences of Wirt, who, indeed, never heard him, but who, being himself a very gifted and a very ambitious advocate,

[1] McRee, *Life of Iredell*, ii. 395.

eagerly collected and keenly scanned the accounts
of many who had heard him : —

"He adapted himself, without effort, to the character
of the cause ; seized with the quickness of intuition its
defensible point, and never permitted the jury to lose
sight of it. Sir Joshua Reynolds has said of Titian,
that, by a few strokes of his pencil, he knew how to
mark the image and character of whatever object he
attempted ; and produced by this means a truer representation than any of his predecessors, who finished
every hair. In like manner Mr. Henry, by a few
master-strokes upon the evidence, could in general
stamp upon the cause whatever image or character he
pleased ; and convert it into tragedy or comedy, at his
sovereign will, and with a power which no efforts of his
adversary could counteract. He never wearied the jury
by a dry and minute analysis of the evidence ; he did
not expend his strength in finishing the hairs ; he produced all his high effect by those rare master-touches,
and by the resistless skill with which, in a very few
words, he could mould and color the prominent facts of
a cause to his purpose. He had wonderful address, too,
in leading off the minds of his hearers from the contem-
plation of unfavorable points, if at any time they were
too stubborn to yield to his power of transformation.
. . . It required a mind of uncommon vigilance, and
most intractable temper, to resist this charm with which
he decoyed away his hearers ; it demanded a rapidity
of penetration, which is rarely, if ever, to be found in
the jury-box, to detect the intellectual juggle by which
he spread his nets around them ; it called for a stub-
bornness and obduracy of soul which does not exist, to

sit unmoved under the pictures of horror or of pity
which started from his canvas. They might resolve, if
they pleased, to decide the cause against him, and to
disregard everything which he could urge in the defence of his client. But it was all in vain. Some feint
in an unexpected direction threw them off their guard,
and they were gone; some happy phrase, burning from
the soul; some image fresh from nature's mint, and
bearing her own beautiful and genuine impress, struck
them with delightful surprise, and melted them into
conciliation; and conciliation towards Mr. Henry was
victory inevitable. In short, he understood the human
character so perfectly; knew so well all its strength and
all its weaknesses, together with every path and by-way
which winds around the citadel of the best fortified
heart and mind, that he never failed to take them,
either by stratagem or storm."[1]

Still further, in the way of critical analysis,
should be cited the opinion of a distinguished
student and master of eloquence, the Rev. Archibald Alexander of Princeton, who, having more
than once heard Patrick Henry, wrote out, with a
scholar's precision, the results of his own keen
study into the great advocate's success in subduing
men, and especially jurymen: —

"The power of Henry's eloquence was due, first, to
the greatness of his emotion and passion, accompanied
with a versatility which enabled him to assume at once
any emotion or passion which was suited to his ends.
Not less indispensable, secondly, was a matchless per-

[1] Wirt, 75–76.

fection of the organs of expression, including the entire apparatus of voice, intonation, pause, gesture, attitude, and indescribable play of countenance. In no instance did he ever indulge in an expression that was not instantly recognized as nature itself; yet some of his penetrating and subduing tones were absolutely peculiar, and as inimitable as they were indescribable. These were felt by every hearer, in all their force. His mightiest feelings were sometimes indicated and communicated by a long pause, aided by an eloquent aspect, and some significant use of his finger. The sympathy between mind and mind is inexplicable. Where the channels of communication are open, the faculty of revealing inward passion great, and the expression of it sudden and visible, the effects are extraordinary. Let these shocks of influence be repeated again and again, and all other opinions and ideas are for the moment absorbed or excluded; the whole mind is brought into unison with that of the speaker; and the spell-bound listener, till the cause ceases, is under an entire fascination. Then perhaps the charm ceases, upon reflection, and the infatuated hearer resumes his ordinary state.

"Patrick Henry, of course, owed much to his singular insight into the feelings of the common mind. In great cases he scanned his jury, and formed his mental estimate; on this basis he founded his appeals to their predilections and character. It is what other advocates do, in a lesser degree. When he knew that there were conscientious or religious men among the jury, he would most solemnly address himself to their sense of right, and would adroitly bring in scriptural citations. If this handle was not offered, he would lay bare the sensibility of patriotism. Thus it was, when he succeeded in rescu-

ing the man who had deliberately shot down a neighbor;
who moreover lay under the odious suspicion of being a
Tory, and who was proved to have refused supplies to a
brigade of the American army." [1]

Passing now from these general descriptions to
particular instances, we may properly request Dr.
Alexander to remain somewhat longer in the wit-
ness-stand, and to give us, in detail, some of his
own recollections of Patrick Henry. His testimony, accordingly, is in these words: —

"From my earliest childhood I had been accustomed
to hear of the eloquence of Patrick Henry. On this
subject there existed but one opinion in the country.
The power of his eloquence was felt equally by the
learned and the unlearned. No man who ever heard
him speak, on any important occasion, could fail to admit his uncommon power over the minds of his hearers.
. . . Being then a young man, just entering on a profession in which good speaking was very important, it
was natural for me to observe the oratory of celebrated
men. I was anxious to ascertain the true secret of their
power; or what it was which enabled them to sway the
minds of hearers, almost at their will.

"In executing a mission from the synod of Virginia,
in the year 1794, I had to pass through the county
of Prince Edward, where Mr. Henry then resided.
Understanding that he was to appear before the circuit
court, which met in that county, in defence of three
men charged with murder, I determined to seize the
opportunity of observing for myself the eloquence of
this extraordinary orator. It was with some difficulty

[1] J. W. Alexander, *Life of A. Alexander*, 191–192.

I obtained a seat in front of the bar, where I could have a full view of the speaker, as well as hear him distinctly. But I had to submit to a severe penance in gratifying my curiosity; for the whole day was occupied with the examination of witnesses, in which Mr. Henry was aided by two other lawyers. In person, Mr. Henry was lean rather than fleshy. He was rather above than below the common height, but had a stoop in the shoulders which prevented him from appearing as tall as he really was. In his moments of animation, he had the habit of straightening his frame, and adding to his apparent stature. He wore a brown wig, which exhibited no indication of any great care in the dressing. Over his shoulders he wore a brown camlet cloak. Under this his clothing was black, something the worse for wear. The expression of his countenance was that of solemnity and deep earnestness. His mind appeared to be always absorbed in what, for the time, occupied his attention. His forehead was high and spacious, and the skin of his face more than usually wrinkled for a man of fifty. His eyes were small and deeply set in his head, but were of a bright blue color, and twinkled much in their sockets. In short, Mr. Henry's appearance had nothing very remarkable, as he sat at rest. You might readily have taken him for a common planter, who cared very little about his personal appearance. In his manners he was uniformly respectful and courteous. Candles were brought into the court-house, when the examination of the witnesses closed; and the judges put it to the option of the bar whether they would go on with the argument that night or adjourn until the next day. Paul Carrington, Junior, the attorney for the State, a man of large size, and uncommon dignity of person and manner, and also an accomplished lawyer, professed his willingness to proceed immediately, while the testimony was fresh in the minds of all. Now for the first time I heard Mr. Henry make anything of a speech; and though it was short, it satisfied me of one thing, which I had particularly desired to have decided : namely, whether like a player he merely assumed the appearance of feeling. His manner of addressing the court was profoundly respectful. He would be willing to proceed with the trial, ' but,' said he, ' my heart is so oppressed with the weight of responsibility which rests upon me, having the lives of three fellow citizens depending, probably, on the exertions which I may be able to make in their behalf (here he turned to the prisoners behind him), that I do not feel able to proceed to-night. I hope the court will indulge me, and postpone the trial till the morning.' The impression made by these few words was such as I assure myself no one can ever conceive by seeing them in print. In the countenance, action, and intonation of the speaker, there was expressed such an intensity of feeling, that all my doubts were dispelled; never again did I question whether Henry felt, or only acted a feeling. Indeed, I experienced an instantaneous sympathy with him in the emotions which he expressed; and I have no doubt the same sympathy was felt by every hearer.

"As a matter of course, the proceedings were deferred till the next morning. I was early at my post; the judges were soon on the bench, and the prisoners at the bar. Mr. Carrington . . . opened with a clear and dignified speech, and presented the evidence to the jury. Everything seemed perfectly plain. Two brothers and a brother-in-law met two other persons in pursuit of a slave, supposed to be harbored by the brothers. After some altercation and mutual abuse, one of the brothers, whose name was John Ford, raised a loaded gun which he was carrying, and presenting it at the breast of one of the other pair, shot him dead, in open day. There was no doubt about the fact. Indeed, it was not denied. There had been no other provocation than opprobrious words. It is presumed that the opinion of every juror was made up from merely hearing the testimony; as Tom Harvey, the principal witness, who was acting as constable on the occasion, appeared to be a respectable man. For the clearer understanding of what follows, it must be observed that said constable, in order to distinguish him from another of the name, was commonly called Butterwood Harvey, as he lived on Butterwood Creek. Mr. Henry, it is believed, understanding that the people were on their guard against his faculty of moving the passions and through them influencing the judgment, did not resort to the pathetic as much as was his usual practice in criminal cases. His main object appeared to be, throughout, to cast discredit on the testimony of Tom Harvey. This he attempted by causing the law respecting riots to be read by one of his assistants. It appeared in evidence that Tom Harvey had taken upon him to act as constable, without being in commission; and that with a posse of men he had entered the house of one of the Fords in search of the negro, and had put Mrs. Ford, in her husband's absence, into a great terror, while she was in a very delicate condition, near the time of her confinement. As he descanted on the evidence, he would often turn to Tom Harvey — a large, bold-looking man — and with

the most sarcastic look would call him by some name
of contempt; 'this Butterwood Tom Harvey,' 'this
would-be constable,' etc. By such expressions, his contempt for the man was communicated to the hearers.
I own I felt it gaining on me, in spite of my better
judgment; so that before he was done, the impression
was strong on my mind that Butterwood Harvey was
undeserving of the smallest credit. This impression,
however, I found I could counteract the moment I had
time for reflection. The only part of the speech in
which he manifested his power of touching the feelings
strongly, was where he dwelt on the irruption of the
company into Ford's house, in circumstances so perilous
to the solitary wife. This appeal to the sensibility of
husbands — and he knew that all the jury stood in this
relation — was overwhelming. If the verdict could
have been rendered immediately after this burst of the
pathetic, every man, at least every husband, in the
house, would have been for rejecting Harvey's testimony, if not for hanging him forthwith." [1]

A very critical and cool-headed witness respecting
Patrick Henry's powers as an advocate was Judge
Spencer Roane, who presided in one of the courts
in which the orator was much engaged after his
return to the bar in 1786 : —

"When I saw him there," writes Judge Roane, "he
must necessarily have been very rusty; yet I considered
him as a good lawyer. . . . It was as a criminal lawyer
that his eloquence had the finest scope. . . . He was a
perfect master of the passions of his auditory, whether
in the tragic or the comic line. The tones of his voice,

[1] J. W. Alexander, *Life of Archibald Alexander*, 183–187.

to say nothing of his matter and gesture, were insinuated into the feelings of his hearers, in a manner that baffled all description. It seemed to operate by mere sympathy, and by his tones alone it seemed to me that he could make you cry or laugh at pleasure. Yet his gesture came powerfully in aid, and, if necessary, would approach almost to the ridiculous. . . . I will try to give some account of his tragic and comic effect in two instances that came before me. About the year 1792, one Holland killed a young man in Botetourt. . . . Holland had gone up from Louisa as a schoolmaster, but had turned out badly, and was very unpopular. The killing was in the night, and was generally believed to be murder. . . . At the instance of the father and for a reasonable fee, Mr. H. undertook to go to Greenbrier court to defend Holland. Mr. Winston and myself were the judges. Such were the prejudices there, as I was afterwards informed by Thomas Madison, that the people there declared that even Patrick Henry need not come to defend Holland, unless he brought a jury with him. On the day of the trial the court-house was crowded, and I did not move from my seat for fourteen hours, and had no wish to do so. The examination took up a great part of the time, and the lawyers were probably exhausted. Breckenridge was eloquent, but Henry left no dry eye in the court-house. The case, I believe, was murder, though, possibly, manslaughter only; and Henry laid hold of this possibility with such effect as to make all forget that Holland had killed the storekeeper, and presented. the deplorable case of the jury's killing Holland, an innocent man. He also presented, as it were, at the clerk's table, old Holland and his wife, who were then in Louisa, and asked what must be the feel-

ing of this venerable pair at this awful moment, and
what the consequences to them of a mistaken verdict
affecting the life of their son. He caused the jury to
lose sight of the murder they were then trying, and weep
with old Holland and his wife, whom he painted, and
perhaps proved to be, very respectable. All this was
done in a manner so solemn and touching, and a tone so
irresistible, that it was impossible for the stoutest heart
not to take sides with the criminal. . . . The result of
the trial was, that, after a retirement of an half or
quarter of an hour, the jury brought in a verdict of not
guilty! But on being reminded by the court that they
might find an inferior degree of homicide, they brought
in a verdict of manslaughter.

"Mr. Henry was equally successful in the comic line.
. . . The case was that a wagoner and the plaintiff were
travelling to Richmond, and the wagoner knocked down
a turkey and put it into his wagon. Complaint was
made to the defendant, a justice; both the parties were
taken up; and the wagoner agreed to take a whipping
rather than be sent to jail. But the plaintiff refused.
The justice, however, gave him, also, a small whipping;
and for this the suit was brought. The plaintiff's plea
was that he was wholly innocent of the act committed.
Mr. H., on the contrary, contended that he was a party
aiding and assisting. In the course of his remarks he
thus expressed himself: 'But, gentlemen of the jury,
this plaintiff tells you that he had nothing to do with the
turkey. I dare say, gentlemen, — not until it was
roasted!' and he pronounced the word — 'roasted' —
with such rotundity of voice, and comicalness of manner
and gesture, that it threw every one into a fit of laughter at the plaintiff, who stood up in the place usually

allotted to the criminals; and the defendant was let off with little or no damages." [1]

Finally, we must recall, in illustration of our present subject, an anecdote left on record in 1813, by the Rev. Conrad Speece, highly distinguished during his lifetime, in the Presbyterian communion: —

"Many years ago," he then wrote, "I was at the trial, in one of our district courts, of a man charged with murder. The case was briefly this: the prisoner had gone, in execution of his office as a constable, to arrest a slave who had been guilty of some misconduct, and bring him to justice. Expecting opposition in the business, the constable took several men with him, some of them armed. They found the slave on the plantation of his master, within view of the house, and proceeded to seize and bind him. His mistress, seeing the arrest, came down and remonstrated vehemently against it. Finding her efforts unavailing, she went off to a barn where her husband was, who was presently perceived running briskly to the house. It was known he always kept a loaded rifle over his door. The constable now desired his company to remain where they were, taking care to keep the slave in custody, while he himself would go to the house to prevent mischief. He accordingly ran towards the house. When he arrived within a short distance of it, the master appeared coming out of the door with his rifle in his hand. Some witnesses said that as he came to the door he drew the cock of the piece, and was seen in the act of raising it to the position of firing. But upon these points there was not an

[1] MS.

entire agreement in the evidence. The constable, standing near a small building in the yard, at this instant fired, and the fire had a fatal effect. No previous malice was proved against him; and his plea upon the trial was, that he had taken the life of his assailant in necessary self-defence.

"A great mass of testimony was delivered. This was commented upon with considerable ability by the lawyer for the commonwealth, and by another lawyer engaged by the friends of the deceased for the prosecution. The prisoner was also defended, in elaborate speeches, by two respectable advocates. These proceedings brought the day to a close. The general whisper through a crowded house was, that the man was guilty and could not be saved.

"About dusk, candles were brought, and Henry arose His manner was . . . plain, simple, and entirely unassuming. 'Gentlemen of the jury,' said he, 'I dare say we are all very much fatigued with this tedious trial. The prisoner at the bar has been well defended already; but it is my duty to offer you some further observations in behalf of this unfortunate man. I shall aim at brevity. But should I take up more of your time than you expect, I hope you will hear me with patience, when you consider that blood is concerned.'

"I cannot admit the possibility that any one, who never heard Henry speak, should be made fully to conceive the force of impression which he gave to these few words, 'blood is concerned.' I had been on my feet through the day, pushed about in the crowd, and was excessively weary. I was strongly of opinion, too, notwithstanding all the previous defensive pleadings, that the prisoner was guilty of murder; and I felt anxious to know how the matter would terminate. Yet when Henry had uttered these words, my feelings underwent an instantaneous change. I found everything within me answering, — 'Yes, since blood is concerned, in the name of all that is righteous, go on; we will hear you with patience until the rising of to-morrow's sun!' This bowing of the soul must have been universal; for the profoundest silence reigned, as if our very breath had been suspended. The spell of the magician was upon us, and we stood like statues around him. Under the touch of his genius, every particular of the story assumed a new aspect, and his cause became continually more bright and promising. At length he arrived at the fatal act itself: 'You have been told, gentlemen, that the prisoner was bound by every obligation to avoid the supposed necessity of firing, by leaping behind a house near which he stood at that moment. Had he been attacked with a club, or with stones, the argument would have been unanswerable, and I should feel myself compelled to give up the defence in despair. But surely I need not tell you, gentlemen, how wide is the difference between sticks or stones, and double-triggered, loaded rifles cocked at your breast!' The effect of this terrific image, exhibited in this great orator's peerless manner, cannot be described. I dare not attempt to delineate the paroxysm of emotion which it excited in every heart. The result of the whole was, that the prisoner was acquitted; with the perfect approbation, I believe, of the numerous assembly who attended the trial. What was it that gave such transcendent force to the eloquence of Henry? His reasoning powers were good; but they have been equalled, and more than equalled, by those of many other men. His imagination was exceedingly quick, and commanded all the stores of nature, as materials for illustrating his subject. His voice and delivery were inexpressibly happy. But his most irresistible charm was the vivid feeling of his cause, with which he spoke. Such feeling infallibly communicates itself to the breast of the hearer."[1]

[1] Howe, *Hist. Coll. Va.* 222-223.

CHAPTER XXI

IN RETIREMENT

IN the year 1794, being then fifty-eight years old, and possessed at last of a competent fortune, Patrick Henry withdrew from his profession, and resolved to spend in retirement the years that should remain to him on earth. Removing from Prince Edward County, he lived for a short time at Long Island, in Campbell County; but in 1795 he finally established himself in the county of Charlotte, on an estate called Red Hill, — an estate which continued to be his home during the rest of his life, which gave to him his burial place, and which still remains in the possession of his descendants.

The rapidity with which he had thus risen out of pecuniary embarassments was not due alone to the earnings of his profession during those few years; for while his eminence as an advocate commanded the highest fees, probably, that were then paid in Virginia, it is apparent from his account-books that those fees were not at all exorbitant, and for a lawyer of his standing would not now be regarded as even considerable. The truth is that, subsequently to his youthful and futile attempts at busi-

ness, he had so profited by the experiences of his
life as to have become a sagacious and an expert
man of business. " He could buy or sell a horse,
or a negro, as well as anybody, and was peculiarly
a judge of the value and quality of lands." [1] It
seems to have been chiefly from his investments in
lands, made by him with foresight and judgment,
and from which, for a long time, he had reaped
only burdens and anxieties, that he derived the
wealth that secured for him the repose of his last
years. The charge long afterward made by Jefferson, that Patrick Henry's fortune came either from
a mean use of his right to pay his land debts in a
depreciated currency " not worth oak-leaves," or
from any connection on his part with the profligate
and infamous Yazoo speculation, has been shown,
by ample evidence, to be untrue.[2]

The descriptions which have come down to us of
the life led by the old statesman in those last five
years of retirement make a picture pleasant to look
upon. The house at Red Hill, which then became
his home, " is beautifully situated on an elevated
ridge, the dividing line of Campbell and Charlotte,
within a quarter of a mile of the junction of Falling
River with the Staunton. From it the valley of the
Staunton stretches southward about three miles,
varying from a quarter to nearly a mile in width,
and of an oval-like form. Through most fertile
meadows waving in their golden luxuriance, slowly

[1] Spencer Roane, MS.
[2] *Hist. Mag.* for 1867, 93; 369–370.

winds the river, overhung by mossy foliage, while on all sides gently sloping hills, rich in verdure, enclose the whole, and impart to it an air of seclusion and repose. From the brow of the hill, west of the house, is a scene of an entirely different character: the Blue Ridge, with the lofty peaks of Otter, appears in the horizon at a distance of nearly sixty miles." Under the trees which shaded his lawn, and "in full view of the beautiful valley beneath, the orator was accustomed, in pleasant weather, to sit mornings and evenings, with his chair leaning against one of their trunks, and a can of cool spring-water by his side, from which he took frequent draughts. Occasionally, he walked to and fro in the yard from one clump of trees to the other, buried in revery, at which times he was never interrupted." [1] "His great delight," says one of his sons-in-law, "was in conversation, in the society of his friends and family, and in the resources of his own mind." [2] Thus beneath his own roof, or under the shadow of his own trees, he loved to sit, like a patriarch, with his family and his guests gathered affectionately around him, and there, free from ceremony as from care, to give himself up to the interchange of congenial thought whether grave or playful, and even to the sports of the children. "His visitors," writes one of them, "have not unfrequently caught him lying on the floor, with a group of these little ones

[1] Howe, *Hist. Coll. Va.* 221.
[2] Spencer Roane, MS.

climbing over him in every direction, or dancing around him with obstreperous mirth, to the tune of his violin, while the only contest seemed to be who should make the most noise." [1]

The evidence of contemporaries respecting the sweetness of his spirit and his great lovableness in private life is most abundant. One who knew him well in his family, and who was also quite willing to be critical upon occasion, has said : —

"With respect to the domestic character of Mr. Henry, nothing could be more amiable. In every relation, as a husband, father, master, and neighbor, he was entirely exemplary. As to the disposition of Mr. Henry, it was the best imaginable. I am positive that I never saw him in a passion, nor apparently even out of temper. Circumstances which would have highly irritated other men had no such visible effect on him. He was always calm and collected; and the rude attacks of his adversaries in debate only whetted the poignancy of his satire. . . . Shortly after the Constitution was adopted, a series of the most abusive and scurrilous pieces came out against him, under the signature of Decius. They were supposed to be written by John Nicholas, . . . with the assistance of other more important men. They assailed Mr. Henry's conduct in the Convention, and slandered his character by various stories hatched up against him. These pieces were extremely hateful to all Mr. Henry's friends, and, indeed, to a great portion of the community. I was at his house in Prince Edward during the thickest of them. . . . He evinced no feeling on the occasion, and far less

[1] Cited in Wirt, 380–381.

condescended to parry the effects on the public mind. It was too puny a contest for him, and he reposed upon the consciousness of his own integrity. . . . With many sublime virtues, he had no vice that I knew or ever heard of, and scarcely a foible. I have thought, indeed, that he was too much attached to property, — a defect, however, which might be excused when we reflect on the largeness of a beloved family, and the straitened circumstances in which he had been confined during a great part of his life." [1]

Concerning his personal habits, we have, through his grandson, Patrick Henry Fontaine, some testimony which has the merit of placing the great man somewhat more familiarly before us. " He was," we are told, " very abstemious in his diet, and used no wine or alcoholic stimulants. Distressed and alarmed at the increase of drunkenness after the Revolutionary war, he did everything in his power to arrest the vice. He thought that the introduction of a harmless beverage, as a substitute for distilled spirits, would be beneficial. To effect this object, he ordered from his merchant in Scotland a consignment of barley, and a Scotch brewer and his wife to cultivate the grain, and make small beer. To render the beverage fashionable and popular, he always had it upon his table while he was governor during his last term of office ; and he continued its use, but drank nothing stronger, while he lived." [2]

Though he was always a most loyal Virginian,

---

[1] Spencer Roane, MS.   [2] Fontaine, MS.

he became, particularly in his later years, very unfriendly to that renowned and consolatory herb so
long associated with the fame and fortune of his
native State.

"In his old age, the condition of his nervous system
made the scent of a tobacco-pipe very disagreeable to
him. The old colored house-servants were compelled
to hide their pipes, and rid themselves of the scent of
tobacco, before they ventured to approach him. . . .
They protested that they had not smoked, or seen a
pipe; and he invariably proved the culprit guilty by following the scent, and leading them to the corn-cob pipes
hid in some crack or cranny, which he made them take
and throw instantly into the kitchen fire, without reform-
ing their habits, or correcting the evil, which is likely to
continue as long as tobacco will grow."[1]

Concerning another of his personal habits, during the years thus passed in retirement at Red
Hill, there is a charming description, also derived
from the grandson to whom we are indebted for the
facts just mentioned: —

"His residence overlooked a large field in the bottom
of Staunton River, the most of which could be seen from
his yard. He rose early; and in the mornings of the
spring, summer, and fall, before sunrise, while the air
was cool and calm, reflecting clearly and distinctly the
sounds of the lowing herds and singing birds, he stood
upon an eminence, and gave orders and directions to his
servants at work a half mile distant from him. The
strong, musical voices of the negroes responded to him.

[1] Fontaine, MS.

During this elocutionary morning exercise, his enunciation was clear and distinct enough to be heard over an
area which ten thousand people could not have filled;
and the tones of his voice were as melodious as the notes
of an Alpine horn." [1]

Of course the house-servants and the field-serv-
ants just mentioned were slaves; and, from the beginning to the end of his life, Patrick Henry was
a slaveholder. He bought slaves, he sold slaves,
and, along with the other property — the lands, the
houses, the cattle — bequeathed by him to his heirs,
were numerous human beings of the African race.
What, then, was the opinion respecting slavery
held by this great champion of the rights of man?
" Is it not amazing " — thus he wrote in 1773 —
" that, at a time when the rights of humanity are
defined and understood with precision, in a country
above all others fond of liberty, in such an age, we
find men, professing a religion the most humane,
mild, meek, gentle, and generous, adopting a principle as repugnant to humanity as it is inconsistent
with the Bible and destructive to liberty? . . .
Would any one believe that I am master of slaves
of my own purchase? I am drawn along by the
general inconvenience of living without them. I
will not, I cannot, justify it; however culpable my
conduct, I will so far pay my ' devoir' to virtue as
to own the excellence and rectitude of her precepts,
and to lament my want of conformity to them. I
believe a time will come when an opportunity will

[1] Fontaine, MS.

be offered to abolish this lamentable evil: everything we can do is to improve it, if it happens in our day; if not, let us transmit to our descendants, together with our slaves, a pity for their unhappy lot, and an abhorrence of slavery. We owe to the purity of our religion, to show that it is at variance with that law which warrants slavery."[1] After the Revolution, and before the adoption of the Constitution, he earnestly advocated, in the Virginia House of Delegates, some method of emancipation; and even in the Convention of 1788, where he argued against the Constitution on the ground that it obviously conferred upon the general government, in an emergency, that power of emancipation which, in his opinion, should be retained by the States, he still avowed his hostility to slavery, and at the same time his inability to see any practicable means of ending it: "Slavery is detested: we feel its fatal effects, — we deplore it with all the pity of humanity. . . . As we ought with gratitude to admire that decree of Heaven which has numbered us among the free, we ought to lament and deplore the necessity of holding our fellow-men in bondage. But is it practicable, by any human means, to liberate them without producing the most dreadful and ruinous consequences?"[2]

During all the years of his retirement, his great fame drew to him many strangers, who came to pay their homage to him, to look upon his face, to

[1] Bancroft, ed. 1869, vi. 416–417.
[2] Elliot, *Debates*, iii. 455–456; 590–591.

listen to his words. Such guests were always received by him with a cordiality that was unmistakable, and so modest and simple as to put them at
once at their ease. Of course they desired most of
all to hear him talk of his own past life, and of the
great events in which he had borne so brilliant a
part; but whenever he was persuaded to do so, it
was always with the most quiet references to himself. "No man," says one who knew him well,
" ever vaunted less of his achievements than Mr.
H. I hardly ever heard him speak of those great
achievements which form the prominent part of his
biography. As for boasting, he was entirely a
stranger to it, unless it be that, in his latter days,
he seemed proud of the goodness of his lands, and,
I believe, wished to be thought wealthy. It is my
opinion that he was better pleased to be flattered
as to his wealth than as to his great talents. This
I have accounted for by recollecting that he had
long been under narrow and difficult circumstances
as to property, from which he was at length happily
relieved ; whereas there never was a time when his
talents had not always been conspicuous, though he
always seemed unconscious of them." [1]

It should not be supposed that, in his final with-
drawal from public and professional labors, he
surrendered himself to the enjoyment of domestic
happiness, without any positive occupation of the
mind. From one of his grandsons, who was much
with him in those days, the tradition is derived

[1] Spencer Roane, MS.

that, besides "setting a good example of honesty, benevolence, hospitality, and every social virtue," he assisted "in the education of his younger children," and especially devoted much time "to earnest efforts to establish true Christianity in our country."[1] He gave himself more than ever to the study of the Bible, as well as of two or three of the great English divines, particularly Tillotson, Butler, and Sherlock. The sermons of the latter, he declared, had removed "all his doubts of the truth of Christianity;" and from a volume which contained them, and which was full of his pencilled notes, he was accustomed to read "every Sunday evening to his family; after which they all joined in sacred music, while he accompanied them on the violin."[2]

There seems to have been no time in his life, after his arrival at manhood, when Patrick Henry was not regarded by his private acquaintances as a positively religious person. Moreover, while he was most tolerant of all forms of religion, and was on peculiarly friendly terms with their ministers, to whose preaching he often listened, it is inaccurate to say, as Wirt has done, that, though he was a Christian, he was so "after a form of his own;" that "he was never attached to any particular religious society, and never . . . communed with any church."[3] On the contrary, from a grandson who

[1] Fontaine, MS.
[2] J. W. Alexander, *Life of A. Alexander*, 193; Howe, *Hist. Coll. Va.* 221.
[3] Wirt, 402.

spent many years in his household comes the tradition that "his parents were members of the Protestant Episcopal Church, of which his uncle, Patrick
Henry, was a minister;" that "he was baptized
and made a member of it in early life;" and that
"he lived and died an exemplary member of it."[1]
Furthermore, in 1830, the Rev. Charles Dresser,
rector of Antrim Parish, Halifax County, Virginia, wrote that the widow of Patrick Henry told
him that her husband used to receive "the communion as often as an opportunity was offered, and
on such occasions always fasted until after he had
communicated, and spent the day in the greatest
retirement. This he did both while governor and
afterward."[2] In a letter to one of his daughters,
written in 1796, he makes this touching confes-
sion : —

"Amongst other strange things said of me, I hear it
is said by the deists that I am one of the number; and,
indeed, that some good people think I am no Christian.
This thought gives me much more pain than the appellation of Tory; because I think religion of infinitely
higher importance than politics; and I find much cause
to reproach myself that I have lived so long, and
have given no decided and public proofs of my being a
Christian. But, indeed, my dear child, this is a character which I prize far above all this world has, or can
boast."[3]

[1] Fontaine, MS.
[2] Meade, *Old Churches*, etc. ii. 12.
[3] Wirt, 387.

While he thus spoke, humbly and sorrowfully, of his religious position as a thing so little known to the public that it could be entirely misunderstood by a portion of them, it is plain that no one who had seen him in the privacy of his life at home could have had any misunderstanding upon that subject. For years before his retirement from the law, it had been his custom, we are told, to spend " one hour every day . . . in private devotion. His hour of prayer was the close of the day, including sunset; . . . and during that sacred hour, none of his family intruded upon his privacy." [1]

As regards his religious faith, Patrick Henry, while never ostentatious of it, was always ready to avow it, and to defend it. The French alliance during our Revolution, and our close intercourse with France immediately afterward, hastened among us the introduction of certain French writers who were assailants of Christianity, and who soon set up among the younger and perhaps brighter men of the country the fashion of casting off, as parts of an outworn and pitiful superstition, the religious ideas of their childhood, and even the morality which had found its strongest sanctions in those ideas. Upon all this, Patrick Henry looked with grief and alarm. In his opinion, a far deeper, a far wiser and nobler handling of all the immense questions involved in the problem of the truth of Christianity was furnished by such Eng-

[1] Fontaine, MS.

lish writers as Sherlock and Bishop Butler, and, for popular use, even Soame Jenyns. Therefore, as French scepticism then had among the Virginia lawyers and politicians its diligent missionaries, so, with the energy and directness that always characterized him, he determined to confront it, if possible, with an equal diligence; and he then deliberately made himself, while still a Virginia lawyer and politician, a missionary also, — a missionary on behalf of rational and enlightened Christian faith. Thus during his second term as governor he caused to be printed, on his own account, an edition of Soame Jenyns's "View of the Internal Evidence of Christianity;" likewise, an edition of Butler's "Analogy;" and thenceforward, particularly among the young men of Virginia, assailed as they were by the fashionable scepticism, this illustrious colporteur was active in the defence of Christianity, not only by his own sublime and persuasive arguments, but by the distribution, as the fit occasion offered, of one or the other of these two books.

Accordingly when, during the first two years of his retirement, Thomas Paine's "Age of Reason" made its appearance, the old statesman was moved to write out a somewhat elaborate treatise in defence of the truth of Christianity. This treatise it was his purpose to have published. "He read the manuscript to his family as he progressed with it, and completed it a short time before his death." When it was finished, however, being "diffident about his own work," and impressed, also, by the great ability of the replies to Paine which were then appearing in England, "he directed his wife to destroy" what he had written. She "complied literally with his directions," and thus put beyond the chance of publication a work which seemed, to some who heard it, to be "the most eloquent and unanswerable argument in the defence of the Bible which was ever written." [1]

Finally, in his last will and testament, bearing the date of November 20, 1798, and written throughout, as he says, "with my own hand," he chose to insert a touching affirmation of his own deep faith in Christianity. After distributing his estate among his descendants, he thus concludes: "This is all the inheritance I can give to my dear family. The religion of Christ can give them one which will make them rich indeed." [2]

It is not to be imagined that this deep seclusion and these eager religious studies implied in Patrick Henry any forgetfulness of the political concerns of his own country, or any indifference to those mighty events which, during those years, were taking place in Europe, and were reacting with tremendous effect upon the thought, the emotion, and even the material interests of America. Neither did he succeed in thus preserving the retirement which he had resolved upon, without having

[1] Fontaine, MS. Also Meade, *Old Churches*, etc. ii. 12; and Wm. Wirt Henry, MS.

[2] MS. Certified copy

to resist the attempts of both political parties to
draw him forth again into official life. All these
matters, indeed, are involved in the story of his
political attitude from the close of his struggle for
amending the Constitution down to the very close
of his life, — a story which used to be told with
angry vituperation on one side, perhaps with some
meek apologies on the other. Certainly, the day
for such comment is long past. In the disinter-
estedness which the lapse of time has now made
an easy virtue for us, we may see, plainly enough,
that such ungentle words as " apostate" and " turn-
coat," with which his name used to be plentifully
assaulted, were but the missiles of partisan excitement; and that by his act of intellectual readjust-
ment with respect to the new conditions forced
upon human society, on both sides of the Atlantic,
by the French Revolution, he developed no occasion for apologies, since he therein did nothing
that was unusual at that time among honest and
thoughtful men everywhere, and nothing that was
inconsistent with the professions or the tendencies
of his own previous life. It becomes our duty,
however, to trace this story over again, as con-
cisely as possible, but in the light of much historical evidence that has never hitherto been presented
in connection with it.

Upon the adoption, in 1791, of the first ten
amendments to the Constitution, every essential
objection which he had formerly urged against that
instrument was satisfied; and there then remained

no good reason why he should any longer hold himself aloof from the cordial support of the new government, especially as directed, first by Washington, and afterward by John Adams, — two men with whom, both personally and politically, he had always been in great harmony, excepting only upon this single matter of the Constitution in its original form. Undoubtedly, the contest which he had waged on that question had been so hot and so bitter that, even after it was ended, some time would be required for his recovery from the soreness of spirit, from the tone of suspicion and even of enmity, which it had occasioned. Accordingly, in the correspondence and other records of the time, we catch some glimpses of him, which show that even after Congress had passed the great amendments, and after their approval by the States had become a thing assured, he still looked askance at the administration, and particularly at some of the financial measures proposed by Hamilton.[1] Nevertheless, as year by year went on, and as Washington and his associates continued to deal fairly, wisely, and, on the whole, successfully, with the enormous problems which they encountered; moreover, as Jefferson and Madison gradually drew off from Washington, and formed a party in opposition, which seemed to connive at the proceedings of Genet, and to encourage the formation among us of political clubs in apparent

[1] For example, D. Stuart's letter, in *Writings of Washington*, x. 94-96; also, *Jour. Va. House Del.* for Nov. 3, 1790.

sympathy with the wildest and most anarchic doctrines which were then flung into words and into deeds in the streets of Paris, it happened that Patrick Henry found himself, like Richard Henry Lee, and many another of his companions in the old struggle against the Constitution, drawn more and more into support of the new government.

In this frame of mind, probably, was he in the spring of 1793, when, during the session of the federal court at Richmond, he had frequent conversations with Chief Justice Jay and with Judge Iredell. The latter, having never before met Henry, had felt great dislike of him on account of the alleged violence of his opinions against the Constitution; but after making his acquaintance, Iredell thus wrote concerning him: " I never was more agreeably disappointed than in my acquaintance with him. I have been much in his company; and his manners are very pleasing, and his mind, I am persuaded, highly liberal. It is a strong additional reason I have, added to many others, to hold in high detestation violent party prejudice." [1]

In the following year, General Henry Lee, then governor of Virginia, appointed Patrick Henry as a senator of the United States, to fill out an unexpired term. This honor he felt compelled to decline.

In the course of the same year, General Lee, finding that Patrick Henry, though in virtual sym-

[1] McRee, *Life of Iredell*, ii. 394–395.

pathy with the administration, was yet under the impression that Washington had cast off their old friendship, determined to act the part of a peacemaker between them, and, if possible, bring together once more two old friends who had been parted by political differences that no longer existed. On the 17th of August, 1794, Lee, at Richmond, thus wrote to the President : —

"When I saw you in Philadelphia, I had many conversations with you respecting Mr. Henry, and since my return I have talked very freely and confidentially with that gentleman. I plainly perceive that he has credited some information, which he has received (from whom I know not), which induces him to believe that you consider him a factious, seditious character. . . . Assured in my own mind that his opinions are groundless, I have uniformly combated them, and lament that my endeavors have been unavailing. He seems to be deeply and sorely affected. It is very much to be regretted; for he is a man of positive virtue as well as of transcendent talents; and were it not for his feelings above expressed, I verily believe, he would be found among the most active supporters of your administration. Excuse me for mentioning this matter to you. I have long wished to do it, in the hope that it would lead to a refutation of the sentiments entertained by Mr. Henry." [1]

To this letter Washington sent a reply which expressed unabated regard for his old friend; and this reply, having been shown by Lee to Henry, drew from him this noble-minded answer: —

[1] *Writings of Washington*, x. 560–561.

RED HILL, 27 June, 1795.

MY DEAR SIR, — Your very friendly communication of so much of the President's letter as relates to me, demands my sincere thanks. Retired as I am from the busy world, it is still grateful to me to know that some portion of regard remains for me amongst my countrymen; especially those of them whose opinions I most value. But the esteem of that personage, who is contemplated in this correspondence, is highly flattering indeed.

The American Revolution was the grand operation, which seemed to be assigned by the Deity to the men of this age in our country, over and above the common duties of life. I ever prized at a high rate the superior privilege of being one in that chosen age, to which Providence intrusted its favorite work. With this impression, it was impossible for me to resist the impulse I felt to contribute my mite towards accomplishing that event, which in future will give a superior aspect to the men of these times. To the man, especially, who led our armies, will that aspect belong; and it is not in nature for one with my feelings to revere the Revolution, without including him who stood foremost in its establishment.

Every insinuation that taught me to believe I had forfeited the good-will of that personage, to whom the world had agreed to ascribe the appellation of good and great, must needs give me pain; particularly as he had opportunities of knowing my character both in public and in private life. The intimation now given me, that there was no ground to believe I had incurred his censure, gives very great pleasure.

Since the adoption of the present Constitution, I have generally moved in a narrow circle. But in that I have never omitted to inculcate a strict adherence to the principles of it. And I have the satisfaction to think, that in no part of the Union have the laws been more pointedly obeyed, than in that where I have resided and spent my time. Projects, indeed, of a contrary tendency have been hinted to me; but the treatment of the projectors has been such as to prevent all intercourse with them for a long time. Although a democrat myself, I like not the late democratic societies. As little do I like their suppression by law. Silly things may amuse for awhile, but in a little time men will perceive their delusions. The way to preserve in men's minds a value for them, is to enact laws against them.

My present views are to spend my days in privacy. If, however, it shall please God, during my life, so to order the course of events as to render my feeble efforts necessary for the safety of the country, in any, even the smallest degree, that little which I can do shall be done. Whenever you may have an opportunity, I shall be much obliged by your presenting my best respects and duty to the President, assuring him of my gratitude for his favorable sentiments towards me.

Be assured, my dear sir, of the esteem and regard with which I am yours, etc.,

PATRICK HENRY.[1]

After seeing this letter, Washington took an opportunity to convey to Patrick Henry a strong practical proof of his confidence in him, and of his cordial friendship. The office of secretary of state

[1] *Writings of Washington.* x. 562–563.

having become vacant, Washington thus tendered the place to Patrick Henry: —

MOUNT VERNON, 9 October, 1795.

DEAR SIR, — Whatever may be the reception of this letter, truth and candor shall mark its steps. You doubtless know that the office of state is vacant; and no one can be more sensible than yourself of the importance of filling it with a person of abilities, and one in whom the public would have confidence.

It would be uncandid not to inform you that this office has been offered to others; but it is as true, that it was from a conviction in my own mind that you would not accept it (until Tuesday last, in a conversation with General Lee, he dropped sentiments which made it less doubtful), that it was not offered first to you.

I need scarcely add, that if this appointment could be made to comport with your own inclination, it would be as pleasing to me, as I believe it would be acceptable to the public. With this assurance, and with this belief, I make you the offer of it. My first wish is that you would accept it; the next is that you would be so good as to give me an answer as soon as you conveniently can, as the public business in that department is now suffering for want of a secretary.[1]

Though Patrick Henry declined this proposal, he declined it for reasons that did not shut the door against further overtures of a similar kind; for, within the next three months, a vacancy having occurred in another great office, — that of chief justice of the United States, — Washington

[1] *Writings of Washington*, xi. 81-82.

again employed the friendly services of General Lee, whom he authorized to offer the place to Patrick Henry. This was done by Lee in a letter dated December 26, 1795 : —

" The Senate have disagreed to the President's nomination of Mr. Rutledge, and a vacancy in that important office has taken place. For your country's sake, for your friends' sake, for your family's sake, tell me you will obey a call to it. You know my friendship for you; you know my circumspection ; and, I trust, you know, too, I would not address you on such a subject without good grounds. Surely no situation better suits you. You continue at home, only [except] when on duty. Change of air and exercise will add to your days. The salary excellent, and the honor very great. Be explicit in your reply." [1]

On the same day on which Lee thus wrote to Henry he likewise wrote to Washington, informing him that he had done so ; but, for some cause now unknown, Washington received no further word from Lee for more than two weeks. Accordingly, on the 11th of January, 1796, in his anxiety to know what might be Patrick Henry's decision concerning the office of chief justice, Washington wrote to Lee as follows : —

MY DEAR SIR, — Your letter of the 26th ult. has been received, but nothing from you since, — which is embarrassing in the extreme ; for not only the nomination of chief justice, but an associate judge, and secretary of war, is suspended on the answer you were to

[1] MS.

receive from Mr. Henry; and what renders the want of it more to be regretted is, that the first Monday of next month (which happens on the first day of it) is the term appointed by law for the meeting of the Superior Court of the United States, in this city; at which, for particular reasons, the bench ought to be full. I will add no more at present than that I am your affectionate,

GEO. WASHINGTON.[1]

Although Patrick Henry declined this great compliment also, his friendliness to the administration had become so well understood that, among the Federal leaders, who in the spring of 1796 were planning for the succession to Washington and Adams, there was a strong inclination to nominate Patrick Henry for the vice-presidency, — their chief doubt being with reference to his willingness to take the nomination.[2]

All these overtures to Patrick Henry were somewhat jealously watched by Jefferson, who, indeed, in a letter to Monroe, on the 10th of July, 1796, interpreted them with that easy recklessness of statement which so frequently embellished his private correspondence and his private talk. " Most assiduous court," he says of the Federalists, " is paid to Patrick Henry. He has been offered everything which they knew he would not accept." [3]

A few weeks after Jefferson penned those sneer-

---

[1] Lee, *Observations*, etc. 116.

[2] Gibbs, *Administration of Washington*, etc. i. 337; see, also, Hamilton, *Works*, vi. 114.

[3] Jefferson, *Writings*, iv. 148.

ing words, the person thus alluded to wrote to his daughter, Mrs. Aylett, concerning certain troublesome reports which had reached her : —

" As to the reports you have heard, of my changing sides in politics, I can only say they are not true. I am too old to exchange my former opinions, which have grown up into fixed habits of thinking. True it is, I have condemned the conduct of our members in Congress, because, in refusing to raise money for the purposes of the British treaty, they, in effect, would have surrendered our country bound, hand and foot, to the power of the British nation. . . . The treaty is, in my opinion, a very bad one indeed. But what must I think of those men, whom I myself warned of the danger of giving the power of making laws by means of treaty to the President and Senate, when I see these same men denying the existence of that power, which, they insisted in our convention, ought properly to be exercised by the President and Senate, and by none other ? The policy of these men, both then and now, appears to me quite void of wisdom and foresight. These sentiments I did mention in conversation in Richmond, and perhaps others which I don't remember. . . . It seems that every word was watched which I casually dropped, and wrested to answer party views. Who can have been so meanly employed, I know not, neither do I care; for I no longer consider myself as an actor on the stage of public life. It is time for me to retire ; and I shall never more appear in a public character, unless some unlooked-for circumstance shall demand from me a transient effort, not inconsistent with private life — in which I have determined to continue." [1]

[1] Entire letter in Wirt, 385–387.

In the autumn of 1796 the Assembly of Virginia, then under the political control of Jefferson, and apparently eager to compete with the Federalists for the possession of a great name, elected Patrick Henry to the governorship of the State. But the man whose purpose to refuse office had been proof against the attractions of the United States Senate, and of the highest place in Washington's cabinet, and of the highest judicial position in the country, was not likely to succumb to the opportunity of being governor of Virginia for the sixth time.

CHAPTER XXII

LAST DAYS

THE intimation given by Patrick Henry to his daughter, in the summer of 1796, that, though he could never again engage in a public career, he yet might be compelled by "some unlooked-for circumstance" to make "a transient effort" for the public safety, was not put to the test until nearly three years afterward, when it was verified in the midst of those days in which he was suddenly to find surcease of all earthly care and pain.

Our story, therefore, now passes hurriedly by the year 1797, — which saw the entrance of John Adams into the presidency, the return of Monroe from France in great anger at the men who had recalled him, the publication of Jefferson's letter to Mazzei, everywhere an increasing bitterness and even violence in partisan feeling. In the same manner, also, must we pass by the year 1798, — which saw the popular uprising against France, the mounting of the black cockade against her, the suspension of commercial intercourse with her, the summons to Washington to come forth once more and lead the armies of America against the enemy;

then the moonstruck madness of the Federalists, forcing upon the country the naturalization act, the alien acts, the sedition act; then the Kentucky resolutions, as written by Jefferson, declaring the acts just named to be " not law, but utterly void and of no force," and liable, "unless arrested on the threshold," " to drive these States into revolution and blood;" then the Virginia resolutions, as written by Madison, denouncing the same acts as "palpable and alarming infractions of the Constitution;" finally, the preparations secretly making by the government of Virginia[1] for armed resistance to the government of the United States.

Just seven days after the passage of the Virginia resolutions, an eminent citizen of that State appealed by letter to Patrick Henry for some written expression of his views upon the troubled situation, with the immediate object of aiding in the election of John Marshall, who, having just before returned from his baffled embassy to Paris, was then in nomination for Congress, and was encountering assaults directed by every energy and art of the opposition. In response to this appeal, Patrick Henry wrote, in the early part of the year 1799, the following remarkable letter, which is of deep interest still, not only as showing his discernment of the true nature of that crisis, but as furnishing a complete answer to the taunt that his mental faculties were then fallen into decay: —

[1] Henry Adams, *Life of J. Randolph*, 27-28.

TO ARCHIBALD BLAIR.

RED HILL, CHARLOTTE, 8 January, 1799.

DEAR SIR, — Your favor of the 28th of last month I have received. Its contents are a fresh proof that there is cause for much lamentation over the present state of things in Virginia. It is possible that most of the individuals who compose the contending factions are sincere, and act from honest motives. But it is more than probable, that certain leaders meditate a change in government. To effect this, I see no way so practicable as dissolving the confederacy. And I am free to own, that, in my judgment, most of the measures lately pursued by the opposition party, directly and certainly lead to that end. If this is not the system of the party, they have none, and act ' ex tempore.'

I do acknowledge that I am not capable to form a correct judgment on the present politics of the world. The wide extent to which the present contentions have gone will scarcely permit any observer to see enough in detail to enable him to form anything like a tolerable judgment on the final result, as it may respect the nations in general. But, as to France, I have no doubt in saying that to her it will be calamitous. Her conduct has made it the interest of the great family of mankind to wish the downfall of her present government; because its existence is incompatible with that of all others within its reach. And, whilst I see the dangers that threaten ours from her intrigues and her arms, I am not so much alarmed as at the apprehension of her destroying the great pillars of all government and of social life, — I mean virtue, morality, and religion. This is the armor, my friend, and this alone, that renders us invincible. These are the tactics we should study. If we lose these, we are conquered, fallen indeed. In vain may France show and vaunt her diplomatic skill, and brave troops : so long as our manners and principles remain sound, there is no danger. But believing, as I do, that these are in danger, that infidelity in its broadest sense, under the name of philosophy, is fast spreading, and that, under the patronage of French manners and principles, everything that ought to be dear to man is covertly but successfully assailed, I feel the value of those men amongst us, who hold out to the world the idea, that our continent is to exhibit an originality of character ; and that, instead of that imitation and inferiority which the countries of the old world have been in the habit of exacting from the new, we shall maintain that high ground upon which nature has placed us, and that Europe will alike cease to rule us and give us modes of thinking.

But I must stop short, or else this letter will be all preface. These prefatory remarks, however, I thought proper to make, as they point out the kind of character amongst our countrymen most estimable in my eyes. General Marshall and his colleagues exhibited the American character as respectable. France, in the period of her most triumphant fortune, beheld them as unappalled. Her threats left them, as she found them, mild, temperate, firm. Can it be thought that, with these sentiments, I should utter anything tending to prejudice General Marshall's election ? Very far from it indeed. Independently of the high gratification I felt from his public ministry, he ever stood high in my esteem as a private citizen. His temper and disposition were always pleasant, his talents and integrity unques-

tioned. These things are sufficient to place that gentleman far above any competitor in the district for Congress. But, when you add the particular information
and insight which he has gained, and is able to communicate to our public councils, it is really astonishing that
even blindness itself should hesitate in the choice. . . .
Tell Marshall I love him, because he felt and acted as
a republican, as an American. . . . I am too old and
infirm ever again to undertake public concerns. I live
much retired, amidst a multiplicity of blessings from
that Gracious Ruler of all things, to whom I owe un-
ceasing acknowledgments for his unmerited goodness to
me ; and if I was permitted to add to the catalogue one
other blessing, it should be, that my countrymen should
learn wisdom and virtue, and in this their day to know
the things that pertain to their peace. Farewell.

I am, dear Sir, yours,

PATRICK HENRY.[1]

The appeal from Archibald Blair, which evoked
this impressive letter, had suggested to the old
statesman no effort which could not be made in
his retirement. Before, however, he was to pass
beyond the reach of all human appeals, two others
were to be addressed to him, the one by John
Adams, the other by Washington, both asking him
to come forth into the world again; the former
calling for his help in averting war with France,
the latter for his help in averting the triumph of
violent and dangerous counsels at home.

On the 25th of February, 1799, John Adams,
shaking himself free of his partisan counsellors, —

[1] *Writings of Washington*, **xi**. 557–559.

all hot for war with France, — suddenly changed
the course of history by sending to the Senate the
names of these three citizens, Oliver Ellsworth,
Patrick Henry, and William Vans Murray, " to be
envoys extraordinary and ministers plenipotentiary
to the French republic, with full powers to discuss
and settle, by a treaty, all controversies between
the United States and France." In his letter of
the 16th of April declining the appointment, Patrick Henry spoke of himself as having been " confined for several weeks by a severe indisposition,"
and as being " still so sick as to be scarcely able to
write this." " My advanced age," he added, " and
increasing debility compel me to abandon every
idea of serving my country, where the scene of
operation is far distant, and her interests call for
incessant and long continued exertion. . . . I cannot, however, forbear expressing, on this occasion,
the high sense I entertain of the honor done me
by the President and Senate in the appointment.
And I beg you, sir, to present me to them in
terms of the most dutiful regard, assuring them
that this mark of their confidence in me, at a crisis
so eventful, is an agreeable and flattering proof of
their consideration towards me, and that nothing
short of an absolute necessity could induce me to
withhold my little aid from an administration whose
ability, patriotism, and virtue deserve the gratitude
and reverence of all their fellow citizens." [1]

Such was John Adams's appeal to Patrick

[1] *Works of John Adams*, ix. 162; viii. 641–642.

Henry and its result. The appeal to him from Washington — an appeal which he could not resist, and which induced him, even in his extreme feebleness of body, to make one last and noble exertion of his genius — happened in this wise. On the 15th of January, 1799, from Mount Vernon, Washington wrote to his friend a long letter, marked "confidential," in which he stated with great frankness his own anxieties respecting the dangers then threatening the country : —

"It would be a waste of time to attempt to bring to the view of a person of your observation and discernment, the endeavors of a certain party among us to disquiet the public mind with unfounded alarms; to arraign every act of the administration; to set the people at variance with their government; and to embarrass all its measures. Equally useless would it be to predict what must be the inevitable consequences of such a policy, if it cannot be arrested.

"Unfortunately, — and extremely do I regret it, — the State of Virginia has taken the lead in this opposition. . . . It has been said that the great mass of the citizens of this State are well-affected, notwithstanding, to the general government and the Union; and I am willing to believe it, nay, do believe it. But how is this to be reconciled with their suffrages at the elections of representatives, . . . who are men opposed to the former, and by the tendency of their measures would destroy the latter? . . . One of the reasons assigned is, that the most respectable and best qualified characters among us will not come forward. . . . But, at such a crisis as this, when everything dear and valuable to us

is assailed; when this party hangs upon the wheels of
government as a dead weight, opposing every measure
that is calculated for defence and self-preservation, abet-
ting the nefarious views of another nation upon our
rights; . . . when measures are systematically and per-
tinaciously pursued, which must eventually dissolve the
Union, or produce coercion; I say, when these things
have become so obvious, ought characters who are best
able to rescue their country from the pending evil, to
remain at home? Rather ought they not to come forward, and by their talents and influence stand in the
breach which such conduct has made on the peace and
happiness of this country, and oppose the widening of
it? . . .

"I come, now, my good Sir, to the object of my
letter, which is to express a hope and an earnest wish,
that you will come forward at the ensuing elections
(if not for Congress, which you may think would take
you too long from home), as a candidate for representative in the General Assembly of this Commonwealth.

"There are, I have no doubt, very many sensible
men who oppose themselves to the torrent that carries
away others who had rather swim with, than stem it
without an able pilot to conduct them; but these are
neither old in legislation, nor well known in the community. Your weight of character and influence in the
House of Representatives would be a bulwark against
such dangerous sentiments as are delivered there at present. It would be a rallying point for the timid, and
an attraction of the wavering. In a word, I conceive it
to be of immense importance at this crisis, that you
should be there; and I would fain hope that all minor
considerations will be made to yield to the measure." [1]

[1] *Writings of Washington*, xi. 387–391.

There can be little doubt that it was this solemn invocation on the part of Washington which induced the old statesman, on whom Death had already begun to lay his icy hands, to come forth from the solitude in which he had been so long buried, and offer himself for the suffrages of his neighbors, as their representative in the next House of Delegates, there to give check, if possible, to the men who seemed to be hurrying Virginia upon violent courses, and the republic into civil war. Accordingly, before the day for the usual March[1] court in Charlotte, the word went out through all that country that old Patrick Henry, whose wondrous voice in public no man had heard for those many years, who had indeed been almost numbered among the dead ones of their heroic days foregone, was to appear before all the people once more, and speak to them as in the former time, and give to them his counsel amid those thickening dangers which alone could have drawn him forth from the very borders of the grave.

When the morning of that day came, from all the region thereabout the people began to stream toward the place where the orator was to speak. So widespread was the desire to hear him that even the college in the next county — the college of Hampden-Sidney — suspended its work for that day, and thus enabled all its members, the president himself, the professors, and the students, to hurry over to Charlotte court-house. One of those

---

[1] Garland, *Life of John Randolph*, 130.

students, John Miller, of South Carolina, according to an account said to have been given by him in conversation forty years afterward, having with his companions reached the town, —

"and having learned that the great orator would speak in the porch of a tavern fronting the large court-green, . . . pushed his way through the gathering crowd, and secured the pedestal of a pillar, where he stood within eight feet of him. He was very infirm, and seated in a chair conversing with some old friends, waiting for the assembling of the immense multitudes who were pouring in from all the surrounding country to hear him. At length he arose with difficulty, and stood somewhat bowed with age and weakness. His face was almost colorless. His countenance was careworn; and when he commenced his exordium, his voice was slightly cracked and tremulous. But in a few moments a wonderful transformation of the whole man occurred, as he warmed with his theme. He stood erect; his eye beamed with a light that was almost supernatural; his features glowed with the hue and fire of youth; and his voice rang clear and melodious with the intonations of some grand musical instrument whose notes filled the area, and fell distinctly and delightfully upon the ears of the most distant of the thousands gathered before him." [1]

As regards the substance of the speech then made, it will not be safe for us to confide very much in the supposed recollections of old men who heard it when they were young. Upon the whole,

[1] Fontaine, MS.

probably, the most trustworthy outline of it now
to be had is that of a gentleman who declares that
he wrote down his recollections of the speech not
long after its delivery. According to this account,
Patrick Henry —

"told them that the late proceedings of the Virginian Assembly had filled him with apprehensions and
alarm; that they had planted thorns upon his pillow;
that they had drawn him from that happy retirement
which it had pleased a bountiful Providence to bestow,
and in which he had hoped to pass, in quiet, the remainder of his days; that the State had quitted the sphere
in which she had been placed by the Constitution, and,
in daring to pronounce upon the validity of federal
laws, had gone out of her jurisdiction in a manner not
warranted by any authority, and in the highest degree
alarming to every considerate man; that such opposition, on the part of Virginia, to the acts of the general
government, must beget their enforcement by military
power; that this would probably produce civil war,
civil war foreign alliances, and that foreign alliances
must necessarily end in subjugation to the powers called
in. He conjured the people to pause and consider well,
before they rushed into such a desperate condition, from
which there could be no retreat. He painted to their
imaginations Washington, at the head of a numerous
and well-appointed army, inflicting upon them military execution. 'And where,' he asked, 'are our resources to meet such a conflict? Where is the citizen
of America who will dare to lift his hand against the
father of his country?' A drunken man in the crowd
threw up his arm, and exclaimed that he dared to do

it. 'No,' answered Mr. Henry, rising aloft in all his
majesty, 'you dare not do it: in such a parricidal attempt, the steel would drop from your nerveless arm!'
. . . Mr. Henry, proceeding in his address to the people, asked whether the county of Charlotte would have
any authority to dispute an obedience to the laws of
Virginia; and he pronounced Virginia to be to the
Union what the county of Charlotte was to her. Having denied the right of a State to decide upon the con-
stitutionality of federal laws, he added, that perhaps it
might be necessary to say something of the merits of
the laws in question.[1] His private opinion was that
they were good and proper. But whatever might be
their merits, it belonged to the people, who held the
reins over the head of Congress, and to them alone, to
say whether they were acceptable or otherwise to Virginians; and that this must be done by way of petition;
that Congress were as much our representatives as the
Assembly, and had as good a right to our confidence.
He had seen with regret the unlimited power over the
purse and sword consigned to the general government;
but . . . he had been overruled, and it was now necessary to submit to the constitutional exercise of that
power. 'If,' said he, 'I am asked what is to be done,
when a people feel themselves intolerably oppressed, my
answer is ready, — Overturn the government. But do
not, I beseech you, carry matters to this length without
provocation. Wait at least until some infringement is
made upon your rights, and which cannot otherwise be
redressed; for if ever you recur to another change, you
may bid adieu forever to representative government.
You can never exchange the present government but

[1] The alien and sedition acts.

for a monarchy. . . . Let us preserve our strength for the French, the English, the Germans, or whoever else shall dare to invade our territory, and not exhaust it in civil commotions and intestine wars.' He concluded by declaring his design to exert himself in the endeavor to allay the heart-burnings and jealousies which had been fomented in the state legislature; and he fervently prayed, if he was deemed unworthy to effect it, that it might be reserved to some other and abler hand to extend this blessing over the community." [1]

The outline thus given may be inaccurate in several particulars: it is known to be so in one. Respecting the alien and sedition acts, the orator expressed no opinion at all; [2] but accepting them as the law of the land, he counselled moderation, forbearance, and the use of constitutional means of redress. Than that whole effort, as has been said by a recent and a sagacious historian, " nothing in his life was nobler." [3]

Upon the conclusion of the old man's speech the stand was taken by a very young man, John Randolph of Roanoke, who undertook to address the crowd, offering himself to them as a candidate for Congress, but on behalf of the party then opposed to Patrick Henry. By reason of weariness, no doubt, the latter did not remain upon the platform; but having " requested a friend to report to him anything which might require an answer," he

[1] Wirt, 393–395.
[2] *Hist. Mag.* for 1873, 353.
[3] Henry Adams, *John Randolph*, 29.

stepped back into the tavern. "Randolph began by saying that he had admired that man more than any on whom the sun had shone, but that now he was constrained to differ from him ' *toto cœlo*.' " Whatever else Randolph may have said in his speech, whether important or otherwise, was spoken under the disadvantage of a cold and a hoarseness so severe as to render him scarcely able to "utter an audible sentence." Furthermore, Patrick Henry "made no reply, nor did he again present himself to the people." [1] There is, however, a tradition, not improbable, that when Randolph had finished his speech, and had come back into the room where the aged statesman was resting, the latter, taking him gently by the hand, said to him, with great kindness: "Young man, you call me father. Then, my son, I have something to say unto thee: keep justice, keep truth, — and you will live to think differently."

As a result of the poll, Patrick Henry was, by a great majority, elected to the House of Delegates. But his political enemies, who, for sufficient reasons, greatly dreaded his appearance upon that scene of his ancient domination, were never any more to be embarrassed by his presence there.

---

[1] J. W. Alexander, *Life of A. Alexander*, 188–189. About this whole scene have gathered many myths, of which several first appeared in a Life of Henry, in the *New Edinb. Encycl.* 1817; were thence copied into Howe, *Hist. Coll. Va.* 224–225; and have thence been engulfed in that rich mass of unwhipped hyberboles and of unexploded fables still patriotically swallowed by the American public as American history.

For, truly, they who, on that March day, at Charlotte court-house, had heard Patrick Henry, "had
heard an immortal orator who would never speak
again." [1]   He seems to have gone thence to his
home, and never to have left it. About the middle
of the next month, being too sick to write many
words, he lifted himself up in bed long enough to
tell the secretary of state that he could not go on
the mission to France, and to send his dying blessing to his old friend, the President. Early in
June, his eldest daughter, Martha Fontaine, living
at a distance of two days' travel from Red Hill,
received from him a letter beginning with these
words: "Dear Patsy, I am very unwell, and have
Dr. Cabell with me." [2]   Upon this alarming news,
she and others of his kindred in that neighborhood
made all haste to go to him. On arriving at Red
Hill "they found him sitting in a large, old-fash-
ioned armchair, in which he was easier than upon a
bed." The disease of which he was dying was intus-
susception. On the 6th of June, all other remedies
having failed, Dr. Cabell proceeded to administer to
him a dose of liquid mercury. Taking the vial in
his hand, and looking at it for a moment, the dying
man said: "I suppose, doctor, this is your last resort?" The doctor replied: "I am sorry to say,
governor, that it is. Acute inflammation of the
intestine has already taken place; and unless it is
removed, mortification will ensue, if it has not already commenced, which I fear." "What will be

[1] Henry Adams.   [2] Fontaine, MS.

the effect of this medicine?" said the old man. "It will give you immediate relief, or" — the kind-hearted doctor could not finish the sentence. His patient took up the word: "You mean, doctor, that it will give relief, or will prove fatal immediately?" The doctor answered: "You can only live a very short time without it, and it may possibly relieve you." Then Patrick Henry said, "Excuse me, doctor, for a few minutes;" and drawing down over his eyes a silken cap which he usually wore, and still holding the vial in his hand, he prayed, in clear words, a simple childlike prayer, for his family, for his country, and for his own soul then in the presence of death. Afterward, in perfect calmness, he swallowed the medicine. Meanwhile, Dr. Cabell, who greatly loved him, went out upon the lawn, and in his grief threw himself down upon the earth under one of the trees, weeping bitterly. Soon, when he had sufficiently mastered himself, the doctor came back to his patient, whom he found calmly watching the congealing of the blood under his finger-nails, and speaking words of love and peace to his family, who were weeping around his chair. Among other things, he told them that he was thankful for that goodness of God, which, having blessed him through all his life, was then permitting him to die without any pain. Finally, fixing his eyes with much tenderness on his dear friend, Dr. Cabell, with whom he had formerly held many arguments respecting the Christian religion, he asked the doctor to observe how great a reality and benefit that religion was to a man about to die. And after Patrick Henry had spoken to his beloved physician these few words in praise of something which, having never failed him in all his life before, did not then fail him in his very last need of it, he continued to breathe very softly for some moments; after which they who were looking upon him saw that his life had departed.

LIST OF PRINTED DOCUMENTS

CITED IN THIS BOOK, WITH TITLES, PLACES, AND DATES OF THE EDITIONS USED.

ADAMS, CHARLES FRANCIS. (See John Adams.)

ADAMS, HENRY, The Life of Albert Gallatin. Philadelphia: 1880.

ADAMS, HENRY, John Randolph. Am. Statesmen Series. Boston: 1882.

ADAMS, JOHN. (See Novanglus, etc.)

ADAMS, JOHN, Letters of, Addressed to his Wife. Ed. by Charles Francis Adams. 2 vols. Boston: 1841.

ADAMS, JOHN, The Works of. Ed. by Charles Francis Adams. 10 vols. Boston: 1856.

ADAMS, SAMUEL, Life of. (See Wm. V. Wells.)

ALEXANDER, JAMES W., The Life of Archibald Alexander. New York: 1854.

American Archives. (Peter Force.) 9 vols. Washington: 1837–1853.

The American Quarterly Review. Vol. i. Philadelphia: 1827.

BANCROFT, GEORGE, History of the United States. 10 vols. Boston: 1870–1874.

BANCROFT, GEORGE, History of the United States. The Author's Last Revision. 6 vols. New York: 1883–1885.

BANCROFT, GEORGE, History of the Formation of the Constitution of the United States of America. 2 vols. New York: 1882.

BLAND, RICHARD, A Letter to the Clergy of Virginia. n. p. 1760.

BROUGHAM, HENRY, LORD, The Life and Times of, Written by himself. 3 vols. New York: 1871.

BURK, JOHN (DALY), The History of Virginia. 4 vols. Petersburg: 1804–1816. Last volume by Skelton Jones and Louis Hue Girardin.

BYRD, WILLIAM, Byrd Manuscripts. 2 vols. Richmond: 1866.

Calendar of Virginia State Papers. Vol. ii. Richmond: 1881.

CAMPBELL, CHARLES, The Bland Papers: Being a Selection from the Manuscripts of Colonel Theodorick Bland, Jr. 2 vols. Petersburg: 1840.

CAMPBELL, CHARLES, History of the Colony and Ancient Dominion of Virginia. Philadelphia: 1860.

Collections of the Connecticut Historical Society. Vol. ii. Hartford: 1870.

Colonel George Rogers Clark's Sketch of his Campaign in the Illinois in 1778-79. Cincinnati: 1869.

COOKE, JOHN ESTEN, Virginia: A History of the People. (Commonwealth Series.) Boston: 1884.

COOLEY, THOMAS M. (See Joseph Story.)

Correspondence of the American Revolution. Edited by Jared Sparks. 4 vols. Boston: 1853.

CURTIS, B. R., Reports of Decisions in the Supreme Court of the United States. Boston: 1855.

CURTIS, GEORGE TICKNOR, History of the Origin, Formation, and Adoption of the Constitution of the United States. 2 vols. London and New York: 1854, 1858.

CURTIS, GEORGE TICKNOR, Life of Daniel Webster. New York: 1872.

DE COSTA, B. F. (See William White.)

DICKINSON, JOHN, The Political Writings of. 2 vols. Wilmington: 1801.

ELLIOT, JONATHAN, The Debates in the Several State Conventions, on the adoption of the Federal Constitution, etc. 5 vols. Philadelphia: 1876.

EVERETT, ALEXANDER H., Life of Patrick Henry. In Sparks's Library of Am. Biography. 2d series, vol. i. Boston: 1844.

FROTHINGHAM, RICHARD, The Rise of the Republic of the United States. Boston: 1872.

GALES, JOSEPH, The Debates and Proceedings in the Congress of the United States. 2 vols. Washington: 1834.

GALLATIN, ALBERT. (See Henry Adams.)

GARLAND, HUGH A., The Life of John Randolph of Roanoke. 2 vols. New York: 1860.

GIBBS, GEORGE, Memoirs of the Administrations of Washington and John Adams, edited from the Papers of Oliver Wolcott. New York: 1846.

GIRARDIN, LOUIS HUE. (See John Burk.)

GORDON, WILLIAM, History of the Rise, Progress, and Establishment of the Independence of the United States of America; including an account of the Late War, and of the Thirteen Colonies from their origin to that period. 3 vols. New York: 1789.

GRIGSBY, HUGH BLAIR, The Virginia Convention of 1776. Richmond: 1855.

HAMILTON, ALEXANDER, Works of. Edited by John C. Hamilton. 7 vols. New York: 1850-1851.

HANSARD, T. C., The Parliamentary History of England. Vol. xviii. London: 1813.

HAWKS, FRANCIS L., Contributions to the Ecclesiastical History of the United States of America. Vol. i. New York: 1836.

HENING, WILLIAM WALLER, The Statutes at Large: Being a Collection of all the Laws of Virginia. 13 vols. Richmond, New York, and Philadelphia: 1819-1823.

HENRY, PATRICK, Life of. (See Wirt, William, and Everett, Alexander H.)

HENRY, WILLIAM WIRT, Character and Public Career of Patrick Henry. Pamphlet. Charlotte Court-house, Va.: 1867.

HENRY, WILLIAM WIRT, Patrick Henry: Life, Correspondence, and Speeches. 3 vols. New York: 1891.

HERRING, JAMES. (See National Portrait Gallery.)

HILDRETH, RICHARD, The History of the United States of America. 6 vols. New York: 1871-1874.

The Historical Magazine, and Notes and Queries Concerning the Antiquities, History, and Biography of America. (Henry B. Dawson.) Vol. ii. 2d series, and vol. ii. 3d series. Morrisania: 1867 and 1873.

HOWE, HENRY, Historical Collections of Virginia. Charleston: 1845.

HOWISON, ROBERT R., A History of Virginia. Vol. i. Philadelphia: 1846. Vol. ii. Richmond, New York, and London: 1848.

IREDELL, JAMES, Life of. (See McRee, G. J.)

JAY, WILLIAM, The Life of John Jay. 2 vols. New York: 1833.

JEFFERSON, THOMAS, Notes on the State of Virginia. Philadelphia: 1825.

JEFFERSON, THOMAS, The Writings of. Ed. by H. A. Washington. 9 vols. New York: 1853–1854.

JEFFERSON, THOMAS, Life of. (See H. S. Randall.)

JONES, SKELTON. (See John Burk.)

Journal of the House of Delegates of the Commonwealth of Virginia. (From 1777 to 1790.) 3 vols. Richmond: 1827–1828.

KENNEDY, JOHN P., Memoirs of the Life of William Wirt. 2 vols. Philadelphia: 1850.

LAMB, GENERAL JOHN, Memoir of. (See Leake, Isaac Q.)

LAMB, MARTHA J. (See Magazine of American History.)

LEAKE, ISAAC Q., Memoir of the Life and Times of General John Lamb. Albany: 1850.

LEE, CHARLES CARTER. (See Lee, Henry, Observations, etc.)

LEE, HENRY, Observations on the Writings of Thomas Jefferson, with Particular Reference to the Attack they contain on the Memory of the late Gen. Henry Lee. In a series of Letters. Second ed., with an Introduction and Notes by Charles Carter Lee. Philadelphia: 1839.

LEE, RICHARD HENRY. (See Richard Henry Lee, 2d.)

LEE, RICHARD HENRY, 2d, Memoir of the Life of Richard Henry Lee. 2 vols. Philadelphia: 1825.

LEE, RICHARD HENRY, 2d, Life of Arthur Lee, LL. D. 2 vols. Boston: 1829.

LEONARD, DANIEL. (See Novanglus, etc.)

LONGACRE, JAMES B. (See National Portrait Gallery.)

MACKAY, CHARLES, The Founders of the American Republic. Edinburgh and London: 1885.

MACMASTER, JOHN BACH, History of the People of the United States. 2 vols. New York: 1883–1885.

McREE, GRIFFITH J., Life and Correspondence of James Iredell. 2 vols. New York: 1857–1858.

MADISON, JAMES, The Papers of. 3 vols. Washington: 1840.

MADISON, JAMES, Letters and Other Writings of. 4 vols. Philadelphia: 1867.

MADISON, JAMES, Life and Times of. (See William C. Rives.)

The Magazine of American History, with Notes and Queries. Ed. by Martha J. Lamb. Vol. xi. New York: 1884.

MAGRUDER, ALLAN B., John Marshall. (Am. Statesmen Series.) Boston: 1885.

MARSHALL, JOHN, The Life of George Washington. 5 vols. Philadelphia: 1804–1807.

MARSHALL, JOHN. (See Magruder, Allan B.)

MAURY, ANN, Memoirs of a Huguenot Family. New York: 1872.

MEADE, WILLIAM, Old Churches, Ministers, and Families of Virginia. 2 vols. Philadelphia: 1872.

The National Portrait Gallery of Distinguished Americans, Conducted by James B. Longacre and James Herring. 2d vol. Philadelphia, New York, and London: 1835.

Novanglus and Massachusettensis ; or, Political Essays Published in the years 1774 and 1775. Boston: 1819.

PERRY, WILLIAM STEVENS, Historical Collections relating to the American Colonial Church. Vol. i. Virginia. Hartford: 1870.

PEYTON, J. LEWIS, History of Augusta County, Virginia. Staunton: 1882.

Prior Documents. A Collection of Interesting, Authentic Papers relative to the Dispute between Great Britain and America, Shewing the Causes and Progress of that Misunderstanding from 1764 to 1775. (Almon.) London: 1777.

The Proceedings of the Convention of Delegates for the Counties and Corporations in the Colony of Virginia, Held at Richmond Town, in the County of Henrico, on the 20th of March, 1775. Richmond: 1816.

RANDALL, HENRY STEPHENS, The Life of Thomas Jefferson. 3 vols. New York: 1858.

RANDOLPH, JOHN. (See Adams, Henry, and Garland, Hugh A.)

REED, WILLIAM B., Life and Correspondence of Joseph Reed. 2 vols. Philadelphia: 1847.

RIVES, WILLIAM C., History of the Life and Times of James Madison. Boston: Vol. i. 2d ed. 1873. Vol. ii. 1870. Vol. iii. 1868.

ROWLAND, KATE MASON, The Life of George Mason, Including his Speeches, Public Papers, and Correspondence, with an Introduction by General Fitzhugh Lee. 2 vols. New York: 1892.

SLAUGHTER, REV. PHILIP, A History of St. Mark's Parish, Culpeper County, Virginia. n. p. 1877.

SPARKS, JARED. (See Corr. Am. Revolution, and Washington, Writings of.)

STORY, JOSEPH, Commentaries of the Constitution of the United States. Ed. by Thomas M. Cooley. 2 vols. Boston: 1873.

TYLER, LYON G., The Letters and Times of the Tylers. 2 vols.
Richmond: 1884–1885.

The Virginia Historical Register and Literary Note-Book. Vol.
iii. Richmond: 1850.

Virginia State Papers, Calendar of. Vol. ii. Richmond: 1881.

WASHINGTON, GEORGE, The Writings of; Being his Correspondence, Addresses, Messages, and Other Papers, Official and Private; Selected and Published from the Original Manuscripts,
with a Life of the Author, Notes, and Illustrations. Edited
by Jared Sparks. 12 vols. Boston and New York: 1834–
1847.

WASHINGTON, GEORGE, Life of. (See John Marshall.)

WASHINGTON, H. A. (See Jefferson, Thomas, Writings of.)

WEBSTER, DANIEL, Life of. (See Geo. Ticknor Curtis.)

WELLS, WILLIAM V., The Life and Public Services of Samuel
Adams. 3 vols. Boston: 1865.

WHITE, WILLIAM, Memoirs of the Protestant Episcopal Church
in the United States of America. Ed. by B. F. De Costa. New
York: 1880.

WIRT, WILLIAM, Sketches of the Life and Character of Patrick
Henry. Third ed., corrected by the Author. Philadelphia:
1818.

WIRT, WILLIAM, Life of. (See Kennedy, John P.)

WISE, HENRY A., Seven Decades of the Union. Philadelphia:
1872.

INDEX

behalf of Washington, the office of chief justice, 403.

Lee, Richard Henry, on committee to protest against Stamp Act, 66; leader of radicals in politics, 95; appointed delegate to Continental Congress, 99; praised by Virginia delegates as the Cicero of the age, 101; meets John Adams and is praised by him, 106; in debate over manner of voting, 112; on committee to prepare address to king, 117; author of draft rejected by Congress, 118; on committee of Virginia convention for organizing militia, 151; on other committees, 152; in second Continental Congress, 173; letter of Pendleton to, describing military situation in Virginia, 178; in convention of 1776, 190; urged by Henry to promote French alliance, 198; favors a democratic constitution, 202; appealed to for aid by Henry, 204; supposed to have been won by Conway cabal, 243, 253; loses popularity in Virginia, 252; barely succeeds in reelection to Congress, 253; consoled by Henry, 253; warned of decay of public spirit in Virginia, 254; Henry's only rival in leadership of General Assembly, 275; compared with Henry by S. Roane, 295–296; opposes a strong central government, 305; not a member of Virginia ratifying convention, 319; opposes ratification of Constitution, 320; his election as senator dictated by Henry, 350, 353; turns from Jefferson to support of Washington, 398.

Lee, Thomas Ludwell, suggested as messenger by Henry, 205.

Legislature of Virginia, first appearance of Henry before Burgesses in election case, 61; corruption of speaker in, 63; motion for a "loan office" in, defeated by Henry, 64; protests against proposed Stamp Act, 65; doubts among members as to course after its passage, 66–68; deliberates on Stamp Act, 68; introduction of Henry's resolutions,

69; opposition of old leaders, 69, 71; debate in, 71–74; passes, then amends resolutions, 74, 75; deplores Boston Port Bill, 97; dissolved by Governor Dunmore, 97; its members call for a Continental Congress, 98; recommend a colonial convention, 99; which meets, 99; appoints delegates to first Continental Congress, 99, 100; adjourns, 100; second convention meets, 134; its determination to prepare for war, 135; causes for objections to Henry's resolutions to arm militia, 136–139; adopts his resolutions to arm militia, and prepares for war, 151, 152; return of Virginia congressional delegates to, 176; thanks them, 176; appoints Henry commander-in-chief with limited powers, 177; meets at Williamsburg, 190; its able membership, 190; struggle for presidency between Pendleton's and Henry's factions, 191; committees and business transacted by, 192, 193; sentiment in, said to favor independence, 193; instructs delegates to Congress to propose independence, foreign alliance, and a confederation, 197; appoints committee to draw up state Constitution and bill of rights, 200; aristocratic and democratic parties in, 201–207; adopts declaration of rights, 207–210; establishes religious liberty, 208, 209; adopts state Constitution, 210; its democratic form, 210, 211; elects Henry governor, 211; General Assembly holds first session, 220; said to have planned to make Henry dictator, 223, 224, 226; confers extraordinary powers on Governors Henry and Jefferson, 228, 231, 233; adjourns, 232; no trace of a plot in, as described by Jefferson, 233–235; reëlects Henry governor, 238, 239; its sessions during 1777 and 1778, 241; elects delegates to Congress, 253; again confers extraordinary powers on Henry, 256; and reëlects him governor, 256; again confers on Henry extraordinary powers, 260; desires to re-

Moses Coit Tyler emerged at the forefront of the new "critical" historical movement with the 1878 publication of his masterful *History of American Literature, 1607-1765*. A professor of English literature at the University of Michigan, and later of American history at Cornell, Tyler also helped found the American Historical Association. His biography of Patrick Henry represents the first scholarly study of the colorful statesman and contains the seeds of Tyler's greatest work, *The Literary History of the American Revolution*.

Lance Banning is Associate Professor of History at the University of Kentucky. He is author of *The Jeffersonian Persuasion*, among other publications.